WALKING AMERICA

The 1993-94 Guide to More Than 400 Walking Trails

Judith Galas and Cindy West

Copyright ©1993 by Judith Galas and Cindy West

All rights reserved, including the right to reproduce this book or parts thereof, in any form, except for the inclusion of brief quotations in a review.

ISBN: 1-56044-145-3

Published by West Press, P.O. Box 1971, Lawrence, Kansas 66044-8971, in cooperation with SkyHouse Publishers, an imprint of Falcon Press Publishing Co., Inc., Helena, Montana.

Design, typesetting, and other prepress work by Falcon Graphics, Helena, Montana.

Cover photo by Shari Hartbauer.

Distributed by Falcon Press Publishing Co., Inc., P.O. Box 1718, Helena, Montana 59624, or call 1-800-582-2665.

Manufactured in The United States of America.

DEDICATION

To the members of this country's volkswalking clubs in thanks for the countless hours they give so that others can enjoy the beauty of America and the joy of exercising, and especially to Jan Jess for pointing us to our first trail.

ACKNOWLEDGMENTS

Few books are the work of only one or two people, and that's especially true of this one. We want to thank the hundreds of people in the American Volkssport Association network and its national office who mailed back our surveys, returned our phone calls, sent along extra tidbits about their communities, or took the time to write us words of encouragement.

We'd also like to thank the many individuals, chambers of commerce, visitors bureaus, and city, state, and federal agencies who so generously answered our requests for photos. Those agencies are too numerous to mention, but a few special photographers are not. Thanks Janet Benson, Ann Fendorf, Jan Jess, Peg Sampson, Ralph Lauterwasser, Kayla Weiner, and Laurie Wood for letting us give you film to shoot on your own time just because we're friends or sisters.

Thanks also to Susan Hyde for sharing some design time, to Judy Eyerly for loading our software, and to Brian Schwegmann for walking us through it.

Finally, thanks to the folks at SkyHouse for helping to make this project run so smoothly.

CONTENTS

Introduction vii

How To Use This Guide ix

The States

Alabama 1
Arizona 2
Arkansas 7
California 8
Colorado 24
Connecticut 32
Delaware 33
District of Columbia 34
Florida 36
Georgia 44
Hawaii 46
Idaho 47
Illinois 49
Indiana 53
Iowa 58
Kansas 59
Kentucky 64
Louisiana 65
Maine 67
Maryland 68
Massachusetts 74
Michigan 78
Minnesota 79
Mississippi 87
Missouri 88
Montana 97
Nebraska 98
Nevada 103
New Hampshire 106
New Mexico 107
New York 108
North Carolina 113
North Dakota 115
Ohio 117
Oklahoma 122
Oregon 126
Pennsylvania 156
Rhode Island 161

v

South Dakota 163
Tennessee 170
Texas 171
Utah 190
Vermont 192
Virginia 193
Washington 198
West Virginia 215
Wisconsin 216
Wyoming 217

What's Volkswalking? 222

Appendix
Bike Routes 225
Cross-Country Ski Trails 226
Swims 226
Wheelchair-accessible Routes 226

Write to Us 229

About the Authors 232

vi

INTRODUCTION

Cindy and I wrote and financed *Walking America* for many reasons. We want others to know about this national, inexpensive resource called volkswalking. We want to help others find all those great trails and to urge them to make walking a regular part of their day, their family life, and their travels. We want to convince others that there's no better way to see America than up close from a sidewalk or a trail and no better way to slow down your life than to take a brisk walk.

We're not athletes, we aren't rich, and we don't have much free time. But what steady walking has taught us is that you can work toward fitness, have fun, and make time for friends and family and even yourself just by going for a 10K volkswalk. Traveling to a new trail also provides great incentive to explore places you've never seen before simply because you know you'll find a walking path when you get there.

"But," you say, "I don't need to go on 10K treks to walk, I don't need volkswalking to find a good trail, and I don't need walking trails to push me to see America." And to that, I'd say, you're right. So why volkswalk?

The answer has a lot to do with human nature. Lots of people walk, but few people regularly push themselves to walk more than a mile. Until we hit the volkswalk trail, we rarely walked more than a mile or two. When you tackle a 10K walk, you're making the decision to exert yourself, and a little exertion is good for our bodies and our spirits.

Lots of people say, "I should walk more," but the person who marks a walking event on the calendar is more likely to take that walk than the person who just talks about it. Anyone can walk 10K in their own neighborhood, but the person most likely to finish the route is the one following the map, the person who traveled to the start point with the idea of being gone about two hours. We've been on a lot of volkswalks, but we've never been on one we didn't finish.

Lots of people want to travel, and they will, they say, just as soon as they find the time, or the money, or an interesting place to visit. At the heart of *Walking America* is the belief that every walking trail is the start of a great adventure. Reading about an interesting walk in our book might be all the incentive you need to stop in a town or nature reserve you never would have thought to visit and then discover something special. Without a volkswalk to entice us, I know we never would have seen Fort Ransom, N.D.; Augusta, Mo.; Bellevue, Neb.; Collinsville, Ill.; or Albert Lea, Minn. But the walks in each of those little-known towns linger in our memories as special. For me, the Fontenelle Forest in Bellevue is one of this country's truly magical places, but I never would have discovered it if I hadn't been looking for a volkswalk within four hours of home.

vii

Chances are you've picked up *Walking America* because you're interested in walking. Chances are that like us you're also interested in finding new ways to exercise, in having more fun with your family and friends and in getting away from home, if only for an afternoon. If that's all true, then maybe you should start *Walking America*.

HOW TO USE THIS GUIDE

The complete description of each walk will give you information we think you'll need before you can decide which walks are best for you and which you'll enjoy.

Dates: Most year-round walks sponsored by the various walking clubs are open from January through December. Some trails are seasonals, because they are open only for a specific time during the year. Weather often plays a role in helping a walking club decide when to open and close its walking trail. If you see "seasonal" after the date, you know the walk will be held only during certain months. The seasonal dates listed in this 1993-94 guide are accurate for 1993. Because seasonal walks frequently start and end their seasons on weekends, the 1994 dates may be slightly off.

📞 If you have a question about a walk, please call the person listed. These contact people agree to have their names and numbers published so walkers can confirm seasonal dates, holiday closings, and directions or can get an opinion on the walk's difficulty. Most of the phone numbers are to people's homes, so be sure to call during reasonable hours.

Description: In this section you'll find out what you'll see on the walk. You'll also learn how difficult the walk might be, how long it is and whether you can expect hills or uneven surfaces. The number in parentheses rates the walk's difficulty.

Distance: All the walks mentioned in *Walking America* are at least 10K or 6.2 miles. A few, however, are longer. We've mentioned a walk's length only when it's longer than 10K.

Difficulty: You'll know how hard a walk is likely to be by looking at the number in the parentheses. On a scale of 1 to 5, the easiest and flattest trails are rated 1 and the most difficult 5.

We think people in wheelchairs or those pushing strollers need to know exactly what the path will be like. They can't find themselves three miles into a walk and suddenly facing steep stairs or gravel paths. *Walking America*'s 1 and 1+ ratings have stroller and wheelchair pushers in mind.

Those pushing strollers should feel comfortable with walks rated no higher than 1+. Those in or pushing wheelchairs should use the trails with a 1 rating. If a walk with a higher rating sounds interesting and feasible, call the contact person for a more detailed description of the trail. We've used information from the walks' sponsors and personal

ix

experience to assess the 1 and 1+ ratings. Please let us know if the ratings are inappropriate.

1   Trail is suitable for wheelchairs and strollers. The trail is relatively flat and curbing problems should be minimal, or easier alternate routes are provided.

1+   Trail is suitable for strollers, but not wheelchairs. You might encounter stairs or patches of uneven surface such as grass or gravel that might be navigated by strollers but not by wheelchairs.

2   Trail is moderately easy. The path might be paved, but it might also be through open fields or woodlands and might not always be maintained. You shouldn't encounter much trouble with hills.

3   Trail has some difficult terrain. The path might be rocky and uneven in spots with one or two substantial hills or sets of steps.

4   Trail may be difficult. Most likely you'll be walking in a natural setting where you wouldn't expect the paths to be maintained and where the trail includes steep or hilly routes.

5   Trail is demanding. You'll walk in rough fields, with uneven surfaces and up steep or unstable inclines, possibly at high altitudes in isolated areas. You should have experience with long-distance walks.

Remember, the ratings are subjective. Cold, heat, winds, rain and high altitude could leach your stamina and turn a #2 walk into a #4.

See and Stay: We know part of the fun of finding a walking trail is discovering a new town or attraction or tasting some delicacy or unearthing a great museum. We've tried to tell you some of the interesting, fun, or educational things each area has to offer. These are recommendations, not endorsements. When people from the area told us about a particularly good restaurant or attraction, we passed the tip along. If a motel, restaurant, or amusement gives a walker's discount, we let you know. If we learned of a convention and visitors bureau that sends out information, we've given you the address. Many of the walk's contact people would be happy to share details about their communities, so if you'd like to know something particular about an area, just ask them.

Hours: If we haven't listed hours, assume the walk is open daily dawn to dusk, or from about 7 A.M. to 7 P.M. If a walk's hours or days are more restrictive than that, we've posted them. Ideally a trail is open seven days a week during daylight hours. Many walks fit that ideal, but many others must fit within the hours of their start/finish points.

Please pay attention to the finish times. Shopkeepers will close at their regular hours even if you haven't returned. Allow yourself enough time to walk and even more time if you plan to sightsee or push a stroller. Also, add extra time for hilly or uneven paths or routes with lots of stoplights and traffic. The average walker, going at a steady but modest pace, can walk a normal 10K (6.2 miles) in about two hours. Unseasoned walkers might need as much as three hours. Everyone should allow about 20 minutes for every extra kilometer over 10.

We haven't listed holiday closings because, depending on the business, holiday closings can change. So, consider the type of start point when deciding to walk on a traditional or federal holiday. Most hotels are open 365 days a year, but it's unlikely a store will be open on Thanksgiving. If there's a chance a start point might be closed, call to check.

Many walking clubs discourage walkers from walking when it's dark. In some areas, walking at night simply isn't safe. In others, such as a forest, you're probably safe from assault, but not from falling over tree roots or down unlighted inclines.

Many walkers do walk at night, if—and these are big IFS—if the streets and sidewalks are well-lighted, if the start/finish point is not inconvenienced, and if they know the area well enough to know they won't get lost and aren't in danger. If you're walking in a strange town, be safe. Walk during daylight.

Many walkers like to get out at sunup, but many walks don't start before 8 A.M.; some start even later. If you want to start your walk before the start point opens, you might be able to register and pick up your start card the day before and then return it when the start point is open for business. Many walks have this as an option, so ask if you can start earlier than the posted time.

Several of these walking clubs also sponsor biking events and a few even offer a chance to swim. *Walking America* isn't about biking, but for those walkers who like to bike, we've let you know where you might find some good trails.

The check mark alerts you to important information such as which trails forbid dogs, which have ticks and chiggers, which might be muddy and which don't have water. Be sure to read the checked information before deciding on a walk.

Dogs: Most of the walking clubs welcome dogs on their trails. When they don't, it's often because the trail goes through a wildlife reserve or buildings pets can't enter.

In our surveys we asked if unleashed dogs were permitted, and the overwhelming response was "no." In some communities leash laws demand that all dogs be leashed, but I suspect many of those who put several underlines under "no," did so because too often loose dogs are a problem. They scare people on the trails, chase other dogs, jump in flower beds, and poop on lawns and sidewalks. In fact, many surveys included handwritten notes similar to this: "Tell people to clean up after their dogs!!!" Enough said.

A word of caution: If you're walking with your dog in neighborhoods and on country roads, you might encounter loose dogs who show curiosity or hostility toward new dogs on their turf. So keep your eyes open for other dogs.

Water: Drink it. An exercising body needs lots of water. Most of these routes go past places where you can get a drink of water or can purchase a beverage. Still, it's good to carry your own water bottle, especially in warm weather. Dogs also need water, so bring along something you can fill with water before and after the walk.

Weather: Most year-rounds are open in all but the most extreme weather. Give some thought to the day's forecast and be prepared to protect yourself from the rain and sun.

Where Is It? We give you the exact address of the place where the walk starts and the phone number, if we know it, so you can call for directions if you get lost. Most of the directions we've included are the ones the sponsoring clubs use to guide people to their walks. When the club gave us more than one set of directions, we chose the one that seemed the most complete or that followed the route most tourists might take.

Sponsor: Each walk is mapped out, advertised, and supervised by a particular volkswalking club. We've given you the name of the club and its address in case you want to request more information or want to learn more about the club. Many clubs modify their walks from year to year. Some drop or add a walk. So, before you plan a vacation around particular walks or decide to go out of your way to find one, contact the club to see if everything has stayed the same.

ALABAMA

MONTGOMERY ◆ *Historic Downtown Walk*

Dates: *January 1-December 31*   *Elwood Hintz (205) 272-5986*

Description (1+): This city walk takes you past historic sights guaranteed to bring Southern history to life. Almost entirely on concrete and asphalt, this walk also takes you past Hank Williams's grave and even offers an easier option for people in wheelchairs.

See and Stay: Visit the many historic buildings related to the Civil War. Stand on the steps of the renovated state capitol where Jefferson Davis was sworn in as the Confederacy's president and where Dr. Martin Luther King ended the Selma-to-Montgomery civil rights march. Old and young will enjoy the nearby zoo, parks and playgrounds, and a boat ride on the Alabama River. Take in a Shakespearean play at the Alabama Shakespeare Festival Theatre.

Where Is It? The walk starts at the Riverfront Inn, 200 Coosa St., in the downtown area. **From the north on I-65:** Exit Clay St. and follow signs to downtown. Clay intersects Herron St., which intersects Coosa, where you will turn left. **From the south on I-65:** Exit at Herron and continue about 6 blks. to Coosa and turn left. Park in the Riverfront Inn lot.

Sponsor: Capital City Wanderers, 3914 Meredith Dr., Montgomery, AL 36109

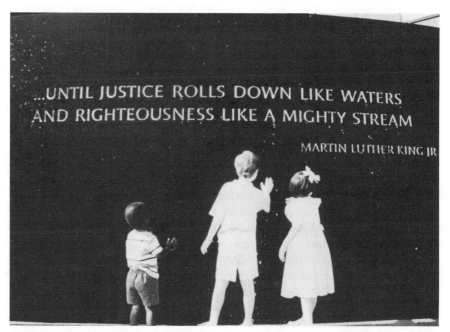

The Civil Rights Memorial remembers those who died in the struggle for racial equality. Courtesy Montgomery Chamber of Commerce.

ARIZONA

FORT HUACHUCA ♦ *Historic Fort Walk*

Dates: January 1–December 31   *Fort Huachuca (602) 533-5962*

Description (1): You'll walk the oldest active U.S. Cavalry post on this 12K walk, which follows sidewalks, streets, and an abandoned railroad bed. The 4,600-ft. elevation may be hard on those pushing wheelchairs or strollers.

See and Stay: Explore the 1800s post, which retains many of its original buildings. The Fort Huachuca Museum, at Boyd and Grierson, depicts the history of the Southwest and army activities in the area.

☑ If you do not have a Department of Defense registration sticker, you will need a visitor's pass. To get one, you must have a valid driver's license, vehicle registration, and proof of insurance. Temperatures can be extreme and thunderstorms are possible from July to September.

Hours: 8 A.M.–5 P.M. Allow about 3 hrs. for this walk.

Where Is It? Start at the Fort Huachuca Golf Course. **From I-10:** Take Exit 302 (SR 90). Follow 90 to the fort's main gate and get a pass, if you need one. Stay in the left lane after passing the gate. The golf course is at the end of Indian Scout Rd., the second road on your left.

Sponsor: Huachuca Wanderers, P.O. Box 588, Ft. Huachuca, AZ 85613

HEREFORD ♦ *Coronado Memorial Walk*

Dates: January 1–December 31   *David Breen (602) 378-1763*

Description (5): All mountain trails, this 11K walk starts at a 5,300-ft. elevation and goes up another 1,600 ft. You'll get breathtaking views and may spot wildlife. Make noise—the bears don't want to see you, either.

Hours: Start 8 A.M.–noon and finish by 5 P.M. Allow 4 hrs.

See and Stay: Sightsee in Bisbee, an old copper town with antique shops and galleries. Food and lodging in Sierra Vista and Bisbee. Thunder Mountain Inn in Sierra Vista offers walker discounts.

☑ No dogs. Bring water and snacks. Expect icy patches in the winter, sun in the summer, and wind on the mountain crest. It's best not to walk alone. Rest rooms are at the start and mid-points. Water is available always at the start, but only at the mid-point in the summer.

Where Is It? Start at the visitor center of the Coronado National Memorial, (602) 458-9333, on Coronado Memorial Hwy. Watch for the brown and white information sign showing the turnoff from Hwy 90 onto Coronado Memorial Hwy.

Sponsor: Thunder Mountain Trekkers, 3288 S. Sky Hawk Dr., Sierra Vista, AZ 85635

ARIZONA

MESA ◆ City Walk

Dates: January 1–December 31   *John Shoemaker (602) 345-1852*

Description (1+): This 11K walk goes along a canal, takes you past a botanical garden and cacti and offers beautiful mountain views.

See and Stay: Look for the Arizona Museum for Youth. This hands-on museum lets kids crawl inside various art forms and even create some of their own. The Mesa Southwest Museum at 53 N. MacDonald St. includes reconstructions of historic Indian dwellings. The Rockin' R Ranch, 6136 Baseline Rd., a re-creation of a western town, offers horse-drawn wagon rides, a petting zoo, and chuckwagon suppers. Ask for the walkers' rate at the Mezona Motor Hotel.

☑ The path is sandy and can be a scorcher in the summer. You'll find water in the parks, but bring head protection. Lone walkers may feel uneasy near the start point.

Where Is It? Start at the Mezona Motel, 250 W. Main St., in Mesa, (602) 834-9233. Take the Superstition Freeway (AZ 360) east to the Country Club exit. Go north to Main, then right on Main to the motel.

Sponsor: Valley Volkssport Association, 18 W. Louis Way, Tempe, AZ 85284

Just how far is a 10K walk?

10K is the minimum distance a volkswalk can be, but some walks are longer than 10K. To figure out how far you're walking, just remember there are .62 miles to every kilometer, so a 10K walk = 10 x .62, or 6.2 miles.

10K = 6.2 miles	11K = 6.8 miles
12K = 7.4 miles	13K = 8.1 miles
14K = 8.7 miles	15K = 9.3 miles

ARIZONA

PHOENIX ◆ Historical Neighborhood Walk
◆ Downtown Walk

Dates: January 1–December 31  *Angel Montalvo (602) 821-5405*

Description (1 +): The historical walk goes past quiet, shady neighborhoods with diverse architecture. It's mostly on sidewalks, except for a short stretch of dirt. On the 13K downtown walk, you'll amble past interesting public art and buildings. Some areas are a little run down, but the walk offers many restaurants and shops, and a stroll through an unusual park built over a parking garage.

Hours: Mon.-Fri., 9 A.M.–5 P.M.; weekends and holidays, 10 A.M. – sunset.

See and Stay: Before or after your walk, ride the carousel in Encanto Park. Be sure to visit the nearby Heard Museum of anthropology and primitive art, which displays Native American baskets, jewelry, pottery, and Kachina dolls. The Phoenix Art Museum, free on Wednesdays, includes medieval, Renaissance, French baroque, and Far Eastern art. In late fall, the museum hosts its annual Cowboy Artists of America exhibition and sale. Hop on the free DASH shuttle bus and ride to the state capitol and adjacent park, which includes the mast of the USS Arizona, now lying in Pearl Harbor. The Mezona Motor Hotel, 250 W. Main St., in nearby Mesa, offers discounts to walkers.

☑ These walks can be scorchers in the summer. Wear a head covering and carry water to supplement the drinks that can be bought along the trails. People walking alone may feel uneasy in the downtown area in the early and late hours.

🚴 This club also offers a 25K and 50K paved bike path, some of it along the banks of an irrigation canal. Bring your own bike. Start point and times are the same as for walkers.

Where Is It? During the week, start at the Norton House, 2700 N. 15th Ave., (602) 262-6412. Park in the lot. On weekends and holidays, start at the Encanto Park Sports Complex in Encanto Park, (602) 261-8443. Park near the start, not at the golf course. **From I-17:** Take the Thomas St. exit east to 15th Ave., then north to Norton House or the Encanto Park Sports Complex; or take McDowell St. exit east to 15th Ave., then north to Norton House or the complex. **From I-10:** Go to Seventh Ave. exit, then north to McDowell, then north to Norton House or the sports complex.

Sponsor: Valley Volkssport Association, 18 W. Louis Way, Tempe, AZ 85284

ARIZONA

SIERRA VISTA ◆ Desert Walk

Dates: January 1–December 31      David Breen (602) 378-1763

Description (2 +): You'll walk through high desert on this 13K walk with a 4,050-ft. elevation. The walk's rating could go higher during extreme heat, heavy rains or snows. Take in the vistas of the Huachuca and Mule mountains, and enjoy the mesquite trees, yucca, cacti and wildlife—coyotes, roadrunners, quail, and hawks.

See and Stay: Visit historic Fort Huachuca or Tombstone, where the famous O.K. Corral gunfight occurred. Veterans Memorial Park in Sierra Vista has playgrounds, a picnic area, and a public swimming pool, open Memorial Day through mid-August. Lodging in the area is reasonable—mostly under $40 for a double—but reservations are always advised. The Thunder Mountain Inn offers walkers a small discount.

☑ Wear jeans or slacks to protect your legs from tall grasses. The bottoms should be loose enough to roll up when you wade across the San Pedro River—the water could be from 1" to 8" deep. Dogs are allowed, but an outbreak of rabid skunks makes leashes and vaccinations a must. It gets hot out here. Bring plenty of water and sun protection, and pace yourself if you're not used to higher elevations.

Where Is It? Pick up your start card at the Thunder Mountain Inn, 1631 S. Hwy 92, (602) 458-7900, south of Sierra Vista. **From I-10:** Take Exit 302 (Fort Huachuca/Sierra Vista) and pick up Rt 90 through Whetstone and Huachuca City. Take the 90 bypass to the intersection with Rt 92 (fifth traffic light). Keep on Rt 92 to the next light. The inn will come up on your left. The walk starts at the San Pedro House, on Rt 90 east of Sierra Vista, at milepost 328. Do not park on Rt 90.

Sponsor: Thunder Mountain Trekkers, 3288 S. Sky Hawk Dr., Sierra Vista, AZ 85635

For more visitor information about Arizona, contact the Arizona Office of Tourism, 1100 W. Washington, Phoenix, AZ 85007, (602) 542-3618.

For information about recreation, such as fishing, hunting, camping, and state parks, contact the Arizona State Parks, 800 W. Washington St., Suite 415, Phoenix, AZ 85007.

☑ A new walk has been added in Tempe. This 12K residential walk starts at Tyke's World Toys & Play Center, 3136 S. McClintock. Call Steve Bartley for details, (602) 491-6017.

ARIZONA

TUCSON ♦ *Historic City Walk*

Dates: January 1–December 31   *Fred or Carolyn Barton (602) 298-4340*

Description (1): Entirely on paved sidewalks, this walk meanders through historic downtown and through the University of Arizona. The city is in a high desert valley, surrounded by four mountain ranges, and is hot from May through September.

See and Stay: Be sure to explore the Arizona State Museum. Its collections of Southwestern archeology are thought to be the most comprehensive in the world. Kids will enjoy the zoo or a ride on the stagecoach in Old Tucson. The Arizona-Sonora Desert Museum, 14 mi. west, exhibits over 200 animals and 300 types of desert plants. The Park Inn Hotel offers walkers a discount.

Where Is It? The walk starts at the Park Inn Hotel, 88 E. Broadway Blvd., (602) 622-4000. **From I-10:** Exit at Congress St. (Exit 258). Turn east into the downtown's center. Go about six traffic lights to Scott Ave. Turn right (south) and the Park Inn will be on your left.

Sponsor: Tucson Volkssport Klub, 270 S. Candlestick Dr., Tucson, AZ 85748

Twin saguaros in bloom in the desert outside Tucson. Photo by Dave Bean, courtesy Metropolitan Tucson Convention & Visitors Bureau.

ARKANSAS

PEA RIDGE ♦ *Country Walk*

Dates: January 2–December 31   *Radine Trees Nehring (501) 787-5930*

Description (1 +): This paved walk in rolling countryside takes you through woods and prairie restoration, and among wildflowers and wildlife, including herds of deer and many birds. One big hill requires strong effort if you're pushing a stroller. Audio recordings along the path tell visitors about the area.

See and Stay: Explore nearby Eureka Springs, a scenic town filled with historic buildings, quaint shops, and tourist attractions. The Traveler's Inn offers discounts off-season. The Battlefield Inn Motel and R.V. Park, (501) 451-1188, in nearby Garfield, is inexpensive, clean, and simple.

Hours: The park is open 8 A.M.- 5 P.M. daily.

☑ Summer visitors should protect against chiggers and ticks and watch for poison ivy. Bathrooms and water only at visitor center.

Where Is It? Pea Ridge National Military Park is on US 62, 10 mi. east of Rogers and 3 mi. west of Garfield. Pick up your start card at The Buss Stop, (501) 359-3430, on Hwy 62, 3 mi. east of the park entrance. Then drive to the walk's start at the park's visitor center and pick up your map. Visitors between 17 and 61 must pay a $1 entrance fee.

Sponsor: Ozark Hill Hikers, Rt. 1, Box 55, Gravette, AR 72736-9611

Open trails and woods beckon walkers near Pea Ridge. Photo by Cindy West.

7

CALIFORNIA

CARLSBAD ◆ City Walk
◆ Beach Park Walk

Dates: January 1–December 31   Irja and Lloyd Graham (619) 758-5667

Description (1 +): Enjoy the ocean views. The city walk follows along the beach and ambles into residential and city areas. The 14K walk looks down at wide-open beaches. You'll walk along old Hwy 101 and encounter two gradual hills and some rutted roadway.

See and Stay: Visit Camp Pendleton, one of the world's leading amphibious training camps. Visitor passes and tour brochures are available at the main gate. East of Oceanside, you'll find Mission San Luis Rey de Francia, one of the state's largest Spanish missions.

🚴 The walking club sponsors a 25K bike path to Encinitas. Bikes can be rented at Carlsbad Cyclery. Call (619) 434-5698 for bike rentals.

🐕 Dogs are not allowed on the beach or seawall. Walkers who would like company should call the Grahams and request a companion. Give about ten-days notice.

Where Is It? Start at the Carlsbad-by-the-Sea Retirement Home, 2855 Carlsbad Blvd., (619) 729-2377. **From I-5:** Take Carlsbad Village (Elm) exit and go west on Carlsbad Village to Carlsbad Blvd. Turn right on Carlsbad Blvd. and go 1 blk. north to Grand.

Sponsor: San Diego County Rockhoppers, 2592 Daily Dr., Fallbrook, CA 92028

CARMEL ◆ City Walk

Dates: January 1–December 31   Art Plummer (408) 384-0218

Description (2): See one of the state's earliest artist colonies on sidewalks and woodchip and dirt paths. At midpoint, you'll hit the beach—the water is cold, even in the summer.

Food and Fun: Catch breakfast at the Power Juice or sample the food in the Barnyard, a shopping and dining complex. Enjoy Carmel's atmosphere and varied architecture. Browse through the shops and galleries. Visit the Mission San Carlos Borromeo del Rio Carmelo, established in 1770, or Point Lobos State Reserve, where you'll find another 10K walk.

Hours: Walk between 7 A.M.–6 P.M.

Where Is It? Start at the Power Juice, (408) 626-6577, in the Crossroads shopping center on Rio Rd. **From Hwy 1 south:** Go to Rio Rd. and turn left onto Rio, then right into the shopping center. The Power Juice is in the row of buildings closest to Rio.

Sponsor: Monterey Peninsula Wanderfreunde, 484 Reindollar, Marina, CA 93933

CALIFORNIA

CITRUS HEIGHTS ♦ Three Town Walks

Dates: January–December 31    Ben or Berta Wilkes (707) 994-4135

Description (1+): These three different walks are on surfaced roads and trails with slight hills.

See and Stay: Citrus Heights is minutes away from Sacramento. Take another 10K walk there or explore the capitol and Old Sacramento on your own.

☑ This area can be hot in the summer, so plan to walk in the morning, if you can.

Hours: Mon.–Thurs., Sat. 10 A.M.–6 P.M.; Fri., 10 A.M.–8 P.M.; Sun. 12–5 P.M.

Where Is It? All the walks start at the SAS shoe store, 7175 Greenback Ln., located in the shopping center. **From I-80:** Exit on Greenback Ln. and go to the store. **From US 50:** Go north on Sunrise, then west on Greenback Ln. to the store.

Sponsor: Golden Bear Paw Prints, P.O. Box 2461, Clearlake, CA 95422-2461

CORONADO ♦ City Walk

Dates: January 1– December 31   Elizabeth Soderholm (619) 437-4454

Description (1): This 12K, mostly flat walk wanders through residential and business areas and takes you to a large park and along the beach.

Food and Fun: Take a 15-min. ferry ride. The San Diego-Coronado Ferry leaves from the Old Ferry Landing at B Ave. and First St. Call (619) 595-1490 for times. Tiffany's Deli and Juice Bar boasts the cheapest sandwiches in town.

☑ Dogs are not allowed on the beach. Parking is limited. Meters have a 2-hr. limit. Bathrooms are not available at the deli, but public restrooms are available on the route.

Hours: Daily between 9 A.M.–5 P.M. The deli is busiest 11:30 A.M.–1 P.M.

Where Is It? Start at Tiffany's Deli, 1120 Adella Ave., (619) 437-1368. **From I-5:** Take the Coronado-San Diego Bay Bridge (Hwy 75) to Coronado. There is a $1 toll for Coronado-bound cars. Cars with two or more persons, stay to the extreme right and pass straight through in the diamond lane. From the bridge, follow the main artery, which becomes Third St. Turn left onto Orange Ave., and go about 1.5 mi. At the light, turn left onto Adella.

Sponsor: San Diego County Rockhoppers, 2592 Daily Dr., Fallbrook, CA 92028

CALIFORNIA

FRESNO ◆ City Walk
◆ Fig Garden Walk

Dates: January 1–December 31   *Dennis Mast (209) 255-5965*

Description (1) (2): You've entered fig, grape, and cotton-growing country and the nation's biggest turkey-raising area. The city walk, with lots of rest rooms and water, is suitable for wheelchairs. The uneven garden walk offers restrooms and water only at the start/finish.

See and Stay: Visit the Fresno Art Museum or the Fresno Metropolitan Museum of Art, History and Science. Nearby Kearney Mansion Museum was the home of one of the country's agricultural pioneers, and Meux Home Museum on Tulare offers original Victorian furnishings. Kids will enjoy the zoo, rides, and Storyland in Roeding Park.

☑ Be prepared for hot, arid summer weather.

Where Is It? **The City Walk:** Start at the IHOP Restaurant, Tulare St. and T St. Traveling north on Hwy 99, take Hwy 41 east to Tulare exit. Turn left across freeway overpass and continue on Tulare to the IHOP on the left side. Traveling south on Hwy 99, take Fresno St. exit and turn left across overpass. Continue to R St. to Tulare. Turn left on Tulare to the IHOP. **The Fig Garden Walk:** Start at the San Joaquin Hotel, 1309 W. Shaw Ave. Traveling north on 99, take Hwy 41 east to the Shaw exit. Turn left and follow Shaw to the 1300 block. The hotel is on your left. Traveling south on Hwy 99, take the Shaw exit and go left across freeway and continue just past West Ave. The hotel will be on your right; park on the side streets.

Sponsor: Big Valley Vagabonds, 3212 E. Tenaya Ave., Fresno, CA 93710

The California Volkssport Association publishes *The Compass*, a 50-page quarterly listing year-round walks and many one-day walking events in California, Arizona, Nevada, and Hawaii, and updates and news about walking in these states. Contact Art Sederholm, 2592 Daily Drive, Fallbrook, CA 92028, (619) 728-1827 for information on how to receive this booklet.

CALIFORNIA

HOMEWOOD ♦ *Lake Tahoe Walk*

Dates: April 15–November 15 (seasonal)   *Barbara Currie (702) 831-0434*

Description(1): This 13K walk on recreational paths and roads will take you along Lake Tahoe and the Truckee River, with views of the Sierra Nevada Mountains. You'll be at an elevation of 6,300 ft., with no significant climb on the route. The walk's sponsors say the path is suitable for wheelchairs.

See and Stay: The area offers camping, fishing, and hiking in the summer. Contact the Lake Tahoe Basin Management Unit, (916) 573-2600, for information. The Heavenly Valley Tram, at the top of Ski Run Blvd., offers a tram ride 2,000 ft. above the lake; several companies offer lake cruises.

Hours: Daily 8 A.M.–5 P.M.

🚲 This club sponsors a 32K or 45K bike path. Bike rentals available.

Where Is It? Start at Tahoe Gear, 5095 W. Lake Blvd. (Hwy 89).
From I-80: Take Hwy 89 to Tahoe City and continue 6 mi. south.
From Hwy 50 (South Lake Tahoe): Take Hwy 89 north for 27 mi. The shop is on the west side, with parking north of the building.

Sponsor: Sierra Nevada Striders, P.O. Box 4344, Incline Village, NV 89450-4344

Named "Big Water" by the Washoe Indians, Lake Tahoe creates a scenic backdrop for walkers. Photo by Richard M. Frieders, courtesy of the Tahoe North Visitors & Convention Bureau.

CALIFORNIA

JACKSON ♦ *Two Town Walks*

Dates: January 1–December 31 Dorothy Williamson (209) 223-3748

Description (1 +) (2): These walks, one 11K with a few small hills and the other 10K with a 15K option, will take you on mostly paved trails with some dirt and gravel. You'll go by parks, historical sites, residential areas, antique shops, and many restaurants.

See and Stay: The Amador County Museum, 225 Church St., features a working scale model of the Kennedy Gold Mine. If you'd like another walk, try the 10K walk in Sutter Creek. The Best Western-Amador Inn gives discounts to walkers.

☑ This area can be hot in the summer, so walk in the morning if you can.

Where Is It? Start at the Best Western, on 200 S. Hwy 49, (800) 543-5221. **From the south:** Take Hwy 88 northeast from Stockton. At Jackson, it joins with Hwy 49 going southeast. **From the north:** Take Hwy 16 east from Sacramento, then Hwy 49 southeast. **From Placerville:** Take Hwy 49 south. The motel is on Main St., where Hwys 49 and 88 separate.

Sponsor: Golden Bear Paw Prints, P.O. Box 2461, Clearlake, CA 95422-2461

LOS GATOS ♦ *Shaded City Walk*

Dates: January 1–December 31 Edith McCoy (408) 264-3280

Description (1 +): You'll encounter a few short hills on this paved walk through Los Gatos, named for the many mountain lions that once inhabited the nearby hills. Restrooms are available on the route and at the motel, only if one of its rooms is vacant at the time.

See and Stay: The Los Gatos Museum has art, science, and nature displays. Oak Meadow Park, at University Ave. and Blossom Hill Rd., houses the Billy Jones Wildcat Railroad and Old Town, with its restored Spanish and Victorian buildings, gardens, shops, and restaurants.

Hours: Start no earlier than 8 A.M.

🚲 The club sponsors a 25K bike path along Los Gatos Creek. Start at Los Gatos Cyclery, (408) 356-1644. No bike rentals.

Where Is It? Start at the Garden Inn Motel, 46 E. Main St., (408) 354-6446. **From Hwy 280 or 101:** Take the Hwy 17 turnoff toward Santa Cruz. Take the Los Gatos-Saratoga exit. Turn left at University Ave. and follow to Main. Turn left on Main; the inn is on the right.

Sponsor: South Bay Striders, 15540 La Pala Ct., Morgan Hill, CA 95037

CALIFORNIA

MILL VALLEY ♦ *Quaint Town Walk*

Dates: January 1–December 31 Bob Glasson (415) 457-1073

Description (2): This walk takes you through this popular tourist town with its lovely homes, woods, and interesting shops. Two hills and a relatively steep downgrade offer some challenge.

See and Stay: Browse through Mill Valley or take the Sausalito walk, which also starts at the recreation center. The Muir Woods National Monument, a 500-acre preserve for the magnificent redwoods, is just off Hwy 1. Visit Mount Tamalpais State Park; a walk to the half-mile summit gives spectacular views of Marin County and the San Francisco Bay area.

☑ Glasson says he would be happy to accompany walkers and serve as a "docent," if you give him some notice. Be prepared for cool, foggy weather, and bring your rain slicker.

Hours: Mon.-Fri., 9 A.M.–5 P.M. Closed Sat. and Sun.

Where Is It? This walk starts at the Mill Valley Parks & Recreation Dept., 180 Camino Alto. **From Hwy 101 north:** Take the Tiburon/Belvedere (131), East Blithedale Ave. exit. Turn right on East Blithedale and go 2 blks. to Camino Alto. Turn left on Camino Alto and go about 1 blk. Turn left into the recreation department's lot. **From Hwy 101 south:** Take the same exit, only turn left at East Blithedale and continue to Camino Alto.

Sponsor: Bay Bandits Volksmarch Club, 59 Convent Ct., San Rafael, CA 94901

MOKELUMNE HILL ♦ *Town Walk*

Dates: January 1–December 31 Dorothy Williamson (209) 274-4339

Description (2+): This walk is on mostly paved paths with some dirt and gravel. There are several short, steep hills. You'll go by parks, historical sites, homes, and a few restaurants.

See and Stay: Try the two walks in Jackson or the walk in Sutter Creek. The Best Western gives discounts to walkers.

Where Is It? Start at the Best Western, 200 S. Hwy 49, (800) 543-5221. **From the south:** Take Hwy 88 northeast from Stockton. At Jackson it joins with Hwy 49 going southeast. **From the north:** Take Hwy 16 east from Sacramento, then Hwy 49 southeast. **From Placerville:** Take Hwy 49 south. The motel is on Main St. where Hwys 49 and 88 separate.

Sponsor: Golden Bear Paw Prints, P.O. Box 2461, Clearlake, CA 95422-2461

13

CALIFORNIA

MONTEREY ◆ City Walk

Dates: January 1–December 31　　　　 Art Plummer (408) 384-0218

Description (1): You'll walk mostly on sidewalks in this picturesque, historic city along the Big Sur coast.

See and Stay: Browse through "Cannery Row" of John Steinbeck fame and visit the galleries and restaurants that have replaced the fish canneries. Visit the Monterey Bay Aquarium, one of the largest in the world, with nearly 600 species in 23 major habitat areas, and a variety of exhibits and aviary. The Monterey State Historic Park offers a seven-acre site of restored buildings that preserve the heritage of old Monterey. You can also visit Carmel and enjoy another walk.

Hours: Daily 9 A.M.–5 P.M.

🚲 This club sponsors a 25K bike path on the Monterey Recreation Trail.

Where Is It? Start at the La Casa Bodega Deli & General Store, 500 Del Monte Ave. **From Hwy 1 South:** Take the Pacific Grove/Del Monte exit toward Fisherman's Wharf. The deli is across from the wharf parking lot. Park on the streets or in nearby lots.

Sponsor: Monterey Peninsula Wanderfreunde, 484 Reindollar, Marina, CA 93933

> The Monterey club hosts a guided walk almost every Sunday, starting at 8:30 A.M., at one of the many lovely spots in the Monterey Bay area. If you're an AVA walker, each walk counts as a separate event. All walkers are welcome. Contact Plummer for each walk's start point.

Walkers enjoy Monterey's Fisherman's Wharf. Photo by Martin Brown, courtesy of the Monterey Peninsula Chamber of Commerce.

CALIFORNIA

MORGAN HILL ◆ City Walk

Dates: January 1–December 31    *Diane or Harold LeGore (408) 779-5013*

Description (1+): This route along shaded residential streets with some sidewalks will wind you down country roads and past historical landmarks. Before the 1700s, this area was home to the Costanoan Indians; the town eventually developed around the Morgan Hill Ranch, a wealthy spread of the late 1800s.

See and Stay: Visit the Wagons to Wings Museum, 15060 Foothill Rd., and see displays of wagons, stagecoaches, and surreys, as well as airplanes, helicopters, and many one-of-a-kind vehicles.

☑ Carry water. No water or restrooms are available at the start/finish, but there are several fast food restaurants near the start of the walk.

Hours: Mon.-Fri., 8:30 A.M.–8 P.M.; Sat., 9:30 A.M.–5:30 P.M.; Sun., 11 A.M.–5 P.M.

Where Is It? Start at Jody's Junction Stationers, 236 Tennant Station, (408) 778-2060. **From Hwy 101:** Take the Tennant Ave. exit, and turn west toward town. After crossing the railroad tracks, turn left at the light at Vineyard Ave. The road curves to the right. Jody's will be on your right in the second group of buildings before you reach the next light.

Sponsor: South Bay Striders, 15540 La Pala Ct., Morgan Hill, CA 95037

If you plan to walk for credit or an award, please note that most of the California walking clubs prefer you pay by check. Those that accept cash ask that you have exact change.

15

CALIFORNIA

NEWHALL ♦ Placerita Canyon Walk

Dates: January 2–December 31    Nature Center (805) 259-7721

Description (2-3): This dirt and rock trail is generally stream gradient with no steep climb. Walkers should not plan to push or pull any strollers or wagons.

See and Stay: If you want some lively entertainment, go to nearby Santa Clarita, which offers Six Flags Magic Mountain, just west of I-5 at 26101 Magic Mountain Pkwy. This 260-acre entertainment complex has more than 100 rides, shows and attractions.

☑ Because of budget cuts, please call Placerita Canyon Nature Center, (805) 259-7721, to confirm hours on dates you want to walk. **Stay on the trails at all times**—poison oak grows profusely along the canyon, and rattlesnakes, though not numerous, are out there. No food available at or near the park. Smoking not permitted on the trails.

Where Is It? Start at the Placerita Canyon Nature Center, 19152 Placerita Canyon Rd. **From I-5:** Take Antelope Valley Fwy (14) toward Palmdale. Look for nature center signs on Antelope Valley Rd.

Sponsor: Hollywood Star Trekkers, 43504 Carol Dr., Lancaster, CA 93535

POINT LOBOS ♦ State Park Walk

Dates: January 1–December 31   Art Plummer (408) 384-0218

Description (3): This walk, primarily on dirt paths, wanders through some of the 1,325 acres of rugged seacoast of the Point Lobos State Reserve. The reserve has a variety of wildlife and sea birds. Half of this reserve is underwater, and harbor seals, gray whales, and the California sea lion and sea otter visit frequently. Save some energy for the flight of 63 steps on the South Shore Trail.

See and Stay: Visit the Monterey Bay Aquarium, with nearly 600 species in 23 habitat areas and an aviary. The Monterey State Historic Park offers a seven-acre site of restored buildings that preserve the heritage of old Monterey. Visit Carmel and enjoy another 10K walk.

☑ Dogs not allowed. Watch for poison ivy and oak. Allow plenty of time to finish before the park closes.

Hours: Walk between 9 A.M. and 5 P.M.

Where is it? Check in at the Power Juice in the Crossroads Shopping Center on Rio Rd.; from there drive to the state park entrance. **From Hwy 1 south:** Go to Rio Rd.; turn left and then right into the shopping center. Power Juice is in the row of buildings closest to Rio Rd.

Sponsor: Monterey Peninsula Wanderfreunde, 484 Reindollar, Marina, CA 93933

CALIFORNIA

REDDING ♦ *Downtown Walk*
♦ *River Walk*

Dates: January 1–December 31   *Beverly Severance (916) 275-2793*

Description (1): The 11K town walk goes through downtown, including the enclosed Downtown Mall and residential streets. The 10K river walk follows the Sacramento River Trail along the south and north river banks and passes over the new suspension bridge. There are some moderate hills on these walks, but the walk's sponsor says both walks are suitable for wheelchairs.

See and Stay: North and west of Redding, visit Whiskeytown-Shasta-Trinity National Recreation Area and pan for gold at Whiskeytown Lake area. Mount Shasta, a dormant volcano with five living glaciers, is in nearby Shasta-Trinity National Forest, covering more than 2.1 million acres. For park reservations call (800) 283-2267.

☑ Summer temperatures can soar close to 120°, so carry water. Beverage and rest stops available along town walk, and water and bathrooms are in two locations along the river walk.

Where Is It? Start at the lab at Mercy Medical Center, Airpark Dr. *From I-5:* Take the Central Redding-Eureka-299 West exit. When 299 ends, continue west on Shasta St. for 7 blks. Turn left at the light at Court St. Continue south for 11 blks., then turn right on Rosaline Ave. and go up the hill. Turn left on Airpark, and follow signs to medical center. Park in the lot or garage. Follow signs to main entrance and ask at the desk for directions to the lab. Please do not phone the hospital. If you're taking the river walk, you'll leave the medical center and drive 2.2 mi. to the start point.

Sponsor: Redding Road Ramblers, 18251 Ranchera Rd., Redding, CA 96003

CALIFORNIA

REDONDO BEACH ♦ *Two King Harbor Walks*

Dates: January 1–December 31   *John and Kathy Shirtz (805) 942-7075*

Description(1): Both walks offer ocean views and city streets. One walk goes along city streets to the Palos Verdes peninsula, coming back along the beach on a paved strand through the Redondo Beach Pier. The second walk goes along the beach on a paved strand to the Manhattan Beach Pier and returns through streets and a walking trail.

Food and Fun: Sample the seafood at the Redondo Beach Pier restaurants or wander down to the International Boardwalk's souvenir shops, amusement center, and fresh fish markets.

Where Is It? Start at the Best Western Sunrise Hotel, King Harbor Marina, 400 N. Harbor Dr. **From the north:** Exit Fwy 405 on either Rosecrans or Artesia Blvd. **From the south:** Exit 405 on Artesia Blvd. Go west on Rosecrans or Artesia to Aviation Blvd. Turn left (south) on Aviation to Pacific Coast Hwy (Sepulveda). Turn left here and go to Herondo. Turn right on Herondo, then left on Harbor Dr. Park behind the hotel, and use the back door to reach the registration desk.

Sponsor: Hollywood Star Trekkers, 43504 Carol Dr., Lancaster, CA 95820

SACRAMENTO ♦ *Capital Walk*

Dates: January 1–December 31   *Del Ebeling (916) 432-0580*

Description (1): Explore the historic and downtown sections of the capital on this 11K walk along mostly flat, paved sidewalks and a piece of recreational trail.

See and Stay: Enjoy the capitol grounds, complete with gardens, orange trees, fish pond, and squirrels. Explore Old Sacramento, redeveloped with museums, restaurants and shops, and ride the *Spirit of Sacramento*, a historic, 110-ft. paddlewheeler departing from the L St. landing for 1-hr. sightseeing cruises. The Sandman Motel offers a walkers' discount.

🚲 This walking club sponsors 30K and 52K bike paths that mostly follow the American River Bike Trail. Check in at the Sandman Motel.

Where Is It? Start at the Sandman Motel, 236 Jibboom, near I-5 and Richards Blvd. **From I-5 north:** Take the Richards Blvd. exit and turn right onto Jibboom. Go to the motel. **From I-5 south:** Take the Richards Blvd. exit and turn left onto Jibboom. Free parking next to motel.

Sponsor: California Volkssport Association, 2592 Daily Dr., Fallbrook, CA 92028

18

CALIFORNIA

SAN JOSE ♦ Downtown Walk

Dates: January 1–December 31   Del or Gretchen Sparks (408) 997-1686

Description (1): This level walk on city streets goes through San Jose State University.

Food and Fun: The San Jose Flea Market covers 120 acres and features thousands of booths and 35 restaurants. Open Wed.–Sun., dawn to dusk. Kids will enjoy the Children's Discovery Museum, at Woz Way and Auzerais St., and Happy Hollow, 1300 Senter Rd., a family park with playground, treehouse, rides and a zoo. Also nearby on Senter, the San Jose Historical Museum has 21 original and restored Victorian buildings.

Hours: No earlier than 8 A.M. Bathrooms at start/finish and checkpoint only with purchase.

☑ Pets are discouraged because this is entirely a city walk.

Where Is It? Go to the Best Western Inn, 455 S. Second St., (408) 298-3500. **From Hwy 17:** Take the First St. exit and go south until you must turn right. Go right 1 blk. and turn left on Market St. Stay on Market to Williams St. and turn left. Go left onto First St. The inn will be on the right side. **From Hwy 280:** Take the Bird Ave. exit and go north. Turn right at San Carlos and proceed to Market. Turn right at Market and go 2 blks. to Williams. Turn left. Go left again on First. Park in lot or on city streets.

Sponsor: South Bay Striders, 15540 La Pala Ct., Morgan Hill, CA 95037

SAN LUIS OBISPO ♦ City Walk

Dates: January 1–December 31   Ed Ritchie (805) 937-4719

Description (1): This mostly paved walk has slight hills and includes historical, residential, and downtown areas with many interesting shops.

See and Stay: Visit Mission San Luis Obispo de Tolosa at Chorro and Monterey Sts. Often called the "Prince of Missions," this 1772 mission is now a parish church. The museum houses Chumash Indian artifacts and items from the early settlers.

Where Is It? Start at the Cuesta Canyon Lodge, 1800 Monterey St., (800) 822-8601. **Going north on US 101:** Take the Grand Ave. exit and turn right. The motel is on the corner of Grand and Monterey. **Going south on US 101:** Take Monterey exit. The motel will be on your right.

Sponsor: Big Valley Vagabonds, 3212 E. Tenaya Ave., Fresno, CA 93710

CALIFORNIA

SAN PEDRO ◆ Coastal Walk
◆ Shoppers Walk

Dates: January 1–December 31  Mike Logan (310) 548-4690

Description (2): Shoppers will enjoy the 11K walk that goes to Ports O' Village on the main channel of Los Angeles Harbor. The other 11K walk goes through coastal residential areas, Point Fermin Park, and Old Fort MacArthur.

See and Stay: Explore the harbor area. The Cabrillo Marine Museum specializes in marine life of Southern California and includes 38 seawater aquariums. The Los Angeles Maritime Museum displays scale models of the Queen Mary and the Titanic. Jump on a life-size boat and take one of the harbor cruises departing from the Village Boat House.

Hours: Daily after 9:30 A.M. Finish Mon.–Thurs. by 8 P.M., Fri. by 7, and weekends by 5.

Where Are They? Start at Marathom's Running Shop, in the Von's Shopping Center, 1424 W. 25th St. **From the north:** Take 405 south to the 110 (Harbor) Fwy. Go west on 110 to San Pedro. At the freeway's end, turn left on Gaffey. Turn right on 25th. Von's is on your right. **From the south:** Take the 405 north to the 110. Go west on the 110 to San Pedro and follow directions above.

Sponsor: Hollywood Star Trekkers, 43504 Carol Dr., Lancaster, CA 95820

Palm trees jut against the skyline on San Pedro's coastal walk. Photo by Laurie Wood.

CALIFORNIA

SAUSALITO ♦ *Quaint Village Walk*

Dates: January 1–December 31   Bob Glasson (415) 457-1073

Description (1): This 12K walk meanders through this tourist mecca, complete with spectacular views of San Francisco and the Golden Gate Bridge.

See and Stay: Visit one of Sausalito's many excellent restaurants, poke around in a shopper's paradise, or take the Mill Valley walk, which also starts at the recreation desk. San Francisco and Muir Woods National Monument are minutes away.

☑ Glasson says he would be happy to accompany walkers and serve as a "docent," if you give him advance notice. Be prepared for cool, foggy weather, and bring your rain slicker.

Hours: Mon.–Fri., 8 A.M.–5 P.M. Closed Saturday and Sunday.

Where Is It? Start at the Mill Valley Parks & Recreation Dept., 180 Camino Alto. **From Hwy 101 north:** Take the Tiburon/Belvedere (131), East Blithedale Ave. exit. Turn right on East Blithedale and go 2 blks. to Camino Alto. Turn left on Camino Alto and go about 1 blk. Turn left into the recreation department's lot. **From Hwy 101 south:** Take the same exit, only turn left at East Blithedale and continue to Camino Alto.

Sponsor: Bay Bandits Volksmarch Club, 59 Convent Ct., San Rafael, CA 94901

STOCKTON ♦ *City Walk*

Dates: January 2–December 31   Eveline Martin (209) 477-6131

Description (1): This seaport offers a walk mostly on sidewalks and pavement through residential and business areas and a park.

Food and Fun: Archie's offers walkers a 10% discount. Just show your start card or AVA books. Kids will enjoy the zoos at Micke Grove Regional Park in Lodi or Pixie Woods Wonderland in Louis Park, offering rides and sets from popular children's stories.

Where Is It? Start at Archie's, 1304 E. Hammer Ln. **From Hwy 99:** Exit on Hammer and go west to West Ln. Turn left on West Ln., then right on the first street (no street sign). Turn right again at the stop sign (Kathleen). Archie's is on the right in the shopping area on the corner of Hammer and West Ln. **From Hwy 5:** Exit on Hammer and drive east to Kathleen and turn right. Archie's is on the left. Do not park right in front of Archie's, but in the outer rows, along the street, or in Kaiser Permanente's lot.

Sponsor: Delta Tule Trekkers, 2022 Vada Way, Stockton, CA 95210

CALIFORNIA

SUTTER CREEK ♦ City Walk

Dates: January 1–December 31   Elizabeth Payne (916) 486-8687

Description (2 +): This walk will take you past historic buildings, shops and restaurants. The trail includes a significant hill and some narrow paths along the highway.

Food and Fun: The Gold Quartz Inn, an elegant getaway, has generous breakfasts, afternoon teas, and a 10% discount for walkers. While on the route, you'll have a checkpoint at Ja-Ba-Do-Da's Eatery, offering refreshments and great food.

☑ Summers can be hot, so start in the morning, if you can.

Hours: Daily between 8 A.M.–5 P.M.

Where Is It? This walk starts at the Gold Quartz Inn, 15 Bryson Dr., (209) 267-9155. **From Sacramento:** Take Hwy 16 east to the Hwy 49 cutoff. Continue south on Hwy 49 to Sutter Creek. The inn is on the extreme south end of Sutter Creek, 1 blk. east of Hwy 49 on Bryson Dr. Please park on the street unless you are staying at the inn.

Sponsor: Worldwide Volkssport Tours, P.O. Box 660931, Sacramento, CA 95866

VACAVILLE ♦ City Walk

Dates: January 1–December 31   Ruth Redd (707) 429-1899

Description (1): This easy walk on sidewalks and pavement will take you past shops and residential areas. Watch for the jack rabbits in the Leisure Town housing area.

Food and Fun: Visit the Vacaville Museum displaying historical artifacts from Solano County and an interpretive garden of native plants. The Nut Tree Factory Outlet of stores is on the route, but you might want to return after your walk. The famous Nut Tree Restaurant offers good food and pleasant grounds for a short stroll.

☑ Summer afternoons can be hot, so walk in the morning or early evening, if you can.

Where Is It? Start this walk by the file cabinet in the main lobby of the Vaca Valley Hospital, 1000 Nut Tree Rd. **From east I-80:** Take the Mason St./Travis AFB exit and turn right at first light onto Elmira Rd. Continue to Nut Tree Rd. Turn left at Nut Tree and continue 2 blks. Hospital is on the right. **From west I-80:** Take the Peabody Rd./Elmira exit. Turn left at light. Turn right at next light onto Elmira and follow directions above.

Sponsor: Vaca Valley Volks, 848 Stonegate Ct., Vacaville, CA 95687

YUBA CITY ♦ Two City Walks

Dates: January 1–December 31   Duane Spence (916) 671-1444

Description (1): Yuba City, the marketing center for this agricultural area, offers two level, paved walks that will take you through residential and business areas. One of the walks is 10K, the other 11K.

Food and Fun: Birders will enjoy a visit to the Gray Lodge Refuge, 15 mi. northwest off Hwy 99. This 8,400-acre refuge is a stopover on the Pacific flyway and the nesting grounds for dove, pheasant, coot, and hawk. Depending on the season, enjoy the locally produced tomatoes, almonds, walnuts, pistachios, apricots, and kiwis.

Hours: Start no earlier than 8 A.M.

Where Are They? Start at the Bonanza Inn (Best Western), 1001 Clark Ave., (916) 674-8824. **From Sacramento:** Go 43 mi. north on Hwy 99. **From Williams:** On I-5, go 33 mi. east on Hwy 20. The inn is located .5 mi. east of the intersection of Hwys 20 and 99.

Sponsor: California Camel Clompers, P.O. Box 5223, Marysville, CA 95901

COLORADO

AURORA ♦ City Walk

Dates: January 1–December 31   Mary Humphrey (303) 690-9601

Description (1 or 1+): This paved city walk offers three return options back to the start—a path along the Highline Canal, the Sixth Ave. Bike Trail, or a path past the golf course. A more accessible option for people in wheelchairs is available. You might see prairie dogs.

Food and Fun: The Aurora History Museum, which is the checkpoint, offers free passes to walkers, and Helga's Deli offers good food.

Hours: Mon., 8 A.M.–6 P.M., Tues.-Fri., 8 A.M.–9 P.M.; Sat., 9 A.M.–9 P.M. Closed Sundays. Try not to start weekdays during busy lunchtime. Finish by dark; the path is unlit.

Where Is It? Start at Helga's German Delicatessen, 728 Peoria St., (303) 344-5488. **From I-225:** Take Exit 9 (Sixth Ave.), turn right onto Peoria St., then right into Hoffman Heights Shopping Village. **From I-70:** Take Exit 281 (Peoria St.) and go 3 mi. south. Turn left into the shopping village. Helga's is on the north side toward the east end.

Sponsor: Rocky Mountain Wanderers, 346 S. Xapary St., Aurora, CO 80012

CAÑON CITY ♦ Arkansas River Walk

Dates: January 1–December 31   Wendy King (719) 942-4394

Description (3): This 11K maintained dirt trail, with moderate hills, follows along the Arkansas River, which begins its 1,900-mi. run to the Mississippi River from here.

See and Stay: Rising 1,053 ft. above the river, the Royal Gorge Bridge, 8 mi. west of town, is said to be the world's highest suspension bridge. Take the incline railway to the bottom of the gorge or the aerial tram across the canyon.

Hours: Start between 7 A.M. and noon; finish by 4 P.M.

☑ Water is only available at the start point.

Where Is It? The walk starts at the Best Western Royal Gorge Motel, 1925 Fremont Dr., Cañon City, (800) 231-7317, or (719) 275-3377. **From the east:** Follow U.S. 50 into Cañon City. You'll pass a Wal-Mart and Burger King on your right, then come to Orchard St. Turn right and then immediately left onto the frontage road. The motel will be on your right.

Sponsor: Falcon Wanderers, P.O. Box 17162, Colorado Springs, CO 80935

COLORADO SPRINGS ♦ Bear Creek Regional ♦ Park Walk

Dates: March 2–November 30 (seasonal) *Pat Gray (719) 684-9462*

Description (3+): This 11K walk on dirt, foot, and horse paths has three significant hills. The park has deer, foxes, birds, rabbits, wildflowers, beautiful shrubs and trees, and a creek.

See and Stay: Enjoy the sightseeing opportunities: the U.S. Air Force Academy, Pikes Peak, Garden of the Gods, Cave of the Winds, Cheyenne Mountain Zoo, and museums.

☑ No dogs. Rain and snow make the trail muddy. Carry water.

Hours: Tues.-Sat., start 9 A.M.–1 P.M.; finish by 4 P.M. Closed Sun. and Mon.

🚴 The walking club sponsors a 25K bike path. Call Gray for details and directions.

Where Is It? The walk starts at Bear Creek Nature Center, (719) 520-6387. **From I-25:** Take Exit 141. At the end of the exit ramp, turn left on Hwy 24 toward the mountains and drive 2 mi. to 26th St. Turn left and drive 1.5 mi. to the center.

Sponsor: Falcon Wanderers, P.O. Box 17162, Colorado Springs, CO 80935

COLORADO SPRINGS ♦ Monument Valley Walk

Dates: January 1–December 31 *Marcile Riber (719) 633-8971*

Description (1+) Dirt trails will wind you through the park, and sidewalks will lead you through the residential areas on this city walk.

See and Stay: Linger in Colorado Springs, where you'll find much to explore. Tour McAllister House, which you'll pass on your walk.

Hours: Mon.-Sat., 9 A.M.–6 P.M.; Sun., 11 A.M.–5 P.M.

Where Is It? Start at the Mountain Chalet, 226 N. Tejon. **From I-25:** Take Exit 142 (Bijou) and go east. At Cascade Ave. turn left. Go to Platte Ave. and turn right. Tejon is the next street. Turn right; the chalet will be on your right. **From US 24 West:** US 24 becomes Platte. When 24 turns south, stay on Platte. Turn left at Tejon; the chalet is on your right. Street parking available within a couple of blocks.

Sponsor: Falcon Wanderers, P.O. Box 17162, Colorado Springs, CO 80935

COLORADO

CREEDE ♦ *Four Mountain Walks*

Dates: June 12– September 26 (seasonal)   B. J. Myers (719) 658-2736

Description (3 and 5): These mountain-setting walks are becoming well-known for absolute beauty in an isolated setting. Creede is the only town in Mineral County, which boasts a population of 560 people. The elevation is over 8,000 ft., and 95% of the county is national forest public access land. The altitude and uneven dirt surfaces make these walks more strenuous than some.

Miners Creek: This path follows a mining road to a little beyond the Boy Scout Camp and retraces its path for the return. Walk starts at 8,850 ft. and tops out at 9,300 ft.

Shallow Creek: Standing in a mountain meadow, you'll take in views of the Upper Rio Grande Valley—the headwaters of the Rio Grande are about 30 mi. above Creede. The path then goes along Shallow Creek, through aspen groves and past beaver ponds.

Phoenix Park: As this trail breaks out of the woods, you'll pass active beaver ponds and two waterfalls. This walk starts at 9,960 ft. and the first quarter is an uphill grade.

East Willow Creek Canyon: This walk, on all dirt roads, is relatively easy, with no steep grades. If you're hearty, you may be able to push a wheelchair or carriage. Use your judgment.

See and Stay: The discovery of silver in the 1890s brought Creede to life. Today visitors come to enjoy the town's mining heritage, historical tours, museums, and shopping. More than 10,000 people see summer productions by the Creede Repertory Theatre. Guest ranches, B&Bs, RV parks, campsites, and motel/hotels provide varied lodging. The Creede-Mineral County Chamber of Commerce, P.O. Box 580, Creede, CO 81130, or (800) 327-2102, mails tourist information on request.

Hours: Daily start between 10 A.M. and noon; finish by 4 P.M. You can arrange to start earlier or finish later by contacting the Abbey Lane Gallery in advance.

☑ **Do not drink the water from the streams.** Giardia, an intestinal parasite that affects people but not pets, has become common in this area. Carry your own water. Rest rooms are available at the city park or at the Abbey Lane Gallery, but only natural pit stops are available on the trails. The gallery keeps good track of walkers to make sure they check in.

Where Is It? Pick up your start cards for these walks at the Abbey Lane Gallery, (719) 658-2736, the last shop on the left, across from the repertory theatre on the main street. You'll be given directions on where to go to start each walk. Creede is in southwestern Colorado on CO Hwy 149, a National Scenic Byway. Hwy 149 intersects with US 160, the main highway connecting I-25 and Durango.

Sponsor: Upper Rio Grande Mountain Walkers, P.O. Box 272, Creede, CO 81130

COLORADO

Spectacular mountain views make the Creede walks popular. Photo by Lucille Buchanan.

Denver has a year-round walk from January 1 to December 31. If you'd like to walk in Denver, call John Burden, (303) 972-9296, for directions to the start point, or write the Rocky Mountain Wanderers, 10118 W. Roxbury Ave., Littleton, CO 80127, and request a brochure on the walk. Be sure to include a self-addressed, stamped envelope with your request.

COLORADO

EVERGREEN ♦ *Elk Meadow Park Walk*

Dates: January 1–December 31   *Kathleen Finley (303) 233-7338*

Description(3): Walk at an altitude of 7,800 ft. in an area surrounded by the Denver Mountain Park System. Enjoy the wildflowers, birds, and magnificent scenery.

See and Stay: Enjoy Evergreen Lake, a 55-acre reservoir offering fishing, boating, and golfing. Visit Hiwan Homestead Museum, a 17-room log lodge known for its twin octagonal towers. Kids will enjoy the hands-on exhibit of 1930s radios.

☑ No water on the trail.

Hours: The store is usually open seven days a week, but hours are seasonal. Call (303) 670-0092 for correct hours on the day you want to walk.

Where Is It? Start at Paragon Sports, 2962 Hwy 74, just south of Pizza Hut. **From I-70:** Take the Evergreen/El Rancho Exit (Hwy 74), through Bergen Park. Turn left at stoplight, Lewis Ridge Rd., and right on frontage road. Paragon is on the hill above the parking lot.

Sponsor: Lakewood on Parade Walkers, 8231 W. 14th Ave., Lakewood, CO 80215

GRAND LAKE ♦ *Mountain Hamlet Walk*

Dates: May 31–September 30 (seasonal)   *George or Lore Lawrence (303) 627-8513*

Description (3+): This 12K walk at high altitude has some dirt and gravel trails. This walk offers mountain majesty, unsurpassed beauty, and abundant wildlife.

See and Stay: Grand Lake offers ample sightseeing, shopping, restaurants, and lodging. Visitors may also enjoy many outdoor activities and Rocky Mountain National Park. The Hideaway Motel, (303) 627-8513, offers a 20% discount for walkers.

Hours: Start daily between 9 A.M. and 1 P.M.; finish by 5 P.M.

☑ After a wet spring, ticks are possible. Walk includes 3 mi. of walking along the shoulder.

Where Is It? Start at the Grand Lake Chamber of Commerce at the intersection of Hwy 34 and Grand, (303) 627-3402. **From Denver on I-70:** Take Exit 232. Go north on US 40 over Berthoud Pass to Granby. At the west end of Granby, 40 and Hwy 34 intersect. Take Hwy 34 north to Grand Lake. **From Denver on I-25:** Exit at Loveland, then take Hwy 34 to Estes Park and on to the west entrance of Rocky Mountain National Park and Grand Lake.

Sponsor: Rocky Mountain Wanderers, 10118 W. Roxbury Ave., Littleton, CO 80127

COLORADO

GREEN MOUNTAIN FALLS ♦ Town Walk

Dates: March 13–December 4 *(seasonal)*   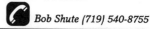 Bob Shute *(719) 540-8755*

Description *(3 +):* This 11K trail, with significant hills, meanders through this mountain community, passing shops and restaurants.

See and Stay: Green Mountain Falls and nearby Colorado Springs are popular tourist areas and offer a variety of sightseeing, shopping, restaurants, and lodging.

☑ Dogs are welcome on the walk, but a strict leash law is enforced.

Hours: Start daily between 8 A.M.–1 P.M.; finish by 5 P.M.

Where Is It? The walk starts at The Market, (719) 684-9874, 10398 Ute Pass Ave. **From Colorado Springs:** Take Exit 141 off I-25 to US 24 West. Follow 24 up Ute Pass to the first Green Mountain Falls exit. The Market is on the right at the four-way stop sign.

Sponsor: Falcon Wanderers, P.O. Box 17162, Colorado Springs, CO 80935

MANITOU SPRINGS ♦ Town Walk

Dates: January 1–December 31   Jo Marner *(719) 685-9727*

Description *(3):* Tucked in the valley against the mountains, Manitou offers a picturesque, but hilly, residential walk at an altitude of 7,000 ft. Many of its older homes look like European castles.

See and Stay: Winding, narrow lanes and an array of quaint shops, restaurants, and interesting lodgings make Manitou a fun stopover. Many of its historic homes are now B & Bs and good restaurants. From May to October, the Pikes Peak Cog Railway leaves from 515 Ruxton Ave. for a 3-hr round-trip journey to Pikes Peak. Children also will enjoy the parks, swimming pool, and museums.

Hours: The store is open 9 A.M.–9 P.M. in the summer and 10 A.M.– 6 P.M. in the winter. Walk during daylight hours before the store closes. In the winter, mountain shadows bring early darkness, so be off the trail by 3 P.M.

Where Is It? This walk starts at Park Place Mall, 733 Manitou Ave., (719) 685-9727. **From I-25:** Take Exit 141 (Hwy 24) and go west. Exit at the Historic Manitou Springs sign and follow Manitou Ave. into town. **From eastbound Hwy 24:** Take the first Manitou exit.

Sponsor: Falcon Wanderers, P.O. Box 17162, Colorado Springs, CO 80935

COLORADO

MANITOU SPRINGS ◆ Garden of the Gods Walk

Dates: January 1–December 31   📞 Jo Marner (719) 685-9727

Description (3): Meander past massive, red sandstone formations in this 940-acre Garden of the Gods park. Marvel at Cathedral Spires and Balanced Rock. Some dirt trails and the altitude (6,412 ft.) might challenge some.

See and Stay: The Colorado Springs/Manitou Springs area offers an assortment of outdoor recreation, unique shopping, and fine or casual dining. Ride the Pikes Peak Cog Railway, which leaves from 515 Ruxton Ave., or tour nearby Cave of the Winds. Photographers should be in the garden at sunrise or sunset for spectacular photos.

Hours: Daily 8 A.M.–8 P.M. in summer; 9 A.M.–4:30 P.M. in winter.

☑ Carry water.

Where Is It? Start at the Garden of the Gods Trading Post, 324 Beckers Ln. **From I-25:** Take Exit 141 (Hwy 24) and go west on 24. Exit at the Historic Manitou Springs sign and turn left onto Manitou Ave. At the first light (Beckers Ln.), turn left and go to the Trading Post. In summer, you can ride the trolley from Manitou Springs to the Trading Post for a small fee.

Sponsor: Falcon Wanderers, P.O. Box 17162, Colorado Springs, CO 80935

MONUMENT ◆ Trail Walk

Dates: January 1–December 31   📞 Mike Nelson (719) 495-0404

Description (3): This 11K trail walk has an altitude of 6,960 ft. and some hills. Enjoy the air and scenic beauty of this mountainous area.

See and Stay: Pikes Peak is the area's main natural attraction and the visible point of the 1.1 million-acre national forest. Drive or take the cog railway to the peak's summit. This forest has many developed campgrounds and opportunities to fish, hunt, hike, and ski. Take the 1.3-mi. hike up to Devil's Head Lookout Tower, the highest point in the Rampart Range.

☑ Leashed pets only.

 This club sponsors a 25K bike trail that also starts at the store.

Hours: Mon.-Fri., 8 A.M.–6 P.M.; Sat., 8 A.M.–5 P.M. Open Sun., 9 A.M.–5 P.M., only in May and June. Water and restrooms on the trail, but no water at start/finish.

Where Is It? Start at the High Country Feed Store. **From I-25 north:** Take Exit 161 (Hwy 105) and go west on 105. **From I-25 south:** Take Exit 161 and turn left onto 105. From Hwy 105, turn west onto Third St. and go to Washington St. Turn left onto Washington and go to the feed store, on your right. Parking is limited at the store and trailhead.

Sponsor: Falcon Wanderers, P.O. Box 17162, Colorado Springs, CO 80935

PUEBLO ◆ City Walk

Dates: January 4–December 31

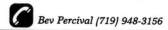 *Bev Percival (719) 948-3156*

Description (2): This walk along city streets, sidewalks, and paved or dirt trails will meander through historic Pueblo, known for its industrial success as well as its 279-acre park system.

See and Stay: Visit a full-size reproduction of Old Fort Pueblo at the El Pueblo Museum and also catch its exhibit on the production of iron and steel. Kids will enjoy the Pueblo Zoological Park, which houses a condor and Bengal tigers and the miniature Happy Time Ranch. Rosemount, a 37-room Victorian mansion gives a peek at what high-society was like in the booming Pueblo of the 1800s.

Hours: Mon.-Sat., 9:30 A.M.–6 P.M.; closed Sun.

Where Is It? Start at Golightly Footwear, 333 S. Union. **From I-25:** Take Exit 98B and First St. Cross Santa Fe Ave. and Main St.; angle left onto Union and go toward the store.

Sponsor: Falcon Wanderers, P.O. Box 17162, Colorado Springs, CO 80840

The U.S. Air Force Academy often has a seasonal volkswalk from May through October. The walk, however, may not be going at this time. If you are in the area and would like to walk at the academy, call Vinda Robison, (719) 472-4356, to see if there is a walk and where it starts. Or write The Falcon Footers, P.O. Box 240, USAF Academy, CO 81130.

CONNECTICUT

WETHERSFIELD ♦ *Historic Town Walk*

Dates: January 4–December 31   *Bill Webb (203) 529-5577*

Description (1 or 1+): This 11K trail passes through the historic part of one of the state's oldest settlements. You'll see 300-year-old houses, the scenic cove, and countless museums. Wheelchairs may have a difficult time in one spot, but the walk offers an easier alternative.

See and Stay: Get a taste of colonial living with a visit to the Buttolph-Williams House at Broad and March Sts. or the Webb-Deane-Stevens Museum, .5 mi. west of I-91, Exit 26, at 211 Main St. These homes, built in the 1700s, have period furniture and distinctive styles.

Where Is It? Start at the Ramada Inn, 1330 Silas Deane Hwy, (800) 228-2828. The inn is located just north of the intersection of I-91 and the Silas Deane Hwy near Exit 24 off I-91. Park in the back lot.

Sponsor: Volkssport Club of West Point, 7 Fernwood St., Wethersfield, CT 06109

Warehouses such as this one, built on the Connecticut River around 1690, stored goods marked for customers inland. Photo courtesy of the Wethersfield Historical Society.

DOVER ◆ *Historic Walk*

Dates: March 1–October 31 (seasonal)   *Ingrid Rockett (302) 697-3008*

Description (1 +): Take this scenic trail through the historic areas of old Dover. Your path will go past stately 18th- and 19th-century homes and historically significant buildings.

See and Stay: Explore Dover, established by William Penn in 1683. Visit the John Dickenson Plantation, an 18th-century plantation that gives a glimpse into our nation's past.

Hours: Mon.-Fri. 8 A.M.–3 P.M.; Sat. 8 A.M.–4 P.M.; Sun. 10 A.M.–3 P.M.

Where Is It? On weekdays start at the Lunch Box Cafe, 820 Silver Lake Blvd. off Walker Rd. On weekends, start at the YMCA, 1137 S. State St. **From I-95 south of Wilmington:** Take Rt 295 east to Rt 13, then south toward Dover. Turn right at the Agricultural Museum toward Alt. Rt 13 (State St.). At second light, turn right onto Walker. At next light (Silver Lake Blvd.) turn right and then left to cafe, Bldg. #820.

Sponsor: Diamond State Trekkers, 11-B N. Railroad Ave., Wyoming, DE 19934

In use only since 1933, Legislative Hall carries the 18th-century style of much of historic Dover. Photo by Ricardo E. Allen, courtesy of Delaware Development Office.

DISTRICT OF COLUMBIA

WASHINGTON, DC ♦ Monument Walk

Dates: January 1–December 31 *Nancy Stenger (703) 664-5457*

Description (1 +): See the sights on this memorable walk: the Lincoln Memorial, Washington Monument, Capitol, White House, and Vietnam Memorial.
Hours: Mon.-Fri., 7:30 A.M.–8 P.M.; Sat., 10 A.M.–7 P.M.; Sun. and holidays, 10 A.M.–4 P.M.
Where Is It? Start at the Columbia Plaza Gourmet, 538 23rd St. NW, (202) 887-8240. Street parking is scarce and limited to 2 hrs. Nearby garage parking could cost between $4 and $12, depending on the day and time. Consider taking the Metro train to the Foggy Bottom Metro stop. Come up the escalator onto 23rd St. Turn right, staying on 23rd, and walk 4 blks., crossing five streets, to Columbia Plaza. At 23rd and Virginia, you'll see a sign for the deli. Turn right into the courtyard at the plaza. The deli is on the right side of the courtyard.
Sponsor: Washington, DC Area Volksmarch Club, 7932 Birchtree Ct., Springfield, VA 22152

WASHINGTON, DC ♦ Rock Creek Walk

Dates: January 1–December 31 *Klaus J. Waibel (301) 681-9084*

Description (2): Half of this 11K walk goes through Rock Creek Park, DC's famous 1,754-acre park. Women should walk with a partner.

☑ Weekday parking's scarce, and tickets are common. If you find a visitor spot, please go and get a permit from the museum staff. Street parking has a 2-hr limit. Try the Metro train. The Takoma Metrorail station on the Red Line is 6 blks. east of Walter Reed Army Medical Center.
Hours: 10 A.M.–2 P.M. daily; finish by 5 P.M. Walk only in daylight.
Where Is It? Start at the Armed Forces Medical Museum, Bldg. 54, Walter Reed Army Medical Center, (202) 576-2348. **From Beltway I-495:** If you're coming from Virginia, take I-495 north beyond the American Legion Bridge, then east to MD Rt 97 (Georgia Ave.). Travel south for about 3 mi. to Elder St. The medical center will be on your right. Turn into the installation, make an immediate right and follow the road to the rear of the hospital. With the rear of the hospital to your left, take the next right turn. Bldg. 54 is 100 yds. to your right. **From downtown:** Take 16th St. or Georgia north. On weekends, only the Elder and Butternut St. gates to the installation are open.
Sponsor: Walter Reed Wandervogel, P.O. Box 59652, Washington, DC 20012

DISTRICT OF COLUMBIA

Rock Creek Park—a bit of nature in the city—follows along Rock Creek in northwest Washington, D.C. Photo courtesy of the Washington, DC Convention & Visitors Association.

FLORIDA

COCOA VILLAGE ♦ Riverside Walk

Dates: January 1–December 31   Ron Barnett (407) 452-9448

Description (1): This scenic village, with period street lamps and storefronts and interesting shops, has a feel of yesterday. You'll walk along the Indian River, with its grand old southern homes and scenic views. Big shade trees will protect you from much of the sun.

See and Stay: Enjoy this beautiful, historic area; visit the many antique and craft stores and restaurants. The Village has special activities planned most every month—call (407) 631-2345 to get a schedule of upcoming market, music, and art show events. The Kennedy Space Center is just up the coast, and Disney World is a quick 50 mi. to the west.

Where Is It? Start at The Bath Cottage, 301 Brevard Ave., (407) 690-2284. **From I-95:** Take the exit for SR 520 and head toward Merritt Island. Brevard intersects 520.

Sponsor: Patrick Pacers, P.O. Box 4360, Patrick AFB, FL 32925

DELAND ♦ City Walk

Dates: January 1–December 31   Lucy Krupp (904) 734-6980

Description (1): Amble along oak-shaded streets on this pretty walk that includes historic architecture, Stetson University, Oakdale Cemetery, and downtown. The path is mostly on sidewalks—most with curb cuts—and some sand and grass.

Food and Fun: Enjoy the local eateries and the downtown. A La Carte, a natural food restaurant, is known for its really good, not rabbit-food, meals. Nearby Ocala National Forest and Lake Woodruff National Wildlife Reserve offer outdoor fun. Rent a houseboat for the day and travel the St. John's River in style. The University Inn offers a discount to walkers.

Where Is It? Start at the University Inn, 644 N. Woodland Blvd., (904) 734-5711. **From I-4:** Take Exit 54 onto County Rd 472, following signs to DeLand via US 17/92. Proceed north 4.3 mi. to University Inn on your left.

Sponsor: Happy Wanderers, P.O. Box 4371, DeLand, FL 32723-4371

FLORIDA

FORT MYERS ♦ City Walk

Dates: January 1–December 31    Bev MacNeill (813) 997-6384

Description (1+): This flat, 11K walk in the "City of Palms" goes through the downtown and Edison Park. Not all curbs are cut and some of the path has no sidewalks, but route is mostly wheelchair-friendly. When you get to the Caloosahatchee River, look for egrets and herons and enjoy tropical plants and flowers year round.

See and Stay: Return to the route to visit the winter homes of neighbors Thomas Edison and Henry Ford or enjoy the Gulf of Mexico and neighboring wildlife reserves. Sheraton Harbor Place offers discounts to walkers. Janury through March is the city's busiest time.

Where Is It? Start at the Sheraton Harbor Place Hotel, 2500 Edwards Dr., the tallest building on the river, (813) 337-0300. **From I-75:** Take Exit 25. Follow Hwy 80 west about 4 mi. This is Palm Beach Blvd., which turns into First St. When the road curves right, it becomes Bay St. Turn right on Lee, right on Edwards. The Sheraton is on the right, at Fowler St., at the Fort Myers Marina. Park in the lot under the hotel.

Sponsor: Meandering Manatees, 666 Brigantine Blvd., North Fort Myers, FL 33917

MELBOURNE ♦ Historic Downtown Walk

Dates: January 1–December 31   Ron Barnett (407) 452-9448

Description (1): Stroll along the tree-lined sidewalks and admire the carefully restored historic buildings on this walk through a renovated downtown with rococo-style architecture. Watch for birds along the Indian River, and feed the ducks in the lake next to the library.

See and Stay: The city offers a variety of water sports—windsurfing, sailing, fishing—in its snug harbor. Visit one of the many shops featuring collectibles, antiques, and art, or grab a bite in one of the cafes. The Brevard Art Center and Museum features local, national, and international artists. If you're heading north, visit the John F. Kennedy Space Center and Cape Canaveral.

Where Is It? Start at the Burger King, 1514 S. Harbor City Blvd. (US 1), (407) 723-7821. **From I-95:** Follow signs to Melbourne. The Burger King is on US 1 just north of SR 192. Park in the lot and go in and ask for the walkers' start box.

Sponsor: Patrick Pacers, P.O. Box 4360, Patrick AFB, FL 32925

FLORIDA

ORLANDO ◆ *Wekiwa Springs Walk*

Dates: *January 1–December 31*  Frank Demolli (407) 330-9677

Description (2): Enjoy Florida's raw, natural beauty in this 6,900-acre park with its fresh water spring and tropical scenery. The well-maintained dirt paths may have fallen trees and roots. You'll see wildlife, maybe even small, non-threatening black bears.

See and Stay: You can swim year-round in the natural springs or picnic in the park before or after your walk, or grab a bite at the park's concession stand. Wekiwa River is considered one of Florida's best canoeing rivers; rent a canoe at the marina. If you want one of the 60 overnight camping sites in the state park, call (407) 884-2009. You won't lack for things to do in the Orlando area. You'll find countless motels, restaurants, and amusements.

☑ No restrooms or water on the trail. Protect yourself against pesky "sketos" and bugs. Call Frank if you'd like a walking companion.

Hours: Start no earlier than 8 A.M.

Where Is It? Start at the concession stand of the Wekiwa Springs State Park, Wekiwa Springs Rd., (407) 884-2009. **From I-4:** Take Exit 49 (Longwood SR 434) west 1 mi. Turn right on Wekiwa Springs Rd. and go 4.2 mi. The park entrance is on your right. Park in the lot on your left and go to the ranger's office to pay the $3.25 entrance fee.

Sponsor: Mid-Florida Milers, 2457 Sherbrooke Rd., Winter Park, FL 32792-5004

Coral Gables may have a walk, bike and swim. Call Ron Brown, (904) 487-4637/224-6756, for information and directions.

Sanibel Island also may have a walk. Call Bev MacNeill, (813) 997-6384, for details.

ORLANDO ◆ *Historic City Walk*

Dates: January 1–December 31  *Frank Demolli (407) 330-9677*

Description (1): Enjoy historic Orlando on this flat, mostly shady, paved walk through parks and business areas and past six lakes. Enjoy the bird life and Church Street Station. More than 700 walkers take this route each year.

See and Stay: Kids will enjoy the playgrounds along the walk's route and the chance to fish in one of the lakes or take a paddle boat out on Lake Eola. The Orlando International Toy Train Museum, (407) 363-9002, features model trains from the early 1900s to the present. Hop the steam train for a ride around the property. Looking for something else to do? Remember, you're in a vacationer's paradise. Disney World is just 20 min. away, and you'll have your pick of countless hotels and restaurants. Camp at Wekiwa Springs State Park.

Hours: Start no earlier than 7 A.M.

☑ Hot in the summer and humid year round. Call Frank if you'd like a walking companion.

Where Is It? Start at the Information Desk of the Orlando Regional Medical Center, 1414 Kuhl Ave., (407) 841-5111. **From I-4:** Take Exit 38 (Anderson St.) east to the second light. Turn right on Orange Ave. At the fifth light, turn right on Copeland Dr., go 1 blk. and left on Kuhl. Go half a block and right on Copeland again. Turn left into second entrance of parking bldg. Parking is available at a nominal fee. Walk half a block to hospital's main entrance.

Sponsor: Mid-Florida Milers, 2457 Sherbrooke Rd., Winter Park, FL 32792-5004

Lake Eola, three blocks from the center of Orlando, is a favorite spot with walkers, joggers, picnickers, and sunbathers. Courtesy of the Orlando/Orange County Convention & Visitors Bureau.

FLORIDA

PENSACOLA ◆ Historic Walk

Date: January 3–December 31 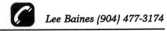 *Lee Baines (904) 477-3174*

Description (1 +): You'll stroll along Pensacola Bay, then through the historic district with its restored 18th- and 19th-century homes, many now housing restaurants, boutiques, and offices. Look for the Spanish names on the graves as you pass through the historic cemetery.

See and Stay: Explore the oldest of Florida's cities, which has flown the flags of Spain, France, England, the Confederate States, and the U.S. Museums and historic points of interest reflect the influence of all five. Contact the Pensacola Tourist Information Center, (904) 434-1234, for free travelers' information.

☑ The start/finish points for the three Pensacola walks only provide necessary materials and maps. Personnel cannot answer questions or make change. The club prefers you pay by check.

Where Is It? You'll find the walking registration materials in the outer lobby of the Pensacola Police Station, 711 N. Hayne St., (904) 435-1900. ***From I-110:*** Take Exit 2 at Cervantes St. and turn left onto Cervantes. Pass Hayne, which is one-way. Turn right at the next street (Alcaniz), and turn right again at Jackson, and right on Hayne. The station will be on your left. After you pick up your map, go to the Visitors Information Center at 1401 E. Gregory St. to start your walk.

PENSACOLA ◆ Naval Air Station Walk

Dates: January 1–December 31 *Carol Raflski (904) 478-3469 (evenings)*

Description (1 +): This scenic, park-like walk on the 75-year-old military installation will take you past the administrative areas and within sight of the training squadrons.

See and Stay: This station is the heart of U.S. naval air training and the home of the Blue Angels. The USS Forrestal, the training carrier, docks here when it's in port, and offers weekend tours. Before or after your walk, explore the museum with more than 100 aircraft, the Skylab Command Module, and simulators visitors can try. Fort Barrancas, one of several forts built by the Spanish, is nearby.

Hours: The station and museum are open daily 9 A.M.–5 P.M.

Where Is It? Start at the National Museum of Naval Aviation. Call (800) 327-5002 if you need directions.

Sponsor: Pensacola Volksmarch Club, P.O. Box 15007, Pensacola, FL 32514, *for both walks*

FLORIDA

PENSACOLA ♦ *Airport Walk*

Dates: January 1–December 31  Judy Regan (904) 477-5340

Description (1 +): Follow sidewalks and paved streets around the Pensacola Regional Airport on this 11K walk through commercial and residential areas.

🚲 This walking club also sponsors a 26K bike path that starts at the Circle K store and runs adjacent to a commercial business district. Helmets required.

Where Is It? Start at the Circle K food store, 2825 Langley Ave., just north of the airport. Ask the clerk for the volksmarch box. Your walking map and self-registration cards are in the box. **From I-10:** Take Exit 6 (US 90), and follow signs for airport.

Sponsor: Pensacola Volksmarch Club, P.O. Box 15007, Pensacola, FL 32514

SAFETY HARBOR ♦ *Historic Town Walk*

Dates: January 1–December 31   Fran Hardy (813) 725-3482

Description (1 +): You'll walk on sidewalks and roads through a harbor town first inhabited 5,000 years ago by Indian Mound builders and in the 16th century by the Spanish. Be prepared to carry a stroller up some steps.

See and Stay: Visit the Safety Harbor Museum at 329 S. Bayshore Dr. Dioramas show the history of the early peoples and their contact with Europeans. On the grounds is an Indian burial gravesite and an ancient well that was part of the area's original mineral springs network. Philippe Park has picnicking, fishing, swimming, and playgrounds and is home to blue herons, egrets, sandpipers, fiddler crabs, and alligators. Endangered manatees are frequently spotted off the marina pier.

☑ Carry water and expect hot weather and sun from March through October.

Hours: Mon.-Sat., start as early as 7 A.M.; no sooner than 8 A.M. on Sun.

Where Is It? Start at the Paradise Restaurant, 443 Main St., (813) 725-1208. **From I-275:** Take the SR 60 exit and go west toward Clearwater. At the first traffic light at the west end of the causeway (SR 60), turn right on Bayshore. Follow Bayshore for 2.5 mi. to Main St. and turn left. The restaurant is 4 blks. down on the right.

Sponsor: Suncoast Sandpipers, P.O. Box 2514, Largo, FL 34649

FLORIDA

TAMPA ◆ *Harbor Walk*

Dates: *January 3–December 31*   *Nina Bartley (813) 839-6269*

Description (1): You'll explore the historical and business sections of downtown Tampa. This walk, on mostly level sidewalks, also includes the longest continuous sidewalk in the U.S., which goes along the bay. Enjoy the birds, boats, marine wildlife, and terrific view.

See and Stay: You'll find plenty to do. Busch Gardens and Adventure Island are 5 mi. north, and the beach is just 30 min. away.

☑ Do not walk during storms. Tampa is the U.S. lightning capital.

Hours: Start no earlier than 7:30 A.M.; finish by 6 P.M. Sunday start after 8 A.M.

Where Is It? Start at Chris's Cookie Shop in the food court at the Harbour Island Shops. **From I-275:** Take Exit 25 and stay in left lane. Follow signs for Ashley St./Tampa St., and Convention Center/Performing Arts Center. Use left lane as you exit onto Tampa. Continue in left lane and follow signs to Harbour Island/Convention Center. The first two hours in the garage under the shops is free. RV and extra parking is in the open area to the southeast.

Sponsor: Suncoast Sandpipers Volkssport Club, P.O. Box 2514, Largo, FL 34649-2514

The Tallahassee Volkssport Club offers a walk and a bike trail from January 1 to December 31. The walk starts at the Holiday Inn, 1.5 mi. southeast on US 27, at 1302 Apalachee Pkwy. For more information on the walk and bike routes, call or write Larry Tepe, (904) 668-0565, 102 N. Westwood Dr., Tallahassee, FL 32304-1411. Be sure to enclose a self-addressed, stamped envelope with your request for information.

FLORIDA

WINTER PARK ♦ Lakes Walk

Dates: January 1–December 31  *Frank Demolli (407) 330-9677*

Description (1+): You'll almost walk on water on this 11K walk that passes six lakes and offers a chance for a boat ride at a reduced walker's rate. You'll also see Mead Garden, an urban oasis with wetlands, creek, and ornamental plants, where you can enjoy a picnic. Call Frank if you'd like a walking companion.

See and Stay: If you didn't take the boat ride during your walk, take it afterward and explore the city's historic canals, Rollins College, and the Kraft Azalea Gardens, and see tropical birds and plants. The city and area also offer endless entertainment and hundreds of hotels and restaurants. Camp in Wekiwa Springs State Park and walk the 10K trail.

🚲 The walking club sponsors a 25K scenic bike path. Start at the information desk of the Winter Park Memorial Hospital Wellness Center, 200 N. Lakemont Ave.

Where Is It? Start at the information desk of the Florida Hospital Medical Center, 601 E. Rollins St., (407) 897-1950. **From I-4:** Take Exit 43 (Princeton St.) east to the first light. Turn left on Orange Ave. to the third light. Turn right on King St. for half a blk. Turn right into Parking Bldg., take ticket, and park. Take elevator to third floor. Turn right from elevator, cross overpass, and take escalator down to main floor. Follow signs to the main lobby. After walk, take parking voucher from the volksmarch box and give to parking attendant for free parking.

Sponsor: Mid-Florida Milers, 2457 Sherbrooke Rd., Winter Park, FL 32792-5004

GEORGIA

ROSWELL ◆ Two Park Walks

Dates: January 1–December 31   *Linda Nickles (404) 641-3760*

Description (1): This walk gives you two 10K options. You can follow a scenic walking trail in Roswell Area Park and on shaded sidewalks in the residential areas, or you can travel through the park on your way to downtown's historic district. The walks have some moderate hills, but the walk's sponsor says the paths are wheelchair-friendly.

See and Stay: You can picnic in Roswell Park or take a dip in its 50-m. pool. The Visitor's Center, (404) 640-3253, is happy to help walkers plan their Roswell visit.

Hours: Mon-Sat., 9 A.M.–8:30 P.M.; closed Sundays and holidays.

Where Is It? Start at the Community Activity Bldg. in Roswell Area Park, 10495 Woodstock Rd. See directions below.

Sponsor: Roswell Striders, 38 Hill St., Roswell, GA 30075

ROSWELL ◆ Historic District Walk

Dates: January 1–December 31   *Duncan Brantley (404) 961-0109*

Description (1+): You'll explore the historic district on this walk along sidewalks and roads to several points of interest, including Bulloch Hill, Goulding Hall, the cemetery, and the Roswell Municipal Complex.

Where Is It? Start at The Courtyard by Marriott, 500 Market Blvd. **From I-285 Atlanta:** Go north on Hwy 400. Take Exit 4A, on Holcomb Bridge Rd. For the **Community Activity Bldg.**, go west on Holcomb Bridge Rd. Several traffic lights down, turn left on "Pug" W. L. Mabry Hwy (Rt 9). Turn right at the next light (Woodstock). The park is about 1 mi. down on your right. For the **Marriott**, bear right after Exit 4A and take first right on Market Way to the motel.

Sponsor: Georgia Walkers, 6524 Revena Dr., Morrow, GA 30260

> The Georgia Walkers also offer a walk in Peachtree City, just south of Atlanta. Call Brantley for walk's location and details.

GEORGIA

STONE MOUNTAIN ♦ *Stone Mountain Park*

Dates: March 1–December 31   Duncan Brantley (404) 961-0109

Description (1): In contrast to the hustle of Atlanta, you'll find peace and nature on this walk that begins in a small 19th-century village and then enters the park. The walk has some gentle hills, but the walk's sponsor says you can push strollers or wheelchairs.

See and Stay: Spend some time at the park, which has motel and camping accommodations and access to fishing, boating, and swimming. The cable car and train rides, riverboat cruise, petting farm, and museum will keep you busy. Call (404) 498-5600 for park information.

This club also sponsors a 32K bike route on rural roads and a 300-m. swim in the Mountain Park pool. Pool closed Fridays. Call Brantley, (404) 961-0109, for walk details and Pedal Power about bike rentals.

Hours: Mon.-Thurs., 11 A.M.–7 P.M.; Fri.-Sat., 10 A.M.–6 P.M.; Sun., noon–5 P.M.

Where Is It? Register for all three events at Pedal Power, 1944 Rockbridge Rd., No. 105, (404) 498-BIKE. **From Atlanta on I-285:** Take Exit 30B, Stone Mtn. Fwy, to Athens (US Hwy 78). The first light, after about 8 mi., is West Park Pl. Turn left into right lane for immediate right turn onto Rockbridge Rd. Pedal Power is in the shopping center on your left.

Sponsor: Georgia Walkers, 6524 Revena Dr., Morrow, GA 30260

The Roswell Striders offer walkers a pleasant stroll through the Roswell Area Park. Photo courtesy of the Roswell Recreation & Parks Department.

45

HAWAII

HONOLULU ♦ Manoa Valley Walk

Dates: March 13–December 31 (Reconfirm dates in '94) *Barbara Mateo (808) 247-5059*

Description (2): This route through residential areas, the University of Hawaii, and past a Chinese cemetery, includes three hills and some grassy shoulders.

See and Stay: Hawaii is a vacation paradise. No doubt you already know what you plan to do once you arrive. If you'd like some additional information, call or write the Hawaii Visitors Bureau, (808) 923-1811, 2270 Kalakaua Ave., Honolulu, HI 96815. If you'd like to enjoy more of the island's natural beauty and outdoor attractions, contact the National Park Service headquarters, Kuhio Federal Bldg., Honolulu, HI 96813, (808) 541-2693, about parks on Maui and Hawaii. Oahu has 16 campgrounds—13 at city beach parks and 3 at state parks. All are free, but you'll need a permit from the City Parks Department.

☑ Water at start/finish point.

Where Is It? Start at the McDonald's restaurant of Manoa Market Place, 2915 E. Manoa Rd., (808) 988-2219. **From H-1:** Take Exit 24B, University Ave., and follow University toward the mountains. At the intersection of University/Oahu Ave./East Manoa Rd., turn right onto East Manoa and continue to the Manoa Market Place Shopping Center. East Manoa is the fifth traffic intersection from Exit 24B. **By bus:** Take Bus #6 (University/Woodlawn) from Ala Manoa Shopping Center. Contact "THE BUS" customer service at (808) 531-1611 for time schedules.

HONOLULU ♦ Diamond Head Walk

Description (1 +): This 12K route wanders through Waikiki, around Diamond Head, and along the Ala Wai Canal on sidewalks. People who want to push a wheelchair may have difficulty with a hill.

Hours: Daily from 8 A.M.–6:30 P.M.

Where Is It? Start at the Sheraton Travel & Entertainment Center, Sheraton Waikiki Hotel, 2255 Kalakaua Ave. Go into the main lobby, turn left and you'll find the Travel Center immediately in front of you. The hotel is behind the Royal Hawaiian Shopping Center. You can pay to park in the Sheraton's garage or find free street parking on Ala Wai Blvd., about .5 mi. from the hotel.

Sponsor: Menehune Marchers Club, P.O. Box 31102, Honolulu, HI 96820, for both walks.

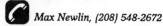

AMERICAN FALLS ◆ Massacre Rocks State Park

Dates: Memorial Day–Labor Day (seasonal)   Max Newlin, (208) 548-2672

Description (3): Six different trails make up this 11K walk in an early campsite of the Oregon Trail. Over 200 species of birds have been sighted here, and mammals, including beaver and coyote, can been seen. The route, on sandy soil with some hills, goes through the campground, along the Snake River, to the old wagon ruts, and through meadows.

See and Stay: Enjoy this 900-acre park in a desert environment. A 52-unit campground offers hookups, a picnic area, nightly summer campfire programs, fishing, boating, and hiking. Nearby American Falls offers restaurants, a laundry, and groceries.

☑ It gets hot in the summer and there's no shade on the trail. Water is available on the trail, but rangers advise you carry some.

Hours: Daily 9 A.M.–5 P.M.

Where Is It? Start at the state park visitors center, 3592 Park Ln., (208) 548-2672. **From I-86:** West of American Falls, take Exit 28 and follow the signs to the state park.

Sponsor: American Falls Volkssport Club, 3592 Park Ln., American Falls, ID 83211

ATHOL ◆ Farragut State Park Walk

Dates: Mid-May–Mid-October (seasonal)   Valerie Olson (208) 263-1441, ext. 102

Description (3): Enjoy views of Pend Oreille (pon-duh-RAY) Lake, spectacular mountains, the tranquility of the meadows and the Coeur d'Alene National Forest on this 11K path. The walk includes some mild hills. Watch for deer, wild turkey, and an occasional bear.

See and Stay: Camp in the state park. Take a cruise on nearby Lake Coeur d'Alene, described by *National Geographic* as one of the world's five most beautiful lakes. Visit Sandpoint, a year-round resort and artists' community. Shop or dine there at Cedar Bridge Public Market, an innovative, contemporary shopping mall created from a city bridge.

☑ Ticks may be a problem in the spring.

Hours: Daily, 8 A.M.–3 P.M.

Where Is It? Start at the headquarters for Farragut State Park, (208) 683-2425. **From I-90:** Take Hwy 95 north and then watch for signs for the state park and office.

Sponsor: Panhandle Pacers, P.O. Box 1448, Sandpoint, ID 83864

IDAHO

Many experienced walkers describe Farragut State Park's year-round walk as "one of the most beautiful walks" they've done. See walk description on previous page. Photo by Al Leiser.

ILLINOIS

BELLEVILLE ◆ *Our Lady of the Snows Walk*

Dates: January 9–November 20   Dan Bainter (618) 398-0294

Description (1 +): Experience the tranquility and scenic beauty of Our Lady of the Snows Shrine on this 11K walk through the landscaped grounds. The entirely paved trail on shrine roadways has some hills that may prove tough on stroller pushers. Only the hardy should attempt to push a wheelchair.

Food and Fun: Enjoy a good meal at the Shrine Restaurant or grab a bite at one of the many restaurants in St. Louis. Visit Union Station—a shopper's and diner's paradise—in downtown St. Louis, or travel up the arch for a panoramic view of the countryside. Still feel like walking? Head to Collinsville and the Cahokia Mounds trail.

Where Is It? Start at the check-in desk at the Pilgrim's Inn, on shrine property and across from the restaurant and gift shop. **From I-64, I-55, or I-70:** Take I-255 south to the Illinois 15 (Belleville) Exit and go south to the shrine's entrance. **From St. Louis:** Cross the interstate bridge (Poplar Street Bridge) into Illinois and follow Rt 15 signs to shrine.

Sponsor: Illinois Trekkers, P.O. Box 25077, Scott AFB, IL 62225-0077

COLLINSVILLE ◆ *Cahokia Mounds Walk*

Dates: January 2–December 31   Tom Boyd (618) 233-6348

Description (1 +): Don't miss the chance to walk one of the U.N.'s World Heritage Sites—there are only 17 in the world. You'll walk on grass, trails, and pavement and along and around mounds that are among the only remnants of a people who lived here from 700 A.D. to 1500 A.D. Take the stairs up Monk's Mound, the largest prehistoric earthen construction in the New World. It contains 22 million cubic feet of dirt; see St. Louis from its top.

See and Stay: Before you walk, see "City of the Sun," shown every 30 min. in the Interpretive Center's auditorium. This free, powerful film will prepare your imagination and help you "see" the civilization that lived here. Everyone will enjoy the center's hands-on exhibits, life-size re-creation of a village, and archeological displays and artifacts.

Hours: The gift shop is open from 9 A.M.–4:45 P.M. daily. State budget cuts, however, are affecting Cahokia. Its hours and days may be reduced in the off-season. Call ahead or write the Cahokia Mounds Historic Site, P.O. Box 681, Collinsville, IL 62234.

ILLINOIS

Where Is It? Start in the Museum Shop in the Interpretive Center, which is at the entrance of Cahokia Mounds, (618) 546-5160. **From I-55/70:** Take Exit 6. Go south and follow signs to Cahokia Mounds. **From I-255:** Take Exit 24 and go west on Collinsville Rd. about 1 mi. to the park entrance.

Sponsor: Illinois Trekkers, P.O. Box 25077, Scott AFB, IL 62225-0077

The base of Monk's Mound covers 14 acres and rises to 100 ft. A massive building—the home of the principal ruler—once stood on the summit. Photo by Cindy West.

ILLINOIS

HILLSBORO ◆ City Walk

Dates: January 2–December 31  Roger Mollett (217) 546-8137

Description (1+): Enjoy a peaceful small town on this walk on mostly level ground on sidewalks and some shoulders of unpaved roads. You'll get a list at the start point of the interesting homes and buildings you'll pass along the way.
Hours: Mon.-Sat., 8 A.M.–5 P.M.; Sun., 8 A.M.–1:30 P.M.
Where Is It? Start at the Red Rooster Inn, (217) 532-6332, 123 E. Seward, just east of the Montgomery County Courthouse in the downtown. **From I-55:** Take Exit 52 at Litchfield and go east on Hwy 16. **From I-70:** Take Exit 45 at Greenville and go north on Hwy 127.
Sponsor: Railsplitter Wanderers, PO Box 6051, Springfield, IL 62708

PETERSBURG ◆ Lincoln's New Salem Walk

Dates: This AVA trail may be closed temporarily   Roger Mollett (217) 546-8137

Description: This popular AVA walk at Lincoln's New Salem State Historic Site has been affected by park road work and state budget cuts. If you'd like to take this well-marked trail past reconstructions of the town's early shops and homes, contact Mollett or write the sponsor for information on the walk's AVA status. It is still possible to visit the park and walk the trails, but AVA walkers might not be able to get credit or purchase awards.
Where Is It? Lincoln's New Salem State Historic Site is about 25 mi. northwest of downtown Springfield along SR 97. **From I-55 south:** Take Exit 109 and follow the signs to Lincoln's New Salem. **From I-55 north:** Take US 36 west to SR 4. Go north on Rt. 4 to 97 and follow the signs to New Salem.
Sponsor: Railsplitter Wanderers, PO Box 6051, Springfield, IL 62708

ILLINOIS

SPRINGFIELD ♦ *Historic Walk*

Dates: January 2–December 31  Mary Pollock (618) 588-4227

Description (1 +): Amble through the city Abraham Lincoln called home. Here he practiced law, married, and was buried. This walk on city sidewalks has some curb cuts. A patch of lawn can be avoided and an elevator in the capitol bypasses steps. People pushing strollers or wheelchairs will face a steep down- and then up-hill ramp in the capitol tunnel.

See and Stay: You'll find many things to see and do. Retrace Lincoln's steps. His home, tomb and nearby New Salem State Park provide interesting and educational tours. Tour the current and the original state capitol. Visit the Dana-Thomas House, one of Frank Lloyd Wright's first prairie homes, complete with more than 100 pieces of original furniture.

☑ Take a "Fun Walk." The walk's sponsor offers two, 3-mile walks. One walk takes you to Lincoln's tomb and the other through parts of town. You can't get AVA credit for either, but these walks may be just the ticket when you want a shorter route.

Hours: Daily 8:30 A.M.–6:30 P.M.

Where Is It? Start at the registration desk of Best Inns of America, 500 N. First St. **From I-55:** Take the Clear Lake Exit and go toward downtown. At Sixth St. turn right and go to Carpenter. Turn left at Carpenter to First. The inn is between Carpenter and Reynolds on First. **From I-72:** Go toward downtown. The highway will become Clear Lake. Take Clear Lake to Sixth and follow above directions. Avoid parking in front of motel.

Sponsor: Illinois Volkssport Assoc., 324 Hazel Ave., Belleville, IL 62223

INDIANA

ANDERSON ◆ Wildlife Walk
◆ University Walk

Dates: January 1–December 31   Bob Kiefert (317) 286-7083

Description (1+): The 10K Blue Trail winds past Shadyside Lakes, Killbuck Wetlands, and river boardwalks. Wildlife abounds. The 11K Red Trail goes to Anderson University, with its tree-lined campus and red-bricked buildings. You'll also catch a glimpse of the rivers.

See and Stay: Enjoy Anderson Lake. Catch a paddle boat at the marina or rent a boat and go fishing. Shoppers will enjoy Mounds Mall, at the junction of the SR 109 bypass and SR 32.

Hours: Start no earlier than 8 A.M.

Where Are They? Start the walks at the Shadyside Marina, 1117 Alexandria Pike, (317) 649-9025. **From north I-69:** Exit at SR 9N and go through Anderson to 100 N Rd. (Lindberg). Go left to Alexandria Pike, and then right on Alexandria to Marina. **From south I-69:** Exit at SR 32W and go toward Anderson. Go right at the SR 9N/SR 32W intersection and then left at 100 N Rd. to Alexandria Pike and then the marina.

Sponsor: White River Ramblers, 501 S. Umbarger Rd., Muncie, IN 47304

AUBURN ◆ Historic City Walk

Dates: January 2–December 31   Su Fennern (219) 925-9064

Description(1): In the early 1900s, Auburn was the home of the Auburn Automobile Co., maker of Cord and Dusenberg cars. Follow the city streets and sidewalks on a walk that will take you past the homes once owned by the auto industry's craftsmen and engineers. Walkers with special needs may choose a shorter route. Ask at the start point.

See and Stay: Explore the Auburn-Cord-Dusenberg Museum with its 140 antique and classic cars displayed in what once was the company's factory showroom. The museum offers a discount to walkers. Write to the Chamber of Commerce, 307 E. Ninth St., Auburn, IN 46706, if you'd like more information about the area.

Hours: Daily, 9 A.M.–6 P.M.

Where Is It? Start this walk at the A-C-D Museum, 1600 S. Wayne, (219) 925-1444. **From I-69:** Take Exit 129 (SR 8). Go east on SR 8 to Van Buren St. Go south on Van Buren to the museum, or follow A-C-D Museum signs.

Sponsor: Auburn Duesey Walkers, 301 N. McClellan St., Auburn, IN 46706-1943

INDIANA

BATESVILLE ♦ Town Walk

Dates: January 1–December 31    Rita Eckstein (812) 934-2446

Description (2): Enjoy a quiet, Midwestern town on this walk that takes you through town and past a park, picnic area, golf course, and an interesting cemetery. Most of the walk is on sidewalks, but some of the trail is over grassy areas and along the shoulder of the road.

See and Stay: Take Hwy 229 north to nearby Metamora, a former Indiana Canal town that still has one of the few operating aqueducts in the nation. Restored buildings contain numerous craft and antique shops, specialty stores, and unique gift shops and restaurants. Stop at Whitewater Canal Historic Site and watch a restored gristmill grind cornmeal, grits, and flour.

Hours: Start no earlier than 9 A.M.

Where Is It? Start at the Sherman House, 35 S. Main St., (812) 934-2407. **From I-74:** Take Exit 149 (Rt 229) and go south 1 mi. to the first stop sign. Turn left 1 blk. on Boehringer to Main. Turn right on Main for 1 blk. and turn left at the 5/3 Bank where you can park. The Sherman House is across the street.

Sponsor: Town & Country Wanderers, 2059 E. County Rd. 1100 N., Batesville, IN 47006

COLUMBUS ♦ Tipton Lakes Walk

Dates: January 1–December 31   Carol Bussell (812) 376-5808

Description (1): This walk through the Tipton Lakes community offers views of peaceful lakes, woods, and lovely homes and landscaping. You'll walk on sidewalks, paved walkways, and nature trails. The portions of the trail not suitable for wheels can be bypassed.

See and Stay: Advanced architectural design is the hallmark of this attractive city. Catch a narrated slide show at the Visitors Center, 506 Fifth St., on the many buildings or reserve space on one of the tour buses. Kids will enjoy the indoor playground at The Commons.

Where Is It? Start at Tipton Lakes Racquet Club, 4000 Goeller Blvd., (812) 342-4495. **From I-65:** Use Exit 68 (SR 46) and go west 1 mi. to first traffic light (Goeller Blvd.). Turn left, then right at first corner (Mimosa). The club is on your right. The racquet club is clearly visible from the intersection of Goeller and SR 46. Park in the lot's far ends.

Sponsor: Columbus Wellness Walkers, 2400 E. 17th St., Columbus, IN 47201

INDIANA

INDIANAPOLIS ♦ Eagle Creek Walk

Dates: January 1–December 31  Clarence Wright (317) 357-8464

Description (3): Enjoy one of the nation's largest developed parks on this walk. The 1,300-acre reservoir and 3,800 acres of land attract deer, birds, and many small mammals. Most of the walk is in the shade. Expect to pay a per-car admission to the park, ranging from $1.75 to $2.25 and 25¢ per person.

See and Stay: Enjoy and explore Indianapolis. Kids will enjoy the Children's Museum, where they'll discover toy trains, an old-fashioned carousel, a 23,000-year-old mummy, and a replica of Tyrannosaurus Rex. The Indianapolis Zoo, a cageless zoo, has one of the world's largest enclosed whale and dolphin pavilions. Visit the Indy Hall of Fame Museum at the Indianapolis Motor Speedway.

Hours: The park opens at 9 A.M. and closes at dusk.

Where Is It? Go to the 71st St. Gate House of Eagle Creek Park, (317) 293-4828, to pick up your start card and maps. The park is at 7840 W. 56th St. on the city's west side. You can catch the 71st St. entrance from I-465 or I-65.

Sponsor: Indy "G" Walkers, P.O. Box 16001, Indianapolis, IN 46216

MARION ♦ Downtown Walk

Dates: August 1–December 31 Bob Marrs (317) 662-7798

Description (1): You'll start this 11K walk in the downtown, but will soon find yourself walking along the Mississinewa River into Matter Park. The river is one of the few in North America that flows north.

Food and Fun: Enjoy a picnic at one of the picnic tables in Matter Park. While you're in the park, visit the Octogenarian Museum, which contains historical artifacts. The Miami Indian Historical Site marks an 1812 battle, the last battle between the settlers and the Miami. Hiking trails cross the former reservation and village.

☑ In 1994, check with Marrs to see if this walk starts earlier in the year.

Where Is It? Start at the Marion Sheraton, 501 E. Fourth St., 2 blks. east of the court house square in downtown. **From I-69:** Take the Marion exit and go west on SR 18 to Marion.

Sponsor: Marion Fussganger, 1124 W. 3rd St., Marion, IN 46952

55

INDIANA

MUNCIE ♦ 'Round Town Walk

Dates: January 1–December 31 *Bob Kiefert (317) 286-7083*

Description (1 +): You'll start downtown and follow a route that includes the banks of the White River, Ball State University campus, the Minnetrista Center, and neighborhoods.

See and Stay: Children will enjoy the hands-on Muncie Children's Museum at 306 S. Walnut Plaza. It includes railroad and farm equipment, antique cars, and other displays. Hotel Roberts, built in the 1920s and on the National Registry of Historic Places, gives special treatment to walkers. Call (317) 741-7777 for reservations.

Where Is It? Start at Hotel Roberts, 420 S. High St. **From I-69:** Exit at SR 32 and take the road east to the center of Muncie. Turn right at High. The hotel is 3 blks. on your left.

Sponsor: White River Ramblers, 501 S. Umbarger Rd., Muncie, IN 47304

NOTRE DAME ♦ Campus Walk

Dates: January 1–December 31 *Jan Bella (219) 277-9682*

Description (1 +): Enjoy the beauty of the grounds and buildings on this picturesque campus that is home to the "Fighting Irish."

See and Stay: In South Bend, catch the Studebaker Exhibit, 520 S. Lafayette, for a peek at vintage cars, the Studebaker archives, and the carriage Lincoln took to the Ford Theatre. If you're heading west on I-80/I-90, get out your swimsuit and sand pails and visit the Indiana Dunes State Park in nearby Chesterton. You can hike or bike along the 9-mi. Calumet Trail. If there's snow on the ground, hit the trail on cross-country skis.

Where Is It? Start at the Jamison Inn, 1404 N. Ivy Rd., (219) 277-9682. **From I-80/I-90:** Take the South Bend exit, Hwy 31, and follow the signs to Notre Dame.

Sponsor: Hoosier Hikers, P.O. Box 11101, South Bend, IN 46634

INDIANA

The distinctive gold dome sets off the Administration Building on the University of Notre Dame campus. Photo courtesy of the Chamber of Commerce of St. Joseph County.

IOWA

AKRON ◆ River Walk

Dates: April 1–December 31 (seasonal)    *Marlene Krause (712) 568-2600*

Description (2): You'll walk along mowed grass, wood chips, and gravel and paved trails as you follow the Big Sioux River, pass through a prairie reserve, and take a tour of the town's historical sites. Watch for eagles, bluebirds, deer, and small mammals. Gnats might pester you along the river.

See and Stay: Get a local birding brochure and go back to the prairie preserve, or enjoy the town's swimming pool, golf course, and tennis courts. You can camp free for up to a week in the Akron City Park.

☑ The Prairie Wanderers have organized several walks along the Big Sioux River. Check the South Dakota chapter for descriptions of those walks.

Where Is It? Start at Casey's General Store, near the intersection of Hwys 12 and 3, (712) 568-3238. **From I-29:** Take Exit 31 (Akron-Spink) and go 13 mi. east. Turn right (south) on Hwy 12 and go about 1 mi. to Casey's. Park on north side of building.

Sponsor: The Prairie Wanderers, 618 13th Ave., Brookings, SD 57006

DES MOINES ◆ Capital Walk

Dates: January 1–December 31    *Jan Adams (515) 277-1524*

Description (1 +): This Midwest capital will surprise you with its bustle, numerous impressive buildings, river views, and enjoyable mix of modern city and historic sights.

See and Stay: Linger in the botanical center and get heady on the aromas and colors. Paid walkers can enter for free.

☑ Please no pets. Pay by check or money order if you wish credit or an award. Trail closed in mid-July for Grand Prix.

Hours: Daily 10 A.M.–5 P.M.

Where Is It? Start the walk at the Des Moines Botanical Center, on the east bank of the Des Moines River, 909 E. River Dr. The dome is visible from I-235. Signs indicate the most direct routes. Park free on site.

Sponsor: Greater Des Moines Volksssport Assoc., 3601 Center, Des Moines, IA 50312

KANSAS

ARKANSAS CITY ◆ Nature Center Walk

Dates: January 1–December 31   *Don Sinclair (316) 358-3131*

Description (2): This nature center walk follows dirt paths and gravel roads. The trail is not marked, but you'll receive a map and instructions at the start point.

See and Stay: Take time to enjoy the nature center, once a 1900s farm managed in ways that protected and enhanced area wildlife. In nearby Arkansas City, visit the Cherokee Strip Land Rush Museum, which depicts the 1893 land run for more than six million acres.

Hours: Tues.-Sat., 9 A.M.–5 P.M.; Sun. 1–5 P.M.; closed Mon.

☑ Restrooms and water only at the nature center. Muddy after rain or snow melt.

Where Is It? Start at the Chaplin Nature Center Visitors Center, about 50 mi. southeast of Wichita and about 5 mi. northwest of Arkansas City. The center is easy to reach via the Kansas Turnpike (I-35). Take I-35 past and south of Wichita. Get off at Exit 4, Hwy 166, to Arkansas City.

Sponsor: Friends of Nature Volkssport Club, Box 129, Grenola, KS 67346

LAWRENCE ◆ City Walk
◆ Levy Walk

Dates: January 1–December 31   *Cindy West (913) 842-4958*

Description (1+) (1): The city walk goes through late 1800s neighborhood, the University of Kansas, and quaint shopping district with uneven sidewalks and curbs. The level levy walk includes 2.5 miles along the Kansas River. Eagles, foxes, and deer are sometimes seen. Good birding, including waterfowl. Unlit trail may be soggy after rain or snow melt.

Food and Fun: This college town has great shopping, abundant lodging, and good restaurants. KU's art and natural history museums are among the best.

☑ Parking can be tight near hotel. Several metered spots, plus the hotel lot, are only for 2 hrs. Stretch the time in unmetered city lots. KU activities such as May graduation and football weekends can make lodging reservations essential.

Where Are They? Walks start at the Eldridge Hotel at Seventh and Massachusetts Sts. **From I-70:** Take East Lawrence exit. Turn left after toll booth and follow highway until it crosses bridge and continue 1 blk. to Seventh St. Hotel is 1 blk. to your left on the corner.

Sponsor: Free State Walkers, 1125 Vermont, Lawrence, KS 66044

KANSAS

LEAVENWORTH ♦ *City Walk*
♦ *Fort Walk*

Dates: January 1–December 31   *Community Center (913) 651-2132*

Description (1 +): The city walk, on mostly level sidewalks, features this historic city's splendid old Victorian homes, including the "Allen House," with its 21 rooms, nine fireplaces, and attic ballroom. The fort walk is a history buff's treasure. Beautifully maintained, this old military post, built in 1827, offers a museum, historic old homes, views of the Missouri River, and wagon ruts from the Santa Fe and Oregon Trails. One steep hill will challenge you, or choose an alternate route. Your fort walking map provides a detailed description of the buildings and their history.

See and Stay: Explore the fort, which maintains much of its turn-of-the-century flavor. Don't miss the antique carriages at the Fort Leavenworth Frontier Army Museum or a peek inside the Memorial Chapel. Ask for the "Jaywalker's Rate" at the Best Western Hallmark Inn, Commanders Inn, Terrace Court Motel, Lansing Inn, Ramada Inn, or Super 8 Motel. Camping available at Riverfront Park by the Leavenworth Bridge.

Hours: The Riverfront Community Center is open Mon.-Fri., 6 A.M.–9 P.M.; Sat., 9 A.M.–7 P.M.; Sun., 1–6 P.M.

Where Are They? Start downtown at the Center, 123 Esplanade, at the east end of Delaware St., (913) 651-2132. **From the north:** Via Hwy 92 or 7/73 West, turn south on Fourth St. and left onto Delaware. **From the south:** Take Hwy 7/73 downtown and turn right on Delaware, which ends at the community center. Ample parking near the center, but avoid the 2-hr. zones.

Sponsor: Kansas Jaywalkers, P.O. Box 3136, Ft. Leavenworth, KS 66027

KANSAS

The Buffalo Soldier Monument honors black soldiers of the late 1800s who were instrumental in opening the West. Courtesy of the Leavenworth Convention and Visitors Bureau.

KANSAS

LENEXA ◆ Neighborhoods Walk

Dates: January 1–December 31   *Marv Blevins (913) 341-8597*

Description (1 +): This walk, with a 20K option, goes through parks, lovely neighborhoods, and along paved bike paths that pass creeks and a small lake. Paths may be secluded in early mornings or late evenings, and might be muddy in spots after heavy rains. Watch for winter ice.

Food and Fun: 10% walkers discount at Holiday Inn, Super 8, Guesthouse Apartment Hotel, Motel 6, Day's Inn, and La Quinta, all at 95th St. and I-35. Panzon's, a restaurant on the walk, serves good Mexican food. RV hookups and camping at Longview Lake, 25 min. away in Missouri.

🚲 A 25K bike trail also is available in Overland Park. Check in at center and drive to start point.

Hours: No earlier than 8 A.M. and no later than 3 hrs. before sundown.

Where Is It? Start at the Lenexa Community Center, 13420 Oak, just off Pflumm Road, (913) 541-0209. **From I-35:** take the 95th St. exit and proceed west to Pflumm. Turn right (north) on Pflumm, then right (east) on Oak to the community center parking lot.

Sponsor: Heart of America Volkssport Club, P.O. Box 4472, Shawnee Mission, KS 66204

TOPEKA ◆ Capital Walk

Dates: January 1–December 31   *Terri Tyler (913) 233-4385*

Description (1): This walk takes in the sights of Kansas's capital, including the historic Victorian Ward-Meade House and gardens, downtown area, shaded neighborhoods, and even a brief peek inside the capitol. Route is entirely on city sidewalks.

See and Stay: Relax in Gage Park between Sixth and Tenth Sts. on Gage Blvd. Its 160 acres include the Topeka Zoological Park, with its gorillas and orangutans; the Reinisch Memorial Rose Garden; and a restored 1908 carousel, which will take you for a melodious spin for just 50¢. The Holiday Inn City Center offers a special volkswalkers' rate.

Where Is It? Start at the Holiday Inn City Center at 914 Madison, at the intersection of Tenth Ave. and I-70. **From the east:** Use the Tenth Ave. exit. **From the west:** Exit at Eighth Ave. and go south 2 blks. to Tenth, turn left and cross over the interstate to the inn.

Sponsor: Sunflower Sod Stompers, P.O. Box 2576, Topeka, KS 66601

KANSAS

WICHITA ♦ Downtown Walk

Date: February 15–December 31

Description (1): This walk will take you through the downtown and along the scenic Arkansas River. You'll pass refurbished older homes, historical sites, and the Wichita-Sedgwick County Historical Museum. Watch for waterfowl along the river and in the parks.

See and Stay: The Old Cow Town Museum, on 17 acres, includes restorations and reproductions of 44 buildings dating from 1865 to 1880, including Wichita's first jail and first residence. Many of the buildings are furnished with period artifacts, and Texas Longhorns graze nearby. Children also will enjoy the Children's Farm at Sedgwick County Zoo and Botanical Gardens and the Wichita Children's Museum with its many hands-on exhibits. The Family Inn offers discounts to walkers.

The club sponsors a 35K bike trail that follows the Arkansas River.

Where Is It? Start at the Family Inn, 221 E. Kellogg, at the intersection of Kellogg (US 54) and Broadway. I-35 (Kansas Turnpike) goes right to Wichita. Exit 50 onto Kellogg will take you to the inn. Exit 45 will connect you with Hwy 15, which travels into the downtown area and intersects with Kellogg a few blocks from Broadway.

WICHITA ♦ Park Walk

Dates: March 20–October 31 (seasonal)   Gene Corns (316) 838-6633

Description (1): This walk through residential areas will take you inside Sedgwick County Park.

A 25K bike path also starts from the YMCA and goes primarily inside Sedgwick County Park.

Where Is It? Start at the Wichita YMCA-West Branch, at 6940 Newell, 1 blk. south of Central and Ridge. **From US 54 (Kellogg):** From the center of town, go west on Kellogg to Ridge. Turn right (north) on Ridge and go to Central. The YMCA will be on your right at the corner.

Sponsor: Wichita Skywalkers Volkssports Club, 3257 N. Charles, Wichita, KS 67204, for both walks.

KENTUCKY

COVINGTON ◆ Historic River Walk
◆ Devou Park Walk

Dates: January 1–December 31 Carol Langen (606) 581-0335

Description (1 +)(3): Both walks offer scenic views of the Ohio River and the Cincinnati skyline. The river walk takes you past Covington Landing, the nation's largest floating restaurant-entertainment complex, and into MainStrasse, a restored German village. The hilly and more challenging Devou Park walk takes you to the city's overlooks and past the Behringer-Crawford Museum. This shady walk is a good summertime choice.

See and Stay: Stop in Goebel Park in the MainStrasse district. This 30-square-blk. area offers shops, restaurants, and homes styled after Old Germany. Catch a concert here in the spring and summer or Oktoberfest in the fall. From Memorial Day to Labor Day, catch a river cruise on the Ohio. The Holiday Inn offers discounts to walkers.

Where Is It? Start at the Holiday Inn-Riverfront, Third and Philadelphia St., (606) 291-4300. **From north or south on I-75:** Take Covington/Fifth Sts. exit (#192). Go east on Fifth to the first light. Turn left on Philadelphia and go to Third, where you'll find the inn.

Sponsor: Northern Kentucky Trotters Walking Club, 1826 Garrard St., Covington, KY 41014

FORT CAMPBELL ◆ Fort Walk

Dates: January 1–December 31 ESTEP Wellness Center (502) 798-4664/4023

Description (2): Located on an army post on the Kentucky/Tennessee border, this walk on paved or graveled roads includes some steep hills and rocky shoulders.

See and Stay: On or near the base, you'll find a nature center, and historic and military museums. Explore Land Between the Lakes, a 170,000-acre wooded peninsula that offers camping, boating, fishing, hunting, hiking, wildlife observation areas, a living-history farm, and other regional attractions and events. Take in another walk just a few miles away in Clarksville, Tenn.

Where Is It? Start on the post at the ESTEP Wellness Center, Bldg. 2270, 14th St. and Kentucky Ave., (502) 798-4664/4023. The fort is between Hopkinsville, Ky., and Clarksville, Tenn., on Hwy 41A. **From I 24: Take Exit 86 west.** Follow 41A to Fort Campbell, Gate #4. **From Clarksville:** Follow 41A to Gate #4. Register at the Welcome Center before entering the post.

Sponsor: Fort Campbell Striding Eagles, ESTEP Wellness Center, Ft. Campbell, KY 42223

LOUISIANA

NEW ORLEANS ◆ *French Quarter Walk*

Dates: January 1–December 31   Debra McDougall (504) 641-5270

Description (1): The 100-square-blk. French Quarter beckons on this walk through the central business district and the historic spots in this city of jazz and jambalaya. Your route also will take you to Canal St., with its many shops, and to the Louisiana Superdome, the world's largest enclosed stadium-arena.

Food and Fun: Linger in "The City That Care Forgot." Indulge your tastebuds in any number of famous restaurants. Find a cozy eatery and sip café au lait and nibble on a beignet, a square-type donut. Admire the art and artists in Jackson Square or watch the barges, tugs, and tankers come into the harbor. Experience the harbor and Mississippi River firsthand by taking one of many riverboat cruises that leave from the wharf each day. Don't miss a stop in Preservation Hall to catch some traditional New Orleans jazz. Catch the St. Charles streetcar in the French Quarter and take a ride into the Garden District and view lovely homes surrounded by flowering shrubs, palms, and oaks. Kids will enjoy the 400-acre Audubon Park and Zoological Gardens.

Hours: Daily 11 A.M. until dusk. Please walk only during daylight hours.

Where Is It? Start this walk at Fritzel's Bar, 733 Bourbon St., (504) 561-0432, in the heart of the French Quarter. **From the west on I-10:** Exit right at Superdome/Claiborne Ave. (Hwy 90 east). Stay on Claiborne to Canal and turn right. Go on Canal until it intersects Bourbon. You can't turn left on Bourbon at this intersection, so go to the first available U-Turn lane and return to Bourbon. **From the east on I-10:** Exit right at French Quarter/Orleans Ave./Vieux Carré (Exit 235A). Turn left on Orleans and go 1 blk. to Claiborne (first traffic signal). Turn right onto Claiborne and go until you reach Canal. Turn left on Canal and proceed as above.

Sponsor: Crescent City Volkssport Club, 233 Putters Ln., Slidell, LA 70460

LOUISIANA

Built in 1794, St. Louis Cathedral is an imposing presence in New Orleans's Jackson Square. See walk description on previous page. Photo by Ron Calamia, courtesy of the Greater New Orleans Tourist & Convention Commission.

MAINE

PORTLAND ◆ Port Walk

Dates: January 1–December 31   *John Tibbetts (207) 774-8306, evenings*

Description (1): Amble in this port city that once was home to Longfellow and that now takes pride in restoring its old landmarks. This walk, entirely on city sidewalks, includes some quaint brick pathways and two hills. The walk's sponsor says it's wheelchair-friendly.

See and Stay: Pop into No. 487 Congress and visit Henry Wadsworth Longfellow's home, or linger in Fort Allen Park for a panoramic view of Casco Bay and the islands. The area known as Stroudwater still looks like it did 250 years ago, when mills, canals, and carefully decorated homes, like the Tate House, dominated the neighborhood. The Convention and Visitors Bureau, 305 Commerical St., Portland, ME 04101, (207) 772-5800, will be happy to give you details about the region.

Where Is It? Start at the Ramada Inn, 1230 Congress St., (207) 774-5611, which is just west of the intersection of I-295 and Congress. **From I-95 northbound:** Take Exit 6A and then the Congress exit. Take the first left to reverse direction and continue under I-295 to the Ramada. **I-95 southbound:** Take Exit 7 and follow the signs to I-295. Take the Congress (west) exit and then go left to reverse direction as above. Park away from the entrance.

Sponsor: Southern Maine Volkssport Association, P.O. Box 722, Westbrook, ME 04098

Wharf Street's interesting shops and brick sidewalks welcome visitors to Portsmouth's Old Port area. Photo courtesy of the Convention & Visitors Bureau of Greater Portland.

MARYLAND

ANNAPOLIS ◆ *Historic City Walk*

Dates: January 7–December 31   *Dick Brandt (410) 544-0396, evenings*

Description (2): This 11K walk takes you through this historic city, whose roots go back to 1649, and onto the Naval Academy. Annapolis has one of the highest concentrations of Colonial buildings in the U.S., so enjoy the architecture and feel of this old port city.

See and Stay: Go to the docks at Main St. and take one of the many Chesapeake Bay cruises. The city dock area also has a wealth of specialty shops. Explore the many historic homes and buildings. The State House, the oldest state capitol in continuous legislative use, briefly served as the U.S. Capitol.

☑ Headsets of any type are not permitted within the U.S. Naval Academy. The walk is closed near the end of May during Commissioning Week when the cadets graduate. Call the USNA, (410) 267-6100, for exact dates. The walk's sponsor says dogs are not encouraged.

Hours: Mon., 7 A.M.–3:30 P.M.; Tues.-Fri.,7 A.M.–5:30 P.M.; Sat., 8 A.M.–4:30 P.M.; Sun., 8 A.M.–1:30 P.M.

Where Is It? Start at Regina's Continental Delicatessen and Restaurant, 26 Annapolis St., (410) 841-5565/268-2662. **From I-95 to Baltimore:** Exit at I-895, through the tunnel to Exit 14 and then Exit 14A (Rt 3). Follow Rt 3 to I-97, Annapolis. I-97 merges into US 50/301. Exit US 50/301 at MD 70 South (Rowe Blvd.), also identified as Exit 24A. Turn left at first traffic light onto Melvin Ave. Go 2 blks. to Annapolis St. Turn right; Regina's is 1 blk. down on the left. Park behind the restaurant or on the streets.

Sponsor: Annapolis Amblers, 1228 Green Holly Dr., Annapolis, MD 21401-4687

MARYLAND

Washington resigned as commander in chief of the Continental Army in the State House, completed in 1779. Courtesy of the Annapolis & Anne Arundel County Conference & Visitors Bureau.

MARYLAND

BALTIMORE ◆ *Waterfront Walks*

Dates: January 7–December 31   Mary Kowalski (410) 282-4953

Description (1): Enjoy the harbor views from Federal Hill and historic landmarks on these walks, one a 10K, the other a 12K. Follow the cobblestone streets and paved paths past the historic sites of the inner city. You'll see Edgar Allen Poe's grave, Babe Ruth's birthplace, and the beautiful Inner Harbor. The 12K also lets you experience the city's colorful ethnic neighborhoods.

Food and Fun: Feast on blue crab, a Baltimore specialty. Revisit and linger in the historic places you've passed on the walk. The City Life Museum waives its fee on Saturday for all volkswalkers. Children will enjoy the Cloisters Children's Museum, (410) 823-2550, where they can learn by doing in a medieval castle. Take Exit 23 off I-695 and follow signs to 10440 Falls Rd. Pop in at the zoo or take a harbor cruise.

Hours: The museum opens at 10 A.M. (noon on Sun.) and closes at 5 P.M. from June to December and at 4 P.M. from January through May. It's always closed Mon.

Where Is It? Start at the Baltimore City Life Museum, 800 E. Lombard St. Enter through courtyard at the rear. **From I-95:** Take Exit 53 onto Rt 395 toward the Inner Harbor. Turn right onto Conway St.; go to the end at Light St. Turn left on Light and stay in the right lane to follow around Harborplace and onto Pratt St. Proceed east on Pratt, cross President (Rt 83) into Little Italy. Take the first left on Albemarle St. to Lombard. Turn left on Lombard; the museum is on your right. You'll find parking lots and metered spots in the area. The meters take only quarters—25¢ buys 15 min.

Sponsor: Star Spangled Steppers, 7905 Omega Ct., Kingsville, MD 21087

MARYLAND

COLUMBIA ♦ *Two City Walks*

Dates: January 7–December 31 *Bruce Taylor (410) 997-4803*

Description (1 +): This planned urban community of nine villages opened in 1967 and will be completed before the year 2000. The walks will take you past four manmade lakes and Columbia Town Centre. The 11K walk goes along the lakes, and includes some natural trails that might be muddy in wet weather. The 25K walk has one significant hill.

See and Stay: Shop at Columbia Mall, with its 195 shops and restaurants. In the summer, catch a concert at the Merriweather Post Pavilion. Columbia is between Baltimore and Washington, so visit the many attractions in those cities.

Hours: You can start by 10 A.M. Mon.-Sat. and by noon on Sun. You must be finished by sunset throughout the year, or earlier on Sat. and Sun. From Mar. to Dec., you must finish by 6:30 P.M. on Sat., and by 4:30 P.M. on Sun. From Jan. to Feb., finish by 5:30 P.M. on Sat. The shop is closed Sundays from Jan. to Feb.

☑ Be sure to allow 4.5 hours to complete Columbia's 25K trail. Feet First offers a 10% discount on walking shoes to walkers, and the Bagel Bin gives walkers a complimentary sandwich if you purchase one.

🚲 The walking club also sponsors three bike trails—one 25K trail and two 50Ks. All are on county-maintained roads. Call Don Weinel, (410) 997-0136, for more information.

Where Is It? Start at Feet First, in the Wilde Lake Village Green Shopping Center, 10451 Twin Rivers Rd., (410) 992-5800. **From I-95:** Take Exit 41B, Rt 175 West, toward Columbia. Follow 175 for 5 mi. to the junction of 175 and Rt 29. Here 175 becomes Little Patuxent Pkwy. Follow the parkway toward Town Center for two traffic signals. Immediately after passing through the intersection of the second signal, move into the right-most traffic lane and follow signs to Gov. Warfield Pkwy. Follow this parkway for two traffic lights to Twin Rivers Rd. Turn right onto Twin Rivers and follow it to Lynx Ln. Turn left onto Lynx. (A gas station and Roy Rogers are at the corner.) You're now in the shopping center. Feet First is located off Lynx behind Giant Food.

Sponsor: Columbia Volksmarch Club, P.O. Box 2251, Columbia, MD 21045

MARYLAND

GAITHERSBURG ◆ Seneca Creek Walk

Dates: January 7–December 31  *Ed Branges (301) 340-9418*

Description (2 +): Get a taste of wilderness in the city on this scenic woodland walk over moderately hilly terrain, through woods, fields, and along a lake. In wet weather a walking stick can offset slippery paths. Watch for deer and beaver, and Canada geese and blue heron along the shores. This trail has attracted thousands of walkers.
   Food and Fun: Kids will enjoy the excellent playground at the walk's half-way point. Pick up a lunch-to-go at the deli and picnic in the park. The Red Roof Inn offers reasonable rates, (800) 843-7663.
   ☑ No dogs allowed in the park.
   Hours: The deli opens at 10 A.M., Mon.-Sat., and at 11 A.M. on Sun. The park gate closes promptly at sunset.
   Where Is It? In Gaithersburg, start at the Gourmet Grog Wine-Beer-Deli, 614 Quince Orchard Plaza. From here you'll drive to the park's entrance at 11950 Clopper Rd., (301) 869-8100. **From the south:** Take Capital Beltway (I-495) to I-270 north to Exit 10 (Clopper Rd./Rt 117). Turn left at the second light, using the inside turnoff lane. Turn right again into Quince Orchard Plaza after passing Friendly's. Park behind the Texaco and walk to the deli next to Ernie's Pub. **From the north:** Take I-270 south to Exit 11B (Quince Orchard Rd./Rt 124 West). Stay in right lane. Turn right into plaza after passing Friendly's.
Sponsor: Seneca Valley Sugarloafers, P.O. Box 3716, Gaithersburg, MD 20885-3716.

LAUREL ◆ Historic District Walk

Dates: January 1–December 31 *Sandra Lynch (301) 725-0918*

   Description (1 +): Laurel was settled in 1669, and this walk through the historic district will take you past old homes, and give you views of the river and lake. You'll pass a former home of Dwight Eisenhower and the spot where George Wallace was shot.
   See and Stay: Visit the Montpelier Mansion, next to the Montpelier Cultural Arts Center. This 18th-century Georgian mansion includes boxwood gardens. The Comfort Suites hotel offers a discount to walkers.
   Where Is It? Start at the Comfort Suites, 14402 Laurel Pl., (301) 206-2600. **From I-95:** Take Exit 33A, Rt 198 East to Laurel. At US Rt 1, turn right and continue south on Rt 1 for about 2 mi. At Mulberry St. turn right. Go a short distance to Laurel Pl. Turn right onto Laurel Pl. Comfort Suites will be on the left. Park in the lot's outer edges.
Sponsor: Freestate Happy Wanderers, P.O. Box 495, Laurel, MD 20725

WHEATON ◆ *Wheaton Regional Park Walk*

Dates: January 1–December 31  Robert Heidenreich (301) 384-1586

Description (2): This trail, almost entirely within Wheaton Regional Park, offers woods, lakes, wildlife, and the Brookside Gardens and conservatory. The walk is particularly beautiful in the spring and at Christmas, when you can really enjoy the flowers in the garden and the conservatory displays. At the end of your walk, you'll discover a super playground and picnic area. A carousel and train ride are available seasonally. This popular walk attracts about 2,000 walkers a year.

Food and Fun: The deli carries a good selection of sandwiches and drinks. Or rest your feet and take a trolley ride at the National Capital Trolley Museum on Bonifant Rd., (301) 384-6088. There you'll find two carhouses filled with antique streetcars.

🚲 The walking club also sponsors a 25K bike path that starts in the park. Kids under 18 must wear helmets. Bike rentals at Ski Chalet of Kensington. Call Sandra Lynch, (301) 725-0918, for more details.

☑ Dogs are not allowed in the gardens. You can make a mail request for the alternate map that avoids the gardens.

Hours: Mon.-Sat., 10 A.M.–7 P.M., or sunset. Sun., 11 A.M.–6 P.M., or sunset.

Where Is It? Start at Wheaton Park Wine & Deli, 12039 Georgia Ave., (301) 949-8191. **From I-95/I-495:** Take Exit 31A (Rt 97, Georgia Ave.) north to Wheaton for about 2.8 mi. You'll pass Viers Mill Rd., University Blvd., and Arcola Ave. The deli is in a small shopping center on your right. Look for a Super Fresh Food Market. The deli is to the far left of the center.

Sponsor: Freestate Happy Wanderers, P.O. Box 495, Laurel, MD 20725

You're in a walker's paradise. Within 1 hr. of the White House, you'll find 11 AVA paths: these seven in Maryland, two in DC, and two in Virginia.

MASSACHUSETTS

CONCORD ♦ *Historic Walk*

Dates: April 15–December 15 (seasonal)   Charlie Smith (508) 263-5093

Description (1 +): Meander through history and the literary past on this walk that takes you to the homes of Ralph Waldo Emerson and Nathaniel Hawthorne; to Old North Bridge, site of the "shot heard 'round the world"; to the Minute Man National Historical Park; and to the town center. You'll encounter some stairs.

See and Stay: Enjoy Concord with its stately New England elegance, fine homes, interesting museums, and historic sites. Sleepy Hollow Cemetery contains the graves of Hawthorne, Emerson, Thoreau, and the Alcotts. Walden Pond is 1.5 mi. south on SR 126. Tired of walking? Rent a canoe from the South Bridge boathouse on SR 62.

Where Is It? Start at the main desk of the Howard Johnson Lodge, Rt. 2 and Elm St., (508) 369-6100. The lodge is midway between routes 128/I-95 and I-495. **From Rt 128/I-95:** Take Rt 2 west. Watch for Emerson Hospital on the left and turn right at the second traffic light past the hospital. The lodge will be on the right. **From I-495:** Take Rt 2 east. Watch for Concord Reformatory on the right. Keep in left lane and turn left at the traffic light. The lodge is on the left.

Sponsor: The Walk 'n Mass Volkssport Club, 1 Mohawk Dr., Acton, MA 01720

DANVERS ♦ *Village Witch Walk*

Dates: January 1–December 31   William Jenkins (508) 468-2104

Description (1 +): Explore this lovely town, which witnessed witchcraft hysteria in the 1600s. You'll walk past original home sites, the new memorial to the victims who refused to confess, the Peabody Library, and Clark Farm, offering wonderful annuals and perennials.

See and Stay: Explore Danvers and then complete your introduction to the witch trials by visiting nearby Salem, the site of the 1692 witch trials and home of the Salem Witch Museum, (508) 744-1692.

Where Is It? Start at the Danvers YMCA on Pickering St. **From Rt 62 east:** As 62 narrows to two-way traffic, you will go uphill and the road will curve left. As you start down, look to your right for Vineyard St. and take it. Then take an immediate left onto Pickering. The YMCA will be .5 mi. on the right. **From I-95 southbound:** Take the Rt 1 exit. Take Rt 62 east and proceed as above. **From the west:** Take I-90 east or I-93 south to I-95/128 north. Continue on I-95/128 north to split. Bear right on I-95. Then take Exit 49 onto Rt 62 east.

Sponsor: Massachusetts State Volkssport Association, 3 Arthur Ave., South Hamilton, MA 01982

MASSACHUSETTS

MARTHA'S VINEYARD ♦ *Oak Bluffs Walk*
♦ *Edgartown Walk*

Dates: Mid-May to Mid-October (seasonal) Leo Convery (508) 627-3721

Description (1) (2): The 10K Oak Bluffs Walk follows the shore around East Chop and then tours the Camp Meeting Grounds. The 12K Edgartown walk visits historical areas, passes sea captains' homes, and tours the downtown and the docks.

See and Stay: Linger on this charming island, walk the beaches, or shop in Oak Bluffs' bustling shopping district. Visit one of the wildlife refuges, where you can avoid the crowds. The Oak Bluffs State Lobster Hatchery is open to the public during the summer.

 This walking club also sponsors a 26K bike path along shoreline and country roads. For bike rentals check with the Oak House staff.

Where Is It? Start at the Oak House Inn B&B, Seaview Ave., Oak Bluffs, (508) 693-4187. The ferry from Woods Hole or Falmouth goes to Oak Bluffs, on the island. The Oak House is a .25 mi. walk from the dock. Call for ferry schedules: Woods Hole, (508) 548-3788, or Falmouth, (508) 548-4800. **To Woods Hole:** Take I-495 south over Bourne Bridge. Follow Rt 28 south to Woods Hole and then on to Falmouth.

Sponsor: The Walk 'n Mass Volkssport Club, 72 Kennedy Dr., North Chelmsford, MA 01863

SALEM ♦ *Historic Walk*

Dates: Spring to Fall (seasonal) U.S. Park Service Visitor Center (508) 741-3648

Description (1 +): See historic buildings on this walk that goes past Salem State College; Pioneer Village, a living history museum; Derby Wharf, with its views of Salem Harbor; the House of the Seven Gables and Hawthorne's birthplace; and beautiful Salem Common.

See and Stay: Lose yourself in history in this area, and enjoy the museums and historic sites. Try the AVA walks in nearby Concord, Sudbury, Danvers, and Topsfield. Tired of walking? Go to the docks and take a harbor cruise or go on a whale watch.

Hours: The Visitor Center is open from 9:15 A.M.–5 P.M., or until 6 P.M. in mid-season.

Where Is It? Start at the information counter of the U.S. National Park Service's Visitor Center in Museum Place. Continue with directions for Salem Shore Walk.

Sponsor: Friendship Walk Club, 174 Derby St., Salem, MA 01970

MASSACHUSETTS

SALEM ♦ *Shore Walk*

Dates: January 1–December 31  *William Jenkins (508) 468-2104*

Description (1 +): This walk will take you past the shore of Collins Cove and continue to Salem Willows, with its island views. You'll go on to the House of the Seven Gables and the Witch Trial Memorial and pass Town Hall, Witch House, Witch Dungeon, and the Witch Museum.

Where Is It: Start at the front desk of the historic Hawthorne Hotel on Salem Common, (508)744-4080. **To Salem from I-95/128 going west and north around Boston:** Where I-95 and Rt 128 split, continue on 128 to Exit 26 in Peabody. At the bottom of the exit ramp, turn right onto Lowell St., which jogs and becomes Boston St. Go past McDonald's. At the second set of lights, turn left onto Bridge St. Go under the overpass and half way around the traffic circle. Turn right at flashing light onto Winter St. At the Salem Common turn right. At the light turn right onto Essex St., then take next right into parking garage. Park free on Sat. and Sun.

Sponsor: Massachusetts State Volkssport Association, 3 Arthur Ave., South Hamilton, MA 01982

SUDBURY ♦ *Wayside Inn Walk*

Dates: April-December (seasonal)   *Betty Foley (508) 443-4857*

Description (1): This 11K walk goes along country roads and lanes to the restored Wayside Inn, made famous by Longfellow's poem "Tales of a Wayside Inn."

Food and Fun: Grab a bite at the Wayside Inn, the oldest continuously operated inn in the U.S., or at the start point, before exploring this region rich in Colonial history and famous literary figures such as Nathaniel Hawthorne and Louisa May Alcott.

The walking club offers a 35K bike path from May-Nov. in nearby Lincoln. The path goes to Walden Pond, a wildlife sanctuary, and Great Meadows National Park. Start at the Lincoln Guide Service in Lincoln. Call Betty Foley (508) 443-4857 about details and rentals.

Where Is It? Start at the Coach House Inn, 738 Boston Post Rd., Rt 20, (508) 443-2223, between routes 128 and 495. **From I-95:** Take Exit 26 and follow Rt 20 west for 10 mi. The inn will be on the right. **From I-495:** Go north to the Marlborough exit and Rt 20. Follow 20 for 8 mi. into Sudbury. The inn will be on your left about 2 mi. into Sudbury.

Sponsor: The Walk 'n Mass Volkssport Club, 72 Kennedy Dr., North Chelmsford, MA 01863

MASSACHUSETTS

TOPSFIELD ◆ *Wildlife Sanctuary Walk*

Dates: March 17–December 5 (seasonal)   Mary Saratora (508) 777-0148, evenings

Description (2): Enjoy the Ipswich River Wildlife Sanctuary on this walk through fields and forests and along marshes and swamps. The park, which covers 3,000 acres, is free to Audubon members; non-members must pay $3 for adults and $2 for children and seniors.

Hours: May-Oct. 9 A.M.–5 P.M.; from Nov.–April open 10 A.M.–4 P.M. Closed Mondays.

☑ Dogs not allowed. Rest rooms and water available only at start point.

🚲 There's a seasonal 25K bike path in nearby South Hamilton, Mar.-Dec. Start at the Bay Road Bike Store, 18 Bay Rd. (Rt 1A), (508) 468-1301. Helmets required.

Where Is It? Start at the office of the Audubon Society home in the wildlife sanctuary, (508) 887-9264. **From I-95:** Exit at Rt 97 and go south. Cross Rt 1 at the lights and continue south on 97. Take the second left (Perkins Row), and follow the Audubon signs.

Sponsor: The Walk 'n Mass Volkssport Club, 72 Kennedy Dr., North Chelmsford, MA 01863

MICHIGAN

Marquette ◆ Lake Superior Walk

Dates: January 20–December 31   Julie Ballaro (906) 346-2580

Description (1): Nature lovers will enjoy this walk with a 20K option. The path goes along Lake Superior and includes Presque Isle, home to many birds and mammals, such as swans, geese, deer, raccoons, and muskrats. The Upper Peninsula's scenery is beautiful, even in the winter. Mostly flat and on cement walkways, this trail is great for anything on wheels.

See and Stay: Linger to enjoy the scenery, visit the Maritime Museum and the lighthouse, take a boat ride, or see the largest wooden dome in the world at Northern Michigan University. In the winter, Presque Isle is groomed for cross-country skiing and snowshoeing. You'll find several motel chains in the area. Anyone affiliated with the military can arrange to stay on K.I. Sawyer AFB-MI.

Hours: Daily between 9 A.M. and 4:30 P.M.

☑ Dogs are not allowed on Presque Isle. This walk is windy, even in the summer, and cold in the winter, when you should dress warmly and watch for snow and ice.

🚲 The club sponsors a 25K bike trail. Call Ballaro for details.

Where Is It? The walk starts at the Marquette Welcome Center, at U.S. Hwy 41, 5 min. south of Marquette, (906) 249-9066. **From Wisconsin:** Pick up Hwy 41 on Wisconsin's east side and follow it to Marquette. **From Michigan:** I-75 goes north across the Mackinac Bridge and on to Rt 28. Take Rt 28 west, where it intersects Hwy 41 just east of Marquette.

Sponsor: Yooper Troopers Volksclub, 410 SPTG/MWO, K. I. Sawyer AFB, MI 49843

PLEASE PAY BY CHECK

You never have to pay a club to walk its volkswalk trails. Many walkers, however, like to buy the award the club offers. These awards usually are medals, multi-colored patches, cane shields, hat pins, or sun catchers, and usually cost about $5. Walkers who don't want an award, but who are keeping an official log of their walks and who want their walking books stamped, must pay about $1.50. Clubs prefer you pay by check, and some insist on it. A check is more secure and usually gives the name and address of everyone who's walked the trail. Remember, even if you're walking for free, you should fill out a start card. Clubs need to know how many walkers enjoy their trails each year.

MINNESOTA

ALBERT LEA ♦ Myre Big Island State Park

Dates: Memorial Day to Labor Day (seasonal) Jerry Katzenmeyer (507) 373-5084

Description (3): This gently rolling walk over natural trails will take you through a mixture of open and wooded areas and along a lake. Watch for the many wildflowers and pelicans.

See and Stay: The park has full-service camping. Stop in Albert Lea and visit the Freeborn County Museum and Historical Village, featuring furnished original 19th-century buildings. Browse through the log cabin, general store, schoolhouse, and blacksmith shop.

☑ Protect against ticks and mosquitoes. The humidity can be high.
Hours: Daily from 8 A.M.–5 P.M.
Where Is It? Start at the park office, (507) 373-5084. The park is located 3 mi. southeast of Albert Lea on Hwy 38. I-90 and I-35 intersect just north of Albert Lea, and both interstates have signs directing you to the park. Exit 11 on I-35 is the most convenient approach. Ask the park staff where to park.
Sponsor: Minnesota State Park Volkssport Assoc., 500 N. Lafayette, St. Paul, MN 55155

BROOKLYN CENTER ♦ Two Trails

Dates: April 1–December 31   Donna Seline (612) 529-0552

Description (1): A north and a south trail go through a natural setting in the middle of a metro area just north of Minneapolis. The 11K south trail goes through parks, residential areas, and past a creek on mostly paved and shady trails. The 10K north trail follows a creek and goes around a lake, and offers a good chance to see wildlife and birds.

See and Stay: Explore the Twin Cities. Visit the Minnesota Zoological Gardens with 1,700 animals and 2,000 plant varieties. At the smaller Como Park Zoo in St. Paul, rent tandem bikes or paddle around in a canoe or rowboat.

☑ Directions are available for physically disabled walkers.
Hours: Mon.-Fri., 8:30 A.M.–10 P.M.; Sat., 8:30 A.M.–9 P.M.; Sun., noon–8 P.M.
Where Are They? Start at the Brooklyn Center Community Center, 6301 Shingle Creek Pkwy, (612) 569-3400, .5 mi. north of the Brookdale Shopping Center. **From I-94 or I-694:** Take the Shingle Creek Pkwy exit. From the east, turn right onto the parkway. The center is on the right just after you cross the freeway. From the west, the center is straight across the parkway at the bottom of the ramp. Park in the lot.
Sponsor: Minnesota State Volkssport Assoc., 221 26th Ave. N., St. Cloud, MN 56303

MINNESOTA

BURNSVILLE ♦ *City Walk*

Dates: April–December   Milt or Vicki Luoma (612) 890-7560/894-3213

Description (1): This level walk, entirely on city sidewalks, travels through a residential area with views of open fields.

See and Stay: Just south of the Twin Cities, Burnsville offers many motels and restaurants.

Where Is It? Start at the Red Roof Inn, I-35W and Burnsville Pkwy, (612) 890-1420. **From I-35W:** Exit at Burnsville Pkwy and turn west on parkway. Turn left onto frontage road (Aldrich Ave.). The inn is on the right. **From I-35E:** Exit at County Rd. 11, turn north, and follow it to parkway. Turn left on Burnsville Pkwy to Pleasant Ave. Turn left onto Aldrich, and the inn is on your right.

☑ The Twin Cities Volksmarchers also sponsors a walk in St. Paul and a bike path. For information about the start point for the walk and bike route, call or write Dennis Mashuga, (612) 4521-4808/342-8634, 1839 Walsh Ln., Mendota Heights, MN 55118.

Sponsor: Twin Cities Volksmarchers, 1839 Walsh Ln., Mendota Heights, MN 55118

LAKE BRONSON ♦ *Lake Bronson State Park*

Dates: Memorial Day–Labor Day (seasonal) Garry Barvels (218) 754-2200

Description (2): This fairly flat, all natural, mowed trail will take you through open prairie and wooded areas and along a lake. Watch for deer and moose, bald eagles and wildflowers.

See and Stay: This 2,983-acre park offers boating and boat rental, swimming, picnicking, and fishing. Camp along the lake or in semi-secluded sites.

☑ Stay on the trail to avoid ticks and poison ivy. Water available only at start point.

Hours: 8 A.M.–5 P.M.

Where Is It? Register at the park's contact station, (218) 754-2200, and get your directions to the start point. The park is located in the northwest corner of the state, near the Canadian border. **From Thief River Falls:** Go north on Hwy 59 and watch for the state park signs.

Sponsor: Minnesota State Park Volkssport Association, 500 N. Lafayette, St. Paul, MN 55155

> You'll have to pay $4 for a two-day permit to each Minnesota state park or an $18 annual fee that gives you unlimited entry to any state park during the year.

MINNESOTA

LAKE CITY ♦ *Frontenac State Park*

Dates: May 22–October 24 *(seasonal)*
  Weekends and holidays only

 Harry Roberts (612) 345-3401

Description (3): The first .5 mi. of this 11K trail is uphill; it then traverses ridges and bluffs and goes down ravines before flattening out for the last third of the walk. You'll be rewarded with one of the most beautiful vistas of the Mississippi River. The surface is mostly sod with some hardpack. Watch for the many birds that migrate over the area.

See and Stay: Take a cruise on Lake Pepin, or enjoy fishing and river views from Lake City or nearby Red Wing. Both towns offer an array of craft shops and antique stores. Red Wing, famous for its boots and pottery, has self-guided tours through its historic district.

☑ This trail is open only weekends and holidays from 8 A.M.–8 P.M. You can walk weekdays only upon special request with the park staff. Protect yourself against ticks and flies during late summer.

Where Is It? Start at the winter warming house parking lot after registering at the Frontenac State Park office, (612) 345-3401. The park is southeast of Minneapolis/St. Paul, on the Mississippi River and 10 mi. southeast of Red Wing on US Hwy 61.

Sponsor: Minnesota State Park Volkssport Assoc., 500 N. Lafayette, St. Paul, MN 55155-4039

Hilly paths in Frontenac State Park lead walkers along the bluffs and to views of the Mississippi River. Photo by Ann Fendorf.

81

MINNESOTA

LANESBORO ♦ *River Root State Park*

Dates: Memorial Day–Labor Day (seasonal)   *Bill Sermeus (507) 467-2154*

Description (1): This out-and-back trail goes past the historic Lanesboro Dam, along the old railroad bed, through rock cuts and woods, and past hills, fields, and farms. The asphalt surface and only one steep hill make this an excellent walk for anyone with disabilities. Watch for wild turkey, vultures, deer, fox, songbirds, and an occasional rattlesnake.

See and Stay: Lanesboro's downtown is on the National Historic Register, and the town provides maps for walking and car tours through this lovely area. Camp in the city park, where you'll find a large playground and fishing ponds and a storyteller on summer weekends.

☑ Start no earlier than 7 A.M. Protect against gnats and mosquitoes. Hazardous wild parsnip grows along the trail, so stay on the asphalt. Carry water.

Where Is It? Register at Mrs. B's Bed & Breakfast, 101 S. Parkway, (507) 467-2154, at the intersection of CR 8 and Parkway, on your left as you come into town. You'll get directions to the trail's start. **From I-90:** Take the exit for Rochester that goes south on Hwy 52 to Fountain. Turn east on CR 8 to Lanesboro.

Sponsor: Minnesota State Park Volkssport Assoc., 500 N. Lafayette, St. Paul, MN 55155

MANKATO ♦ *Betsy-Tacy Walk*

Dates: January 24–December 31 *Audrey or Earl von Holt (507) 625-5375*

Description (2): If you're familiar with the Betsy-Tacy children's book series by Maud Hart Lovelace, you'll love picking out the locations so familiar in these Mankato-based books. The walk, mostly on city streets, also includes a wood-chip path through a wood.

See and Stay: Visit the 1,145-acre Minneopa State Park, 4 mi. west, featuring two large waterfalls in a deep gorge and a 1860s gristmill. In town, Sibley Park, a wooded 100 acres next to the Blue Earth and Minnesota rivers, offers a botanical garden and picnic grounds.

🚲 This club also sponsors a bike trail. Start at the Cliff Kyes Motel, 1727 Riverfront Dr., (507) 388-1638. Call the von Holts for details.

Where Is It? Start in the main lobby of the Holiday Inn-Downtown, 101 Main St., (507) 345-1234. Mankato is southwest of the Twin Cities on Hwy 169.

Sponsor: Riverbend Striders, 1709 Linda Ln., North Mankato, MN 56003

MCGREGOR ♦ Savanna Portage State Park

Dates: Early June through Labor Day (seasonal)    Ron Kuschel (218) 426-3271

Description (2): You'll walk mostly through pine and hardwood forests on this walk around a lake that includes a portion of the historic Savanna Portage. Enjoy the abundant wildflowers, songbirds, and wildlife, including deer, raccoon, and, maybe, bear.

See and Stay: Camp in the state park or at Sandy Lake Lock and Dam, which has a swimming beach. Visit the Rice Lake National Wildlife Refuge 5 mi. south off Hwy 65. This 18,104-acre refuge shelters deer, black bear, grouse, ducks, and geese. Picnic or hike there.

☑ Protect against flies, mosquitoes, and ticks. Trail may be wet in low areas.

Hours: From 8 A.M.–5 P.M.

Where Is It? Start at the park office, (218) 426-3271, and get your directions to the start point. From McGregor, the park is 7 mi. north on Hwy 65, then 10 mi. northeast on County State Aid Hwy 14.

Sponsor: Minnesota State Park Volkssport Assoc., 500 N. Lafayette, St. Paul, MN 55155-4039

MONTICELLO ♦ Lake Maria State Park

Dates: April 24–October 17 (seasonal)    Mark Crawford (612) 878-2325

Description (2): This walk goes through rolling terrain and wooded areas on hardpack and grass. Enjoy scenic overlooks and small lakes and ponds. Watch for wildlife—deer, beaver, fox, and waterfowl.

See and Stay: Camp in the park, which offers hiking, boating and boat rental, and picnicking in its 1,580 acres. RV camping is available 10 mi. away; ask at the visitor center. Drive about 20 mi. to nearby St. Cloud and enjoy Munsinger Gardens, which displays more than 40,000 plants along the Mississippi River.

☑ The trail is open 8 A.M.–5 P.M. only, Fri.-Sun. and holidays. Water only at start/finish point. Protest yourself against insects and be prepared for mud after it rains.

Where Is It: Start at the Trail Interpretive Center, (612) 878-2325. The park is located about 35 mi. west of the Twin Cities, just south of I-94. The park can be reached from the north via County State Aid Highway 8 and Wright County 111, and from the south via CSAH 39 and 111. Watch for brown state park signs.

Sponsor: Minnesota State Park Volkssport Assoc., 500 N. Lafayette, St. Paul, MN 55155

MINNESOTA

RUSHFORD ♦ *Root River Trail State Park*

Dates: Memorial Day–Labor Day (seasonal) *Larry Neilson (507) 864-7720*

Description (2): Walk in hardwood forests in a spot once called "Little Switzerland." This trail of mowed grass and hard pack follows along the river and winds close to rolling wooded hills, fields, and farms. Watch for wildlife—songbirds, deer, vultures, and wild turkey.

See and Stay: Enjoy Rushford—one of the state's oldest settlements. Slip your own or a rented canoe into the Root River. Browse through the antique shops, play golf, or take a dip in the municipal pool. The Ernie Tuff Museum at the junction of I-90 and SR 43 has a complete 1890s country store. Kids will love the dreamland castle playground in Rush Creek Park.

☑ Start no earlier than 7 A.M. Protect against bugs—ticks, flies, and mosquitoes. The trail can get muddy or weedy. Come prepared for hot weather and humidity. Carry water. Wrens like to nest in one of the trail boxes, so please be careful when taking a card.

Where Is It? Check in at Larry's Mobil Station, at the junction of Hwys 16 and 43, (507) 864-7720, and get directions to the start. Rushford is 10 mi. south of I-90 on Hwy 43.

Sponsor: Minnesota State Park Volkssport Assoc., 500 N. Lafayette, St. Paul, MN 55155-4039

The Minnesota Department of Natural Resources coordinates a statewide recreational trail system. The state now has 12 multi-use trails—seven of which are seasonal AVA trails. If you'd like to know more about walking trails and camping facilities, contact the Minnesota Department of Natural Resources, Trails and Waterways Unit, Information Center, Box 40, 500 Layafette Rd., St. Paul, MN 55146. If you're from out of state, call (612) 296-4776, or (800) 652-9747 from within Minnesota.

The DNR also sponsors a hiking club for those who want to hike the state parks. Ask the DNR about the membership kit and the various goodies and perks that come with joining.

ST. CLOUD ♦ River Walk

Dates: *January 28–December 31*   David Hunt (612) 253-4762

Description (1) (1 +): Walk along the Mississippi River and through four parks and gardens, scenic residential areas, the downtown, and the university campus. You'll see fine architectural examples of the world-famous granite industry located in this area. Two sections along the park paths have alternate directions for people pushing wheelchairs. They will encounter some sidewalks without curb cuts.

See and Stay: See what's going on at the St. Cloud State University campus or at the convention center. Take a paddleboat ride. Visit Stearns County Heritage Center at 235 33rd Ave. S. This county historical museum also offers 8 mi. of marked nature trails with interpretive stations. For more information on area attractions, contact the St. Cloud Convention and Visitors Bureau, P.O. Box 487, St. Cloud, MN 56302, or call (612) 251-2940.

☑ Be prepared for the weather—cold, snowy and icy in the winter and humid in the summer. Protect yourself against mosquitoes, the unofficial state bird.

Where Is It? Start at the Sunwood Inn & Convention Center, 1 Sunwood Plaza, (612) 253-0606, downtown. St. Cloud is northwest of the Twin Cities off I-94. Exit at signs for Hwy 23 (Division St.). Turn north on Fourth Ave. S. and go to Sunwood Inn.

Sponsor: Central Minnesota Volkssports, 221 26th Ave. N., St. Cloud, MN 56303

☑ This club may add a second walk that will also start from the Sunwood Inn.

The State Passport Club gives patches and perks to those who visit 8, 16, 32, and 64 parks. Ask the DNR for a brochure that explains the program.

The Minnesota Office of Tourism, (800) 657-3700, has a travel information center that will supply you with a wealth of information if you tell them where you plan to walk and visit.

MINNESOTA

ST. PETER ♦ Quaint Town Walk

Dates: January 24–December 31   *Audrey or Earl von Holt (507) 625-5375*

Description (2): Enjoy this quaint town from yesteryear and get a taste of Swedish heritage on this walk. You'll go past a city park, some historical homes and through the lovely Gustavus Adolphus College campus.

See and Stay: Visit the historic Episcopal church, built in 1857. The stained glass windows were transported by oxcart and steamboat from New York and are still intact.

Where Is It? Start at the Americinn Motel, 700 N. Minnesota Ave., (507) 931-6554. St. Peter is just north of Mankato and south of the Twin Cities on Hwy 169.

Sponsor: Riverbend Striders, 1709 Linda Ln., North Mankato, MN 56003

SPRING GROVE ♦ Town Walk

Dates: May through October (seasonal)   *Maribeth Anderson (507) 498-5669*

Description (1+): Enjoy the small town atmosphere and Norwegian heritage on this walk that is mostly on sidewalks and city streets with some grass. You'll go through a park with playground and past many downtown shops and flower gardens.

See and Stay: Enjoy a treat in the Ballard House ice cream parlor or take a dip in the city pool. Spring Grove has quaint restaurants and reasonably priced motels. The full-service Supersaw Valley Campground is just 6 mi. from town in a beautiful, wooded valley.

Hours: Daily 10 A.M.–5 P.M.

Where Is It? Start at the Ballard House, 163 W. Main St., (507) 498-5434, across from the IGA grocery. Spring Grove is located south of I-90 in the southeast corner of the state. **From I-90:** Take either Hwy 44 south to Spring Grove or Hwy 52 south until it connects with 44.

Sponsor: Syttende Mai Komitteens Folkemarsj Stiftelse, P.O. Box 42, Rt 2, Spring Grove, MN 55974

The Minnesota State Park Volkssport Association publishes a booklet listing not only the seasonal walks, but also about 20 scheduled walking and biking events in the state park system. To get a copy, call the Information Center, (612) 296-6157, or write Box 40, 500 Layafette Rd., St. Paul, MN 55146-4039.

MISSISSIPPI

BILOXI ◆ Beach/Downtown Walk

Dates: January 1–December 31   Antje Tinsely (601) 875-7668/4098

Description (1): This easy walk in one of the country's oldest cities passes historic points of interest and landmarks and offers relaxing beach scenery.

See and Stay: Take in the many sights of historic Biloxi, including Jefferson Davis's home, or enjoy the natural setting of the western end of the Gulf Islands National Seashore area. Seasonal boat rides go to West Ship Island and the historic ruins of a Confederate fort.

Hours: Winter: Mon.-Fri., 8 A.M.–5 P.M.; weekends, noon–5 P.M. Memorial Day-Labor Day: Mon.-Fri., 8 A.M.–6 P.M.; Sat., 9 A.M.–6 P.M.; Sun., noon–5 P.M.

Where Is It? Start at the Biloxi Visitor Center, (601) 374-3105, corner of Hwy 90 and Main St. Biloxi is 80 mi. east of New Orleans and 60 mi. west of Mobile. **From I-10:** Take the exit for I-110, which goes direct to Biloxi and ends at Hwy 90, a few blocks west of Main.

Sponsor: Magnolia State Volkssport Club, P.O. Box 5346, Biloxi, MS 39534

OCEAN SPRINGS ◆ Historic City/Beach Walk

Dates: January 1–December 31   Bob Karvorik (601) 388-5485

Description (2): This 12K walk winds through quiet neighborhoods, along the beach, through woods, and down the nature trails of the Gulf Islands National Seashore Park.

Food and Fun: A favorite spot of artists, the town offers a wide selection of shops and galleries. Enjoy the beautiful homes and architecture, explore the beach and park, or feast on the abundant seafood.

Hours: Daily between 9 A.M.–5 P.M., the visitor center's hours.

🚴 A bike path is available. Call Antje Tinsely (601) 875-7668/4098 for information.

☑ Pets are discouraged, and must be leashed if taken.

Where Is It? Start at the Master Grill, (601) 872-2515, on Hwy 90E. Pick up your start cards and walk to Gulf Islands National Seashore Park. Have your card validated at the Visitors Center, and return your cards to the grill when you're finished. **From I-10:** Take the Ocean Springs exit, Exit 50, south to Hwy 90. Go east on Hwy 90E for 2 mi. to Hanley Rd. and the grill.

Sponsor: Magnolia State Volkssport Club, P.O. Box 5346, Biloxi, MS 39534

MISSOURI

AUGUSTA ♦ "KATY" Trail Walk

Dates: January 2–December 31   Larry McKenna (314) 739-3597

Description (1): Created out of an abandoned railroad corridor, this walk with a 20K option, follows a flat, easy, isolated, crushed limestone trail tucked in against the bluffs with views of the Missouri River. You'll see many birds, an occasional eagle, and deer early in the day.

See and Stay: Recognized as the first U.S. "wine district," Augusta invites you to tour its wineries, browse in its antique shops, galleries and many craft stores or sample the fare in its bakery, cheese, coffee, and spice shops or small restaurants. B&Bs also are available

☑ No water or bathrooms on the 10K stretch. Bathrooms located at 20K turnaround.

🚲 The "KATY" makes a great bike path. Some rentals and bike repairs available at the start point.

Where Is It? Start at the KATY Canteen, 5533 Water St., (314) 228-4627, at the Mo. River State Trail Head. Augusta is on Mo Hwy 94, about 15 miles west of the junction of 94 and US 40-61, west of St. Louis and south of I-70. Once in Augusta, follow the Mo. River State Trail signs..

Sponsor: SMTM Volkssport Society, 1300 New Florissant Rd., Florissant, MO 63033-2122

ELLISVILLE ♦ City Parks Walk

Dates: January 2–December 31   Elsie Voyles (314) 527-3070

Description (2): This 12K walk winds through neighborhoods, six city parks and natural trails and has several moderate grades and a short stairway. Enjoy the the abundant foliage in the changing seasons and look for the many birds that populate the area.

See and Stay: Enjoy St. Louis, just 30 minutes away, or Six Flags, just 20 miles away. Ellisville also offers the Chesterfield Mall, movie theaters, playgrounds, and an array of restaurants.

☑ Paved surfaces aren't cleared of ice and snow in the winter.

Where Is It? Start at the video counter in Dierberg's Supermarket, at Clayton and Clarkson roads. **From the east:** Take I-64 (also known as Hwy 40) west through St. Louis. Exit at Hwy 340, Clarkson/Olive exit. Turn left (south) on Clarkson, and go 3.9 miles to Clayton. Dierberg's will be on your right, just past the traffic light. **From the south:** Take I-270 to I-64 and go west to Clarkson/Olive exit. **From the west:** Take Hwy 40 at Wentzville to the Clarkson/Olive exit.

Sponsor: Die Ballwin Wanderfreunde, PO Box 1187, Ballwin, MO 63022-1187

MISSOURI

FERGUSON ◆ Neighborhoods Walk

Dates: January 1–December 31   *Dennis Overcash (314) 831-6858*

Description (2): Century-old large homes, 20th-century neighborhoods and subdivisions, and parks and playgrounds are combined in this suburban walk with a 20K option. The trail is paved, but hilly in spots. Some easier detours are possible for people in wheelchairs.
   Food and Fun: The walk includes a stop at Spencer's Bakery and there are several restaurants along the way. Kids will enjoy Caboose Park, with its two old railroad cabooses.
   Hours: The market is open Mon.-Sat., 8 A.M.–9 P.M.; Sun. 8 A.M.–6 P.M.
   Where Is It? Pick up your map and start card at Paul's Market, 1020 N. Elizabeth St. From there you will go .5 mi. to the January-Wabash Park. **From I-270:** Get off at Exit 28, and go south on Elizabeth Ave. about 1 mi. to the market.
Sponsor: St. Louis-Stuttgart Sister City Committee, 1535 St. Ives Dr., St. Louis, MO 63136

HERMANN ◆ Wine Country Walk

Dates: March 1 –December 31   *Tom Cabot (314) 486-2747*

Description (1): Explore this old (1836) community nestled in the "Rhine Country of Missouri." More than 100 buildings in this picturesque town are on the National Register of Historic Sites. Walkers can sample award-winning wines.
   Food and Fun: Admire the "gingerbread" houses and poke around in the craft and antique stores. The Stone Hill and the Hermannof wineries offer tours. Take the train to Hermann. AMTRAK's "Missouri Mule" stops near the start point, and you'll have time to walk, explore the town, and hop back on the train for home. Contact The Tourism Group, 314 Market, Hermann, MO 65041, (314) 486-2744, for information on accommodations and shops.
   Hours: Mon.-Fri., 9:30 A.M.–5 P.M.; Sat., 9 A.M.–5 P.M.; Sun., 11 A.M.–5 P.M.
   Where Is It? Start at Die Hermann Werks, 214 E. First St. **From I-70:** Take the exit for Hwy 19 and go south to Hermann. Right after you cross the bridge, you'll come to First. Turn left, and the shop will be down on your right. Park in the rear of the building.
Sponsor: Hermann Volkssport Assoc., RR 1, Box 60A, Hermann, MO 65041

MISSOURI

INDEPENDENCE ♦ *Historic City Walk*

Dates: January 1–December 31 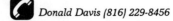 *Donald Davis (816) 229-8456*

Description (1 +): President Harry Truman, pioneers, early Mormons, and Civil War soldiers have all left footprints that can be seen on this walk, which includes more than 30 places of interest. The detailed walking map offers historical information and you can tour several of the visitors sights.

See and Stay: Linger in one of Missouri's most historic cities. Visit the 1859 jail, the Bingham Waggoner Estate, the Mormon Visitors Center, Saints Auditorium, the Truman Home, the Truman Library & Museum, and Vaile Mansion. Opening times and fees are listed on the walking map. You'll find abundant lodging in the Kansas City area.

☑ Tickets to the Truman Home are sold on a first-come basis at the walk's start point. The home looks as if the Trumans had just stepped out. Each 15-min. tour accommodates only eight people.

Hours: The start point is open daily from 8:30 A.M. to 5 P.M.

Where Is It? Start at the Truman Home Ticket and Information Center, 219 N. Main St., (816) 254-2720. **From I-70:** Exit at Noland Rd. Turn north to Truman Rd. Turn west to Main, and park in public lots. Several national park signs help to guide you.

Sponsor: Jacomo Bushedwalkers, P.O. Box 773, Blue Springs, MO 64014-0773

If you want to walk in **Jefferson City**, you can catch a walk that starts at the Days Hotel, 422 Monroe. Call Paul Hoffman, (314) 867-6897, or write him at 1535 St. Ives Dr., St. Louis, MO 63136, for details on this walk. Enclose an SASE with your request for the walk's brochure.

MISSOURI

Independence, home of Harry Truman, offers visitors numerous ways to learn more about their 33rd president. Photo by Judith Galas.

MISSOURI

KNOB NOSTER ◆ Woods Walk

Dates: January 1–December 31 Tom Persian (816) 563-6857

Description (3 +): This walk takes you through the wooded, hilly, natural setting of Knob Noster State Park.

See and Stay: You'll find many motels in the Warrensburg/Knob Noster area. The park offers new campgrounds with electrical hook-ups, grills and picnic facilities. Nearby Kansas City and Independence also provide many attractions.

☑ Absolutely no smoking in the woods. Rain, snow, and ice make the trail slippery, and walking canes can be helpful. Take precautions against ticks and chiggers.

Where Is It? Pick up your directions at Casey's, 609 McPherson St. **From I-70:** Exit at Hwy 23 and go south to Hwy 50. Cross Hwy 50 and go to McPherson and turn right to Casey's. **From Hwy 50:** At a flashing light, turn south off Hwy 50 onto 132 Hwy and go to McPherson and on to Casey's.

Sponsor: "Show -Me" Volksmarch Club, P.O. Box 1255, Warrensburg, MO 64093

LEE'S SUMMIT ◆ Longview Lake Walk

Dates: January 1–December 31   Bobbi Pommer (816) 524-3067

Description (1): This asphalt trail alongside the lake is flat and easy. Enjoy waterfowl and the natural peacefulness of this outdoor setting.

See and Stay: Longview Lake Park offers picnicking facilities, a model airplane field, horse park with bridle trail, and a golf course. The lake is suitable for sailing, fishing, boating, and swimming. Public camping, tent camping as well as electrical hook-ups, is available south of the recreation center off View High Dr. (follow signs).

🚴 The path around the lake is excellent for biking. Register at the center.

Hours: Mon.-Thurs., 6 A.M.–10:30 P.M.; Fri., 6 A.M.–8 P.M.; Sat., 8 A.M.–6 P.M.; Sun., 10 A.M.–6 P.M.

Where Is It? Pick up your directions and start card at Longview Recreation Center, 3801 SW Longview Rd. From there you'll drive to Shelter #14, where the trail begins. **From I-435:** Go to I-470 and travel east to Raytown Rd. Take Raytown Rd. south to 109th St., and 109th east to View High Dr., then south to West 3rd St. Go west to recreation center.

Sponsor: Pace Setters Volkssport Club, 208 N.W. Oldham Parkway, Lee's Summit, MO 64081

MISSOURI

LEMAY ◆ Jefferson Barracks Walk

Dates: January 1–December 31 *Shirley Thompson (314) 352-7118*

Description (1+): This 11K walk passes through Jefferson Barracks National Cemetery, one of the oldest and largest national cemeteries, and Jefferson Barracks Historical Park, once the largest military post in the U.S. You'll enjoy scenic beauty and bluff views of the Mississippi River.
See and Stay: Visit St. Louis or explore the park grounds. Stop at the museum in the 1857 powder magazine, at the ordnance building, and at the restored laborers' house and stable. The house and museum are open Wed.-Sat., 10 A.M.-5 P.M.; Sun. noon-5 P.M. Picnic facilities available.
Where Is It? The walk starts at Hardee's, 2866 Telegraph Rd., (314) 892-1950. **From I-255:** Take Exit 2, Telegraph Rd., Rt 231, and go north about .5 mile. Hardee's will be on the right at Franview Plaza, just past Sheridan Rd.
Sponsor: Missouri Marching Mules, 2428 Country Places Dr., Maryland Heights, MO 63043

ST. CHARLES ◆ "KATY" Trail Walk

Dates: January 1–December 31   *Rex Dix (314) 739-5059*

Description (1): Part of the KATY Trail abandoned railroad corridor, this walk follows a flat, easy, isolated, crushed limestone trail. The walk goes along the bluffs and past a quarry and several wineries. Bird watchers will enjoy an abundance of native birds.
See and Stay: Visit historic St. Charles, offering quaint B&Bs, antique and craft shops, a winery, and riverboat cruises. Noah's Ark, which uses animal decoration to carry out its ark theme, has reasonably priced rooms and offers discounts to American Youth Hostel members at its Lewis and Clark AYH-Hostel. The restaurant offers to-die-for clam chowder.
🚴 The walking club sponsors a level, easy 26K bike path and a 300-m. swim. Register at the front desk. The swim is available Memorial Day through Labor Day.
☑ No water or restrooms available on the trail.
Where Is It? Start at the Noah's Ark Best Western Motel, 1500 S. Fifth St., (314) 946-1000. **From I-70:** Exit at Fifth St. South. Go south past the light into the Noah's Ark parking lot. Proceed around the hotel to the back of the lot, where you will find the inn's entrance.
Sponsor: SMTM Volkssport Society, 1300 New Florissant Rd., Florissant, MO 63033

93

MISSOURI

ST. LOUIS ◆ Sightseeing Walk

Dates: January 1–December 31  Paul Hoffman (314) 867-6897

Description (2): This city walk gives you a sidewalk view of St. Louis's many tourist attractions: See the Arch, walk along the riverfront, browse or eat at Laclede's Landing, and shop 'til you drop at the renovated Union Station. The route is mostly flat, but cobblestones at Laclede's and stairs by the arch make this too difficult for strollers. Bring your camera.

Food and Fun: You won't lack for things to do. Sprawling Forest Park offers the Art Museum, Science Center, History Museum, and one of the country's best zoos—all free. Love Italian food? Visit the restaurants on the "Hill." Take in a major league baseball game or go to one of many live theater performances.

Hours: Start no earlier than 7 A.M.

☑ Dogs not permitted because the trail passes through commercial buildings.

Where Is It? Start at Courtyard by Marriott, 2340 Market, (314) 241-9111. **From I-55/I-70:** Take Memorial Dr. to Market and go 1.5 mi. west to hotel.

ST. LOUIS ◆ Central West End Walk

Dates: January 1–December 31   Paul Hoffman (314) 867-6897

Description (1): Prepare for a sensory experience on this walk through the historic neighborhood the 1904 World's Fair brought to life. Mansion-lined streets, delightful Forest Park, a stretch of boutiques, book stores, galleries, and pubs, the Cathedral of St. Louis, and a multiblock medical complex await you.

☑ Dogs not permitted because the trail passes through commercial buildings.

Hours: Start no earlier than 7 A.M.

Where Is It? Start in the lobby of the Best Western Inn at the Park, 4630 Lindell Blvd., (314) 367-7500. **From Rt 40/I-64:** Take Kingshighway North exit. Go north to Lindell and turn right (east) onto Lindell. The inn is about 1.5 blks. east on right side of street.

Sponsor: The St. Louis-Stuttgart Sister City Committee, 1535 St. Ives Dr., St. Louis, MO 63136, sponsors both walks.

MISSOURI

A tram carries visitors up the 630-ft., stainless steel Gateway Arch to the observation deck. Photo by Cindy West.

MISSOURI

ST. PETERS ◆ *Historic Walk*
◆ *City Walk*

Dates: January 2–December 31   Bob Armstrong (314) 278-6399

Description (1) (1+): The city walk, with a 20K option, is mostly paved and level and includes commercial areas as well as parks with playgrounds. The historic walk goes through parks and the city's old town, which dates back to the mid-1800s. You'll see All Saints Church, built in 1874, and several of the city's historic points of interest. Stairs and some gravel or grass paths make the historic walk unsuitable for strollers or wheelchairs.

See and Stay: Visit nearby St. Louis or historic St. Charles. Babler State Park, a few miles south on the Missouri River, offers camping, picnicking, horseback riding, and a pool and nature center.

The walking club sponsors a 25K bike trail that starts at the Granada Cyclery. Call Armstrong for details.

Where Are They? Both walks start at the video counter in Dierberg's Supermarket, 290 Mid Rivers Mall Dr. **From I-70:** Take Exit 222. Go south on Mid Rivers Mall Dr. about 3 blks. Dierberg's is on the left side. Please park in the north end of the parking lot.

Sponsor: SMTM Volkssport Society, 1300 New Florissant Rd., Florissant, MO 63033-2122

Dogs, listen up.

If you're on the trail with your master, be sure he or she remembers these tips:

• Take me only on walks that welcome me. I can't go in buildings or into wildlife reserves.
• Make sure I don't get too hot. Take a water bowl and fill it up at rest stops.
• If I'm old, small or chubby, give me frequent stops and water breaks.
• Protect me by keeping me on my leash.
• Pick up my droppings. If you carry plastic bags, you just put your hand in the bag, pick up my stool, pull the bag inside out and drop it all in the trash.

MONTANA

VIRGINIA CITY ♦ *Old West Walk*

Dates: May 1–September 30 *(seasonal)*   Melinda Tichenor *(406) 843-5454*

Description (3): You'll get a taste of the Old West on this walk through a reconstructed gold mining town at an elevation of 6,000 ft. The trail, entirely on gravel roads, includes some moderately difficult hills. Watch for eagles, deer, antelope, bear, moose, and coyotes.

See and Stay: Explore the more than 20 reconstructed buildings or tour in a horse-drawn wagon. On summer nights take in a melodrama at the Opera House or catch *The Brewery Follies* vaudeville show at the Gilbert Brewery. Hop on the Alder Gulch Work Train for a trip back to Nevada City to watch a gunfight or an Old West medicine show. The Virginia City campground, (406) 843-5493, has hook-ups and showers.

Hours: 8 A.M.–6 P.M. during May, and until 8 P.M. other months.

☑ Protect against ticks, watch for snakes, and carry water. It can get hot in the summer and muddy when it rains.

Where Is It? Start at Rank's Drug Store, 211 W. Wallace, (406) 843-5454. **From I-15:** Turn off at Dillon and take 41 to Twin Bridges, then 287. **From I-90:** Turn off east of Butte at Whitehall. Take 55 and then 41 to Twin Bridges, then 287. **From West Yellowstone:** Take 287, turning left out of Ennis. **From Bozeman:** Take 84 to Norris, then 287, turning right at Ennis to Virginia City.

Sponsor: Madison County Volkssport Club, P.O. Box 264, Virginia City, MT 59755

Restored buildings capture the look of Montana in the 1860s. Photo by Janet Benson.

97

NEBRASKA

BEATRICE ♦ Church Walk

Dates: January 1–December 31    Jean Miller (402) 228-1783

Description (1 +): You'll pass many churches and beautiful, older homes on this walk along shady sidewalks. Take note of the restored 100-year-old Gage County Courthouse. People pushing strollers may have some difficulty with curbs. Be on the lookout for black squirrels.

See and Stay: Visit Homestead National Monument, one of the first quarter sections of land to be claimed under the 1863 Homestead Act. Located 4 mi. north of Beatrice on SR 4, this site has an original homestead cabin, furnished with pioneer pieces.

Where Is It? Start at the Gas 'N Stop, 1116 N. Sixth St., (402) 223-2522. **From Hwy 77:** Take 77 (Sixth St.) into town; the Gas 'N Shop is located on the east side of the street. **From Hwy 136:** At the intersection of 136 and 77, turn left (north) on Sixth St. and go to the Gas 'N Shop. Please don't park right in front of the store.

Sponsor: Homestead Striders, 1918 Lincoln Blvd., Beatrice, NE 68310

BELLEVUE ♦ Fontenelle Forest Walk

Dates: January 1–December 31   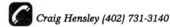 Craig Hensley (402) 731-3140

Description (3 +): You'll wind through an upland deciduous forest of oak, hickory, and basswood on this 12K walk that is hard to match for peaceful grandeur. About 200 species of birds and animals can be found here. Deer are numerous, and wild turkey might startle you as they crash through the brush. This walk on bare ground with exposed tree roots is hilly, and will take you to the forest floor and the circular depressions of a hunting-farming culture that lived along the Missouri River about 600 years ago. A swamp, marsh, farmstead, and magnificent views of the Missouri round out this strenuous but satisfying walk.

Although it's impossible for wheelchairs to navigate this trail, the Fontenelle offers a unique Equal Access Boardwalk that goes .5 mi. into the forest and back along smooth, wide planks with safety rails. This boardwalk is easily traveled by anyone with walking difficulties. The forest sounds have been piped into the nature center, giving everyone the sounds and feel of being in the deep woods. Small mammal and reptile displays and a complete nature gift shop also are in the center.

☑ No dogs. Water and rest rooms only at the start. Could be muddy or icy after rain or snow. The $3 fee is waived if the walker is paying for an AVA award or credit stamp.

Hours: Daily from 8 A.M.–5 P.M. Allow at least 3 hrs. for this walk.

NEBRASKA

Where Is It? Start in the nature center of the Fontenelle Forest, 1111 Bellevue Blvd. N., (402) 731-3140. The center is located just south of Omaha, 2 blks. east of US Hwy 75 and Southroads Shopping Mall. Watch for signs on 75 that show where you turn toward center.

Sponsor: Fontenelle Forest Volkssport Club, 1111 Bellevue Blvd. N, Bellevue, NE 68005

The Fontenelle's half-mile boardwalk gives every nature lover, including those in wheelchairs or with walkers, a chance to experience the forest firsthand. Photo by Mark Dietz.

NEBRASKA

FAIRBURY ◆ *Oregon Trail Walk*

Dates: April 17–October 31 *(seasonal)* Jean Miller (402) 228-1783

Description (2): Pretend you're a pioneer heading to Oregon alongside your wagon and oxen on this walk past wagon ruts and over the prairie grasses. Rock Creek Station State Historical Park rests on 400 prairie acres that are home to a variety of plants and animals.

See and Stay: The park offers oxen-pulled, covered-wagon rides on weekends from Memorial Day through Labor Day, and blacksmith demonstrations. Listen to the slide presentation in the visitors center on the Oregon and California Trails.

☑ No dogs. Be watchful of ticks, chiggers, and poison ivy. This walk won't be repeated in '94.

Hours: Open from April-Oct. Between Memorial Day and Labor Day open daily 9 A.M.–5 P.M. Otherwise open weekends only, Sat., 9 A.M.–5 P.M.; Sun., 1–5 P.M.

Where Is It? Start at the park's visitors center, (402) 729-5777. Rock Creek Station is located near Fairbury and west of Beatrice and Marysville, Kan. **From Beatrice:** Go west on Hwy 136 to the 136/103 intersection. Turn left on 103. Go to the intersection with the cemetery on your left and turn right and follow the blacktop road. Watch for the brown historical markers. The fourth one points to the left. Turn left and go 1 mi. south to the stop sign; turn left. Go to the park entrance.

Sponsor: Homestead Striders, 1918 Lincoln Blvd., Beatrice, NE 68310

FREMONT ◆ *Town Walk*

Dates: January 1–December 31 Mary Benderson (402) 721-1943

Description (1 +): Walk through residential areas on this trail that goes past Midland College, the Louis E. May Museum, and three parks.

See and Stay: Enjoy Fremont Lakes State Recreation Area, which has more than 20 lakes and offers camping, picnicking, hiking trails, fishing, boating and boat rentals. Take a 15-mi. train ride to historic Hooper on the Fremont & Elkhorn Valley Railroad tourist train. Call (800) 942-7245 for reservations and information.

Where Is It? Start at the Holiday Lodge, 1220 E. 23rd St. **From Hwy 77:** Go east onto Hwy 30 toward Fremont. Hwy 30 becomes 23rd St. Look for the lodge after you cross Bell St.

Sponsor: Fremont Volkssport Club, 635 E. 20th, Fremont, NE 68025

NEBRASKA

LINCOLN ◆ Residential Walk
◆ Campus Alternative

Dates: January 1–December 31   *Rose Quackenbush (402) 464-6972*

Description (1): Walk one or both 10K paths. One goes through residential areas and two parks on sidewalks with some curbs. The other goes through the University of Nebraska-Lincoln campus, the downtown, and an historical area.

Food and Fun: The Garden Cafe near the checkpoint on the residential walk offers great food at reasonable prices. Kids will enjoy Folsom Children's Zoo, which has more than 200 animals, a botanical garden, and a miniature railroad. Explore the state capitol or the University of Nebraska State Museum, which houses one of the world's best collections of modern and fossil elephants.

Where Is It? Start at Russ's IGA, 67th and O Sts. **From the west on I-80:** Take Exit 396 to O and turn left (east) and go to 66th. Turn left (north) on 66th to the first intersection. Turn right (east) and park in the shopping center lot. Enter the IGA from the south. **From the east on I-80:** Take Exit 409 to Hwy 6 and turn left (west) on Hwy 6 and go to 84th St. Turn left (south) on 84th and go to O. Turn right (west) on O to 68th. Turn right (north) on 68th to the first intersection and park in the center's lot.

Sponsor: Lincoln Volkssport Club, P.O. Box 83704, Lincoln, NE 68501-3704

OMAHA ◆ Chalco Hills Walk

Dates: January 2–December 31   *Rita Eldrige (402) 558-4061*

Description (1): This smooth asphalt hike/bike trail takes you around Wehrspann Lake, populated with marsh and water birds. Some moderate grades require extra pushing for those with wheelchairs, but the smooth surface and natural surroundings make this walk worth the push. Absolutely no shade.

Hours: Mon.-Fri., 8 A.M.–4:30 P.M.; weekends, noon–4 P.M.

Where Is It? Go to the self-service walk stand in the lobby of the Natural Resources Center of the Chalco Hills Recreation Area, 154th and Giles Rd. **From I-80:** Take Exit 440 to Hwy 50. Follow 50 north to Giles. Turn west into park entrance and follow signs to center.

☑ The club also offers a seasonal walk Mar. 1-Oct. 31. Start at the Nebraska/Omaha Tourist and Visitors Center, 10th and Deer Park; call Rita Eldrige, (402) 558-4061, for details.

Sponsor: Nebraska Wander Freunde Trailblazers, P.O. Box 27434, Omaha, NE 68127

NEBRASKA

SIDNEY ◆ Town Walk

Dates: May 15–October 17 (seasonal) 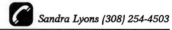 Sandra Lyons (308) 254-4503

Description (2): You'll walk in the heart of Nebraska wheat country. Enjoy the Living Memorial Gardens in Legion Park, with its Pixie Garden in an old children's pool and a map of the U.S. outlined by plants. The Fort Sidney District and its restored buildings will give you a glimpse of days past. On sidewalks and paved streets, this path has some inclines.

See and Stay: Don't miss Cabela's Sporting Goods store, the world's foremost outfitter for fishing, hunting and outdoor gear. The store has more than 500 mounted animals, many caught in dramatic action, and an 8,000-gallon aquarium.

Hours: Mon.-Fri., 6 A.M.–10 P.M.; Sat., 8 A.M.–8 P.M.; Sun., noon–6 P.M. In the summer, the center is closed on Sundays and open from 10 A.M.–4 P.M. Sat.

Where Is It? Start at the Cheyenne County Community Center, 627 Toledo St., (308) 254-7000. Sidney is in the Panhandle off I-80. Take Exit 59 and go north to the Old Post Rd. Turn left and follow the curve of the road until it intersects with 11th Ave. Take 11th to Toledo and turn right and go to the center. Use the south entrance.

Sponsor: Panhandle Walkers, 1530 Manor Rd., Sidney, NE 69162

YORK ◆ Town Walk

Dates: March 1–December 31   Yvonne Junge (402) 362-5247

Description (1): This easy town walk will take you through residential areas and Beaver Creek Park on pavement or a well-maintained trail. You won't find a hill, so it should be easy for anyone pushing a stroller or wheelchair.

Food and Fun: Catch a great meal at Chances 'R' Restaurant in a quaint Victorian setting. The Anna Bemis Palmer Museum in the York Community Center traces local history and offers a replica of a vintage bank and period rooms.

Where Is It? Start at Bosselman's Pump and Pantry No. 16, 109 Lincoln Ave. **From I-80:** Take the exit for Hwy 81 or Lincoln Ave. Go north about 2.5 mi. into York. Bosselman's will be at the corner of Second St. and Hwy 81.

Sponsor: Wellness Wanderers, 535 W. Sixth St., York, NE 68467

NEVADA

INCLINE VILLAGE ♦ Lake Tahoe Walks

Dates: April 1–December 31 (seasonal)   *Barbara Currie (702) 831-0434*

Description (1) (3): At an elevation of about 6,000 ft., these walks offer scenic beauty and some challenge. Both walks are on beautiful country roads, paved paths, and dirt shoulders. The walk's sponsor says the 10K walk is suitable for people in wheelchairs. The 12K walk climbs to 7,000 ft.

See and Stay: Explore the gorgeous Lake Tahoe area, nestled in a valley between the Sierra Nevada and Carson Ranges. You'll find plenty to do all around the shoreline: cruises, museums, and tram and cable car rides. While in Incline Village, visit the Ponderosa Ranch, a western theme park with the original Cartwright ranch house from *Bonanza*.

☑ Water and rest rooms are found along some of the route, but you should carry water. These walks will be cancelled when there's ice and snow.

Hours: Mon.-Sat., 10 A.M.–6 p.m.; Sun., noon–5 P.M.

Where Are They? Start at Fleet Feet, 930 Tahoe Blvd. in Raley's Center. **From Hwy 50 in Sacramento area:** Go east until you reach Hwy 28. Turn left and follow 28 to Incline Village. Turn right on Village and then right into the second driveway, which is Raley's Center. **From Hwy 80:** Take Exit 267, Truckee. Follow 267 to Hwy 28 and turn left. Follow 28 to Incline Village. Turn left on Village, and at the second driveway turn right into Raley's Center.

Sponsor: Sierra Nevada Striders, P.O. Box 4344, Incline Village, NV 89450-4344

LAKE TAHOE

Dates: May 15–October 15 (seasonal)   *Barbara Currie (702) 831-0434*

This walk is described in the California section under HOMEWOOD—Lake Tahoe Walk.

Sponsor: Sierra Nevada Striders, P.O. Box 4344, Incline Village, NV 89450-4344

☑ **Cross-Country Skiers:** The Tahoe Trail Trekkers sponsor a 10K cross-country ski trail and an 8K snowshoe trail near Tahoe City. These trails are open from December to April, weather permitting. Call Tahoe Nordic Ski Center, (916) 583-9858/0484, for details before going up.

NEVADA

LAS VEGAS ◆ City Walk
◆ Campus Walk

Dates: January 1–December 31   *Leroy Wilson (702) 399-1231*

Description (1): Paved, level sidewalks and streets make for easy walks in this casino city. The 10K walk passes by the Liberace Museum and through the UNLV campus, and the 13K walk takes in the casino strip. Be sure to catch the illuminated sight of the strip at night.

See and Stay: In addition to gambling, the city offers a variety of attractions. Kids will love the dolphins and erupting volcano at the Mirage and the high-wire gymnastics at Circus Circus. Beat the heat at Wet 'n Wild, with its 500,000-gallon wave pool, or visit one of the museums, such as the Guiness World of Records or Ripley's Believe It Or Not. The Liberace Museum, with the late entertainer's piano collection, cars, and million-dollar wardrobe, offers reduced admission to walkers presenting the coupon from the walk's brochure. The Mardi Gras Inn offers a $39 rate for walkers. Just say you're coming for the volksmarch. There are also a number of RV parks and campsites with casino shuttles.

☑ It's hot here June–Sept., with temps reaching 110°. Walk early or late to avoid the heat.

Where Are They? Start at the Mardi Gras Inn (Best Western), 3500 Paradise Rd., (800) 634-6501. The inn is .5 mi. east of I-15, between the Flamingo and Sahara exits. Park in the lot.

Sponsor: Las Vegas High Rollers & Strollers, P.O. Box 30153, North Las Vegas, NV 89036

The memorabilia-filled Liberace Museum offers a discount to walkers. Photo courtesy of the Liberace Foundation for the Performing and Creative Arts.

NEVADA

RENO ♦ Hilly City Walk

Dates: January 1–December 31   Lucille Gordon (702) 575-2212

Description (2): This hilly walk is along city streets. Walkers may need to pace themselves in Reno's 5,000-ft. altitude.

Food and Fun: Reno has numerous attractions. Enjoy a light meal along the Truckee River in Wheel's Roadhouse Cafe. Linger at the National Automobile Museum with its 200 vintage autos, period costumes, and multimedia show. Enjoy the Fleischmann Planetarium and the Mineral Museum near UNLV. Visit Pyramid Lake, 36 mi. north on SR 445. The lake, once the homeland of the Paiutes, is Nevada's largest natural lake and is surrounded by red and brown sandstone mountains.

Hours: Start no earlier than 8 A.M.

Where Is It? This walk starts at the Gateway Inn, 1275 Stardust St., (702) 747-4220. The inn is near the northwest corner of I-80 and Keystone Interchange. Take the Keystone exit and go north 1 blk. to Seventh. Turn left on Seventh, left at Elgin, and left at Stardust to the motel entrance.

Sponsor: Fernley-Wadsworth Lions, Lopers & Lollygaggers, P.O. Box 492, Fernley, NV 89408

RENO ♦ Auto Museum Walk

Dates: January 1–December 31   Barbara Currie (702) 831-0434

Description (1): This level walk on paved walkways and sidewalks includes a visit to the National Automobile Museum. The walk's sponsor says the path is suitable for wheelchairs, if you keep in mind you're pushing at a higher altitude.

☑ Snow or ice cancels this walk.

Hours: 9:30 A.M.–5:30 P.M. daily.

Where Is It? Start at the National Automobile Museum, 10 Lake St. S., (702) 333-9300. **From Hwy 80:** Travel east from Sacramento to Hwy 395 Business Route (Virginia) in Reno. Go south on Virginia and turn left on Mill to Lake. Museum is on the northwest corner of Lake and Mill. **From Hwy 50:** Head east and turn left on 395. Go north to Reno. Stay on 395 Business Route (Virginia) and turn right on Mill to Lake.

Sponsor: The Sierra Nevada Striders, P.O. Box 4344, Incline Village, NV 89450-4344

NEW HAMPSHIRE

CONCORD ◆ City Walk

Dates: April through November (seasonal) 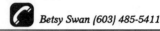 Betsy Swan (603) 485-5411

Description (2): You'll tackle several substantial hills on this walk, but will be rewarded with views of historic sites, including the state house and marvelous old architecture. Be careful at some busy intersections on this urban walk and expect some mud in the spring.

See and Stay: This small state offers a lot of outdoor recreation possibilities. Hike, fish, camp, or picnic in one of 37 state parks. Call or write the N.H. Division of Parks & Recreation, Box 856, Concord, NH 03301, (603) 271-3556, for information. Contact the N.H. Campground Owners Assoc., 30 Bonny St., Nashua, NH 03062, (603) 880-1471, for its camping guide.

Where Is It? Start at the Ramada Inn, 172 N. Main St., (603) 224-9534. **From I-93:** Take Exit 14 and turn left at the ramp, then right onto Main. Extra parking in the rear.

Sponsor: Seacoast Striders Volksmarch, P.O. Box 3151, Portsmouth, NH 03802

PORTSMOUTH ◆ Historic Walk

Dates: April 1–November 30 (seasonal)   Ronald Meattey (603) 332-3006

Description (1): See the historic downtown on this flat 11K walk. Tugboats, gardens, views of the naval shipyard, and many historic homes and churches await you.

See and Stay: Tour the submarine U.S.S. Albacore. Explore the 18 miles of the state's coastline or visit the White Mountain National Forest with massive Mt. Washington. This national forest has a network of shelters, each a day's hike apart. For hiking information contact the Appalachian Mountain Club, Box 298, Pinkham Notch, NH 03581, (603) 466-2725, or WMNF, Box 638, Lanconia, NH 03246, (603) 524-6450.

Hours: Start no earlier than 9 A.M.

Where Is It? Start at the Howard Johnson's Hotel, Interstate Traffic Circle, (800) 654-2000. The hotel is located at the intersections of I-95 (Exit 5) and Routes 1, 4, 16, and the Spaulding Turnpike.

Sponsor: Seacoast Striders Volksmarch, P.O. Box 3151, Portsmouth, NH 03802

NEW MEXICO

CLOUDCROFT ♦ Pines Walk

Dates: January 1–December 31   Robert Turner (505) 434-0405, evenings

Description (3): Smell the pines and enjoy the greenery on this scenic walk through a popular recreation village. You'll be at 9,200 ft. in the Sacramento Mountains, so take your time on the hills and be cautious if you have a heart or blood pressure condition.

See and Stay: Hit a few golf balls on one of the highest courses in North America. The Aspen offers a walker's discount, or treat yourself to a night at The Lodge, an elaborate, historic hotel, (505) 682-2566, built by the railroad for its passengers. Tour Sunspot, the Sacramento Peak Observatory, where the National Science Foundation conducts solar research.

Where Is It? Start at the Aspen Motel and Restaurant, Hwy 82, (505) 682-2526. **From I-25:** Take the exit for Hwys 70/82 to Alamogordo. Turn east where 82 breaks off for Cloudcroft.

Sponsor: Holloman Sun Runners, 3405 Fayne Ln., Alamogordo, NM 88310

☑ The Sun Runners plan to start an "Old Town" walk in nearby Alamogordo. Call Turner for details.

LAS CRUCES ♦ Neighborhood Walk

Dates: January 1–December 31   Bert Holland (505) 526-2219

Description (1+): Follow the blue arrows on this 11K trail on paved surfaces through lovely neighborhoods. The walk offers magnificent views of the Organ Mountains and a panoramic look at the Mesilla Valley. You'll have some moderate inclines and one steep, but short hill.

See and Stay: Visit Fort Selden State Monument, to the north, and get a feel of a frontier military post. Gen. Douglas MacArthur lived here when his father was commanding officer.

Where Is It? Start at Las Cruces Hilton, 705 S. Telshor Blvd., (505) 522-4300. **From southbound I-25:** Take the Las Cruces exit (Lohman Ave.) and keep to the left. Go to the light and turn left onto Lohman. Turn right at the first light onto Telshor Blvd. Then turn left at the first light and go to Hilton's parking lot.

Sponsor: Sun Country Striders, P.O. Box 6787, Las Cruces, NM 88006

NEW YORK

ALBANY ♦ Downtown Walk

Dates: January 2–December 31 *Lois Heyer (518) 477-6236*

Description (1 +): This 11K walk will take you through several historic downtown locations, the Capitol, Governor's Mansion, two parks, City Hall, and museums. People pushing strollers may need some assistance with one hill near the start/finish point.

See and Stay: Explore the Empire State Plaza, an 11-building complex on 98 acres, housing state government offices and cultural facilities. Kids will enjoy the 2-hr., narrated Dutch Apple River Cruises leaving from Broadway and Quay Sts., (518) 463-0220.

Hours: 10 A.M.–4 P.M., daily.

Where Is It? Start at the Albany Urban Cultural Park Visitors Center, 25 Quackenbush Square, corner of Clinton and Broadway, (518) 434-6311. **From I-90:** Go to I-787 and go south to Clinton Ave. exit. Visitor parking is left of exit, and the center is to the right of exit ramp. Park in parking lot. From Mon.-Fri., ignore the "Lot Full" sign and go to the ticket booth. Pay $1.50 to park. Have your ticket stamped at the Visitors Center and your fee will be refunded; booth closed on weekends.

Sponsor: Empire State Capital Volkssporters, P.O. Box 6995, Albany, NY 12206-6995

COOPERSTOWN ♦ Village Walk

Dates: April 24–December 31 *Winifred E. Balz (518) 372-3663*

Description (1 +): You'll get several views of the Susquehanna River on this walk through an historic village. Several homes from the early 1800s, museums, and Lake Otsego add to the charm. Watch for ducks and geese along the shoreline.

See and Stay: Don't miss the National Baseball Hall of Fame on Main St. Visit Fenimore House, home to author James Fenimore Cooper. This city was named for his father. A combination ticket will admit you to the Hall of Fame, Fenimore House, and Farmer's Museum, where artisans work in restored buildings. Enjoy a boat tour of Lake Otsego. Boats leave from the lake's southern tip off Fair St. Glimmerglass State Park, on the lake's northeast side, has camping facilities.

Hours: 8 A.M.–6 P.M., daily.

Where Is It? Go to the A.C.C. Gymnasium, on Susquehanna Ave., (607) 547-2800. Ask for the walk start box. **From I-88:** Take Exit 30 at Herkimer (Rt 28) and go north to Cooperstown. Once in town, go south on Susquehanna Ave. The gym is just over the Susquehanna River.

Sponsor: Empire State Capital Volkssporters, P.O. Box 6995, Albany, NY 12206-6995

NEW YORK

PLATTSBURGH ◆ Lake View Walk

Dates: April 3–October 31   William Wrisley (518) 561-0625, evenings

Description (1): Walk near the Canadian border and in view of Lake Champlain on this residential walk along city streets and sidewalks.

See and Stay: The SUNY Plattsburgh Art Museum in the university library displays the works of illustrator Rockwell Kent, photos by Ansel Adams, and prints and works by Picasso and Cezanne. Take a 2-hr., narrated cruise of Lake Champlain. Juniper Boat Tours leave from the foot of Dock St. Call (518) 561-8970 for schedules. If you're heading to Vermont, catch a Lake Champlain ferry that will scenically transport you to Grand Isle.

Hours: Start no earlier than 8 A.M.

🚲 The club sponsors a 31K bike trail that starts at the Wooden Skit Wheel. Call Wrisley for directions and details. Shop is closed Sundays.

Where Is It? Start at the Howard Johnson's Motor Lodge, I-87 and Rt 3, (518) 561-7750. The lodge is located at the intersection of Rt 3 and I-87. Take Exit 37 off I-87.

Sponsor: Adirondack Wanderers, 3 Roosevelt Ave., Plattsburgh, NY 12901

SARATOGA SPRINGS ◆ Resort Walk

Dates: February 27–December 31 (seasonal)   Ron Hersh (518) 885-6281

Description (1 +): Get a taste of thoroughbred horse racing on this 11K walk through one of racing's most popular resort towns. You'll pass the race track and walk through Yaddo Gardens and two parks with natural springs. The path includes a few minor hills. Call Hersh for information regarding a route for the physically challenged.

See and Stay: Learn about this vibrant resort town at Casino and Congress Park, which includes the story of Saratoga Springs. Visit the National Museum of Dance with its Dance Hall of Fame, or use the picnic pavilions and walking trails at Saratoga Spa State Park, just north on I-87.

Hours: Daily during racing season, July 22-Aug. 24, from 9 A.M.–5 P.M. During the rest of the year, open Tues.-Sat., 10 A.M.–4:30 P.M.; Sun. noon–4:30 P.M. Closed Mon., except when a holiday falls on Mon.

Where Is It? Start at the National Museum of Racing and Hall of Fame, (518)584-0400, at the corner of Union Ave. and Ludlow St. **From I-87:** Get off at Exit 14 (Saratoga Springs/Schuylerville). Go west on Union into Saratoga on Rt 9P north. The museum will be on your right. Park in the rear; enter from Ludlow.

Sponsor: Empire State Capital Volkssporters, P.O. Box 6995, Albany, NY 12206-6995

NEW YORK

SCHENECTADY ♦ *Historic Walk*

Dates: January 30–December 31   *Ellen McNett (518) 372-1270*

Description (1): This 11K trail shows you the highlights of this Mohawk River city, which dates back to 1661. The trail includes the G.E. Realty Plot historic district, with its 130 homes from the early 1900s. Enjoy this district's lovely yards and Union College's formal Jackson Garden and woodland. An informative map will add to your enjoyment of the area.

See and Stay: You might want to return to the G.E. Realty Plot and linger over the architecture in this community planned for G.E.'s executives. Explore in more detail the Stockade area, a 300-year-old neighborhood, or Union College, founded in 1779. Revisit the shops along Jay St.

Hours: Closed Mon. Tues.-Fri., 10 A.M.–4:30 P.M.; weekends, noon–5 P.M.

Where Is It: Start at the Schenectady Urban Cultural Park, at the front desk of the Schenectady Museum, Nott Terrace Heights, (518) 383-7890. **From the New York State Thruway:** Take Exit 25, then take the Crosstown 890 to the Broadway exit. Turn right on Broadway and then right on Millard, which becomes Veeder and then Nott Terrace. Turn right on Nott Terrace Heights.

Sponsor: Empire State Capital Volkssporters, P.O. Box 6995, Albany, NY 12206-6995

WEST POINT ♦ *Academy Walk*

Dates: January 2–December 31   *Farrell Patrick (914) 446-4709*

Description (1 +): This walk is entirely within the scenic U.S. Military Academy on the west bank of the Hudson River. Enjoy the area's natural beauty and the architecturally interesting buildings. Watch out for the cold and wind near the river. An informative walking map will add to your enjoyment of this historic area.

See and Stay: Explore this national historic site and visit the world's largest military museum. See the world's second largest pipe organ in the Cadets Chapel.

Hours: Daily from 7:30 A.M.–3 P.M.

Where Is It? Start at the Hotel Thayer Gift Shop, on the U.S. Military Academy, just outside Thayer Gate, (914) 938-4021. **From I-87 (New York State Thruway):** Exit onto I-84 going east. Take the Newburgh Exit off I-84. Take 9W South to Highland Falls. Take 218 through Highland Falls to Thayer Gate. Park in the hotel's lot.

Sponsor: Volkssport Club of West Point, P.O. Box 30, West Point, NY 10996-0030

NEW YORK

This sculpture in front of the Washington Barracks complex honors 1915 West Point graduate Dwight David Eisenhower, general of the Army and the 34th U.S. president.
Photo courtesy of the U.S. Army, U.S. Military Academy at West Point.

111

NEW YORK

The Niagara Frontier Volkssport Club has offered a seasonal walk in **Niagara Falls**. Contact Roger Black, (716) 627-3104, 5817 Lake View Ter., Lake View, NY 14085, to see when and where the walk starts. Remember to enclose an SASE with your request for a brochure.

The Adirondack Wanderers has offered a seasonal walk in **Ogdensburg**. Contact William P. Wrisley, (518) 297-8464/ 561-0625, 3 Roosevelt Ave., Plattsburgh, NY 12901, to see when and where the walk starts.

NORTH CAROLINA

WINSTON-SALEM ♦ *Three Walks*

Dates: *January 1–December 31* Mona Hunter (919) 766-5055

Description: Moravians, Protestants originally from Bohemia, first settled this town in 1753. These walks offer a rich sampling of the historic and picturesque sights that make up Winston-Salem.

Historic Bethabara Park Walk (3): For this walk you'll go to the start point to register and pick up your map and then head to the Visitor Center at Historic Bethabara Park, the site of the state's first Moravian settlement. The grounds include the church, houses, 40 original foundations, and a reconstructed fort. You'll follow a scenic pathway through historic wooded areas. Some hills, the uneven ground in the cemetery, and the possibility of some trail flooding after rain make this unsuitable for baby strollers. The park is open daily.

Downtown and Old Salem Walk (2): This walk winds through the downtown, quiet neighborhoods and Old Salem, a reconstructed Moravian town. There are some moderate hills and some steps.

Salem Lake Walk (2 +): You'll register at the Visitor Center for this 11K walk and pick up the map that points you to the lake. The trail around the lake is always open, but not the facilities, which are open daily, sunup to sundown, Memorial Day until Labor Day, and closed on Thursdays the rest of the year. From Dec.-Feb. the facilities are open from 9 A.M.–1 P.M.

This club also sponsors a 27K bike path and a 300-meter swim. Pick up start cards and directions at the Visitor Center or the Salem Inn. Call Hunter for more information.

Hours: The Visitor Center in downtown Salem is open Mon.-Fri., 9 A.M.–5 P.M. in winter and until 6 P.M. in summer; 10 A.M.–5 P.M. weekends. Anyone wishing to start any of the walks earlier may pick up a start card at the Salem Inn, 127 S. Cherry, (800) 533-8760 and then return to the Visitor Center after the walk to register and pay any fees.

Where Is It? Start at the Winston-Salem Visitors Center in the City Market Building at 601 N. Cherry, (800) 331-7018. **From I-40:** Follow I-40 to Business I-40. From Business I-40, take the Cherry exit and follow signs north to the center. Be sure you're on Business I-40.

Sponsor: *The Winston Wanderers, P.O. Box 15013, Winston-Salem, NC 27113*

NORTH CAROLINA

The Winston-Salem skyline shows the city's blend of modern buildings and historic neighborhoods snugged in among the trees. Photo courtesy of the Winston-Salem Convention and Visitors Bureau.

NORTH DAKOTA

FARGO ♦ Red River Walk

Dates: April–November (seasonal) Donald or Glenna Scoby (701) 235-3389

Description (2): Amble past magnificent homes with perfectly manicured lawns and through peaceful parks with lovely views of the Red River. Restoration in the downtown area and tree-lined neighborhoods make this a pleasant walk with plenty of shade in the summer.

See and Stay: Bonanzaville U.S.A., 2 mi. west of West Fargo, is a reconstructed pioneer settlement that shows the "Bonanza" farm era. Antique cars, a restored train depot and model train exhibit add to this attraction. Baseball fans must visit the Roger Maris Baseball Museum, commemorating the career of this native son. Ask the Townhouse Inn about its rate for walkers.

☑ The trail along the river may flood in the spring.

Where Is It? Start at the Townhouse Inn, 301 Third Ave. N., (800) 437-4682. **From I-29:** Take the Main St. exit and go east on Main to the downtown.

Sponsor: Red River Volkssport Assoc., 511 Forest Ave. #C, Fargo, ND 58102

Fargo's restored old depot now has a second life as a senior citizen entertainment center. Photo by Jan Jess.

NORTH DAKOTA

FORT RANSOM ♦ State Park Walk

Dates: May 1–October 15 (seasonal) *Wayne Beyer (701) 642-2811*

Description (3): Experience a remote section of the scenic Sheyenne River Valley. Walk under a canopy of elm, green ash, and bur oak; enjoy spectacular prairie vistas; and feel the quiet isolation of walking in a seemingly untouched setting. Fort Ransom is on the way to nowhere, but if you like wildlife and unspoiled natural settings, make it a point to go out of your way for an area that folklore says was once visited by the Vikings.

See and Stay: The park offers primitive and semi-modern camping. Walk-in tent and canoe camping sites can be found along the river. The peaceful Sheyenne is great for canoeing, and canoe rentals are available. Call the park, (701) 973-4331, for information, or write Park Manager, Box 67, Fort Ransom, ND 58033.

☑ The dirt parts of the trail can get muddy. Protect against wood ticks. Carry water.

Hours: Mon.-Sat., 7 A.M.–3 P.M.; Sun., 10 A.M.–3 P.M.

Where Is It? Start at the Fort Cafe, on Main St., in the town of Fort Ransom, (701) 973-2301. The state park is located 30 mi. south of Valley City, 18 mi. northwest of Lisbon, and 2 mi. north of the town of Fort Ransom, along the Walter Hjelle Pkwy. **From I-94:** Take exits 67 or 69 and go south to Hwy 46. Turn east on 46 and look for signs to the park.

Sponsor: Koda Manipe Volkssport Club, 120 N. Fourth St., Wahpeton, ND 58075

WAHPETON ♦ Two States Walk

Dates: May 1–October 15 (seasonal) *Wayne Beyer (701) 642-2811*

Description (2): You'll walk on sidewalks, streets, and asphalt walkways from the friendly town of Wahpeton across the Red River into Minnesota and back.

See and Stay: Kids will enjoy the Chahinkapa Zoo, from the Sioux word for "End of the Woods," which is where you'll be. Chahinkapa Park offers golf, camping, swimming, and picnicking.

Where Is It? Start at the Comfort Inn, 209 13th St. South, (701) 642-1115. **From I-29:** Take Exit 23 (Hwy 13) into Wahpeton. The inn will be on the right side as you enter town.

Sponsor: Koda Manipe Volkssport Club, 120 N. Fourth St., City Hall, Wahpeton, ND 58075

OHIO

COLUMBUS ♦ German Village Walk

Dates: January 4–December 31 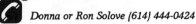 Donna or Ron Solove (614) 444-0424

Description (1 +): You'll explore the historic German Village and the downtown and pass the replica of the *Santa Maria*, Christopher Columbus's flagship. The trail follows city sidewalks. Some of the brick paths may prove hard on stroller-pushers.

Food and Fun: Revisit the restored 19th-century German village, the largest, privately funded, restored historical area in the U.S. You'll find quaint homes and lovely gardens, as well as craft shops, restaurants, and beer gardens within these 233 acres. Spend some time in Columbus. Visit the Columbus Zoo or COSI, Ohio's Center of Science and Industry. The Franklin Park Conservatory will let you tiptoe through the orchids and other exotic plants.

Hours: Weekdays, 9 A.M.–8:30 P.M.; Sat., 9 A.M.–8 P.M.; Sun., 11 A.M.–6 P.M.

Where Is It? Start at the Brown Bag Deli, 898 Mohawk, at the southeast corner of Mohawk and Whittier in the German Village. **From I-70 west:** Take Exit 100B (High St./Rt 23). Turn left at Third St. Take Third to Whittier and turn left. Go to Mohawk. **From I-70 east:** Take Exit 100A (High St./Front St.). Go straight on Livingston Ave. to Third. Proceed as above.

Sponsor: German Village Wander Volk, 115 W. Main St., #300, Columbus, OH 43215

Cincinnati offers two walks from January through December. One, in the Hyde Park suburbs, starts at Bob Roncker's Running Spot, 1993 Madison Rd. The shop is open Mon.-Fri., 11 A.M.–7 P.M., and Sat. from 10 A.M.–4 P.M. For information on this walk, contact Ted Ballman, (513) 385-1279, P.O. Box 39921, Cincinnati, OH 45239-0921.

The other Cincinnati walk starts at the Tischbein Pharmacy, in the Dixie Terminal Bldg., Fourth and Walnut Sts. Contact Angeline Kremer, (513) 761-1482, 507 W. North Bend Rd., Cincinnati, OH 45224. Kremer could also give you information on the walk in **Sharonville**, which starts at the Village Frame Shop, 3320 Creek Rd., on the square.

OHIO

This story-and-a-half cottage is typical of the homes found within Columbus's historic German Village. Photo courtesy of the German Village Society.

MAUMEE ♦ Canal Locks Walk

Dates: March 7–November 24 (seasonal)   *Kitty Hall (419) 885-4703*

Description (1 +): See the old canal locks that once connected Maumee to the larger Erie Canal transportation system and listen to the ongoing sounds of rushing, spilling water. In Side Cut Metropark, you'll walk along the canal towpath and the Maumee River to the Wolcott House Museum Complex and through historic parts of town. Watch for deer along the towpath. Strollers will have to navigate a few steps in the park. A detailed map adds to your enjoyment and the sense of history.

See and Stay: Return after your walk to explore the museum complex, including the Federal-style Wolcott home (circa 1830s), a log home, a saltbox-style farmhouse, and railroad depot with antique cars. Baseball fans will enjoy the Ohio Baseball Hall of Fame.

Hours: Mon.-Sat., 10 A.M.–6 P.M.; Sun., 11 A.M.–6 P.M. Call to check seasonal time changes.

☑ This walk, the only one in northern Ohio, has been receiving rave reviews. If you're in the area, don't miss it.

Where Is It? Start at Jacky's Ice Cream Depot, at the corner of W. Dudley and Allen St., (419) 893-0216. **From I-75:** Go to I-475 and from there use the Maumee exit. Follow Rt 24 east to Conant St. (third light). Turn right onto Conant, then right at the third light onto W. Dudley. The Depot is the stone building on the left at the next corner. Turn left into parking area. Additional parking is on West Mews off W. Dudley.

Sponsor: Maumee Valley Volkssporters, 1315 Hillcrest, Toledo, OH 43612

OHIO

MIDDLETOWN ♦ Park Walk

Dates: January 1–December 31  Bob Hawkins (513) 746-9394

Description (1 +): Visit the historic, old section with its beautiful period homes and parks. Your path will be entirely on sidewalks and a paved jogging path.

See and Stay: Take a dip in the Sunset Park pool. You are midway between Cincinnati and Dayton. In Cincinnati, visit the Zoological Gardens with its rare white Bengal tigers, or the city's Mount Airy Forest with hiking trails in 1,466 acres. In nearby Sharonville, stop at Sharon Woods Village with its restored 19th-century buildings. In Dayton, choose from the U.S. Air Force Museum, showing space capsules and vintage aircraft; the Aullwood Audubon Center and Farm, a 200-acre wildlife refuge; or Carriage Hill Farm, where you can experience a working farm from the 1880s.

Where Is It? Start at the Manchester Inn, 1027 Manchester St., (513) 422-5481. **From I-75:** Take Middletown Exit 32 (SR 122) and follow 122 west to downtown. Watch for Verity Pkwy. After you cross Verity, you'll continue to next light, which is Main St. Turn left on Main and look for the inn's parking signs just past the City Hall parking lot. The next light is Manchester. Park in the city garage on the next block, on the street, or in other lots.

Sponsor: Bulls Run Ramblers, 1809 Galway Circle, Middletown, OH 45042

PIQUA ♦ Historic Walk

Dates: January 1–December 31 Ed Mann (513) 773-1046

Description (1 +): Piqua's roots go way back. The principal village of the Miami Indians rested here, and Fort Pickawillany, an English trading post, was established in 1748. You'll walk through Piqua's historic district, primarily on shady sidewalks.

See and Stay: Visit the Piqua Historical Area. This 174-acre area is the site of a restored farmstead where you'll see demonstrations of pioneer crafts. The Indian Museum displays 18th- and 19th-century clothing and artifacts. Take a mule-drawn canal boat ride.

Hours: Start no earlier than 10 A.M.

Where Is It? Start at the Subway Sandwiches & Salads, in a shopping center at 1563 Covington Ave., (513) 773-4101. **From I-75:** North of Dayton, take the exit for Hwy 36 and go west to Piqua. Park in the shopping center lot, not in front of the shop.

Sponsor: Pickawillany Walkers, 512 Harney, Piqua, OH 45356

OHIO

WEST CARROLLTON ◆ *River Corridor Walk*

Dates: January 1–December 31  Phil or Carol Fretz (513) 859-6518

Description (1 +): You'll have your choice of two trails, both on sidewalks and city streets with a start point close to the Great Miami River. One walk has a hill, the other is flat.

🚴 This club also sponsors a 25K and 50K bike route from the same start point. The trails are mainly along the River Corridor Bikeway.

Hours: Start no earlier than 10 A.M. daily. Closed Sundays from January through March.

Where Is It? Start at Whitman's Bike Shop South, 5641 Marina Dr., on the bikeway across from Roberds, (513) 866-8022. **From I-75 southbound:** Take Exit 47 right to West Carrollton. Turn right on Marina Dr.; the shop is on the left. **From I-75 northbound:** Take Exit 47 for Moraine-Kettering to first light. Go 1 blk. past the light to Winwood Ave. and turn left. Go 1 blk. and turn left on Kettering Blvd. Stay to the right. When road merges go into right lane and turn right on Marina Dr.

Sponsor: Ohio Volkssport Assoc., 721 S. Detroit St., Xenia, OH 45385

WESTERVILLE ◆ *The "Dry" Walk*

Dates: January 2–December 31 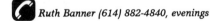 Ruth Banner (614) 882-4840, evenings

Description (1 +): During Prohibition, Westerville was known as the "Dry Capital of the World," and remains "dry" today. You'll pass the Anti-Saloon League Museum and grand homes on Temperance Row. The path includes Astronaut Grove Park, Otterbein College, historic buildings, and an array of antique shops. A detailed walking map adds to the fun.

Food and Fun: After your walk, grab a bite at Rosa's Deli, specializing in great sandwiches and soups. Return to visit the Hanby House, which you passed on the walk, and see this pre-Civil War home of composer—"Up on the House Top"—Benjamin Hanby. Be sure to visit the American Motorcycle Museum.

Hours: Mon.-Fri., dawn to dusk; start after 8 A.M. on Sat., and after 9 A.M. on Sun.

Where Is It? Start at Jerry's Westerville Marathon Service, 155 S. State St., northwest corner of State and Walnut, (614) 882-9879. **From I-70 or I-71:** Take I-270 to Exit 29 (SR 3, Westerville), and go north on 3 (State) to Walnut St. (sixth traffic light).

Sponsor: Westerville Boot-N-Leggers, 728 Waterton Dr., Westerville, OH 43081

OHIO

WILMOT ♦ Wilderness Center Walk

Dates: January 19–December 31 Earl Franks (216) 567-2716

Description (2 +): Woods enthusiasts will love this walk through upland forest, bottomland woods, prairie plantings and marshes. Sigrist Woods Trail wanders among some of Ohio's oldest trees. You'll also find a viewing pier on the lake, a wildlife observation tower, a viewing blind, boardwalks, and bridges over streams.

Hours: The Interpretive Center is open Tues.-Sat., 9 A.M.–5 P.M.; Sun., 1 P.M.–4:45 P.M. Closed Mondays and the Tuesdays following Monday holidays, when the center is open. The trails, however, are open dawn to dusk daily.

✔ No dogs, fires, or camping allowed.

Where Is It? Start at the Interpretive Building Book Store of the Wilderness Center, 9877 Alabama Ave., SW, (216) 359-5235. **From Akron:** Take I-77 south to US 62 at Canton. Take 62 west to Hwy 21. Go south on 21 to US 250. Go west on 250 to Wilmot. The center is 1 mi. west of Wilmot, just north of 250.

Sponsor: Gemütlich Wanderers, 127 N. Second St., Rittman, OH 44270

XENIA ♦ Scenic Trail Walk

Dates: January 1–December 31 Jean Scott (513) 372-6953/1802

Description (1): You'll have two 10K options on this walk. The scenic city path goes through historic, residential, and downtown Xenia. The other option, a bike and pedestrian path, is on the Little Miami Scenic Trail.

Food and Fun: Walkers get a free drink at Friendly Ice Cream, which has good food at family prices. You're close to Dayton and Cincinnati. See "Middletown" in this section for fun things to do in those cities.

🚲 This club sponsors a 30K bike path along the Little Miami Scenic Trail that's part of an 80-mile trail network extending from Eastern Cincinnati to Buck Creek State Park.

Where Is It? Start at Friendly Ice Cream, 608 N. Detroit St. **From I-70:** Going east of Dayton, look for I-675 S to Xenia. From I-675, turn left onto Rt 235 and go until it dead ends at Rt 68. Turn right to Xenia and go through four traffic lights. The shop is on the right.

Sponsor: Xenia Peg Legs, 20 S. Detroit St., Xenia, OH 45385

OKLAHOMA

LAWTON ◆ Prairie Dog Walk

Dates: January 1–December 31   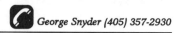 George Snyder (405) 357-2930

Description (1 +): Elmer Thomas Park has one of the largest prairie dog towns in the U.S. Watch these little guys scamper, and come with carrots, bread, and popcorn for the little beggars. Your route also passes Lawton's oldest building (1901), Little Chapel on the Prairie. Watch for migratory birds in the park.

See and Stay: Explore Lawton. Fort Sill Military Reservation, a National Historic Landmark, retains its frontier feel. Several Native American chiefs are buried here, including Geronimo. Hike in the Wichita Mountains Wildlife Refuge, 12 mi. south, and see bison, longhorn cattle, elk, deer, and wild turkey. The Ramada offers its corporate discount to walkers.

 No dogs allowed in the park. Grassy field at start may have springtime ticks.

Where Is It? Start at the Ramada, 601 NW Second St., (405) 355-7155. **From the south and east on I-44:** Take Exit 37 (Gore Blvd.) and go left (west) to Second St. (first light). Turn right (north) to Ferris, the next light. The inn is on your right. **From the north on I-44:** Take Exit 39B (Lawton) and go south .5 mi. The Ramada is on your left.

Sponsor: Holy Family Walkers Volksmarch Club, 1714 NW 49th St., Lawton, OK 73505

NORMAN ◆ University Walk

Dates: January 1–December 31   Nadine Gilchrist (405) 360-8824

Description (1 +): This 11K walk goes through residential areas and the University of Oklahoma campus, mostly on sidewalks with some grassy spots and several curbs.

Food and Fun: Stop by the OU Visitor Information Center, 407 Boyd, for maps and information on things to see on this 3,000-acre campus and university town. The Museum of Art and the Museum of Natural History offer interesting exhibits. This town has a variety of restaurants catering to college tastes and budgets.

Where Is It? Start at the registration desk of the Thunderbird Lodge, 1430 24th Ave. SW, (405) 329-6990. **From I-35:** On the west side of Norman, take Exit 108B (Lindsey exit). Go about .75 mi. east to first signal light at 24th Ave. Turn right (south) on 24th and go about .5 mi. to lodge on your right. Please don't park in front of the motel rooms.

Sponsor: Wandergruppe of Oklahoma City, P.O. Box 26282, Oklahoma City, OK 73126

OKLAHOMA CITY ◆ Two City Walks

Dates: January 1–December 31  *Marvin Baker (405) 329-0808*

Description (1 +): The 10K walk will take you through historic Heritage Hills, with its lovely homes, on to the Capitol complex, and through Bricktown, the entertainment district. You'll find one steep staircase near the end. The 12K walk goes through the Oklahoma City University campus and lovely neighborhoods. Don't be surprised by the oil wells in front of the capitol—this city was nourished by the discovery of oil and several strikes in and around the city still pump oil.

See and Stay: Spend some time in the Crystal Bridge, a 224-ft.-long, seven-story, glass cylinder housing a botanical conservatory. This unusual structure was built as part of the downtown's redesign under the direction of world-famous urban architect I. M. Pei. The city also respects its western heritage and offers The National Cowboy Hall of Fame, the Western Heritage Center, Frontier City, The Center of the American Indian, and many museums. Visit the Oklahoma City Zoo, the oldest zoo in the Southwest. Choose from a great selection of restaurants in Bricktown. You'll also find motel/hotel accommodations in the Oklahoma City/Tulsa areas to be among the cheapest in the country.

Hours: Daily, 9 A.M.–6 P.M.

☑ These are city walks, and you'll see some urban blight as well as signs of renewal and growth. Both walks will give you a sidewalk view of a city that literally sprang up overnight during a one-day land rush.

Where Is It? Start at the Crystal Bridge Botanical Garden in the Myriad Gardens, Reno and Harvey Sts. in the downtown, (405) 297-3995. **From I-40:** Eastbound drivers exit at Walker Ave.; westbound at Robinson Ave. (Exit 150). Head toward downtown area. Park in the free visitor lot on the east side of Myriad Gardens.

Sponsor: Frontier Walkers, P.O. Box 24122, Oklahoma City, OK 73124-0122

OKLAHOMA

SULPHUR ♦ *Nature Center Walk*

Dates: January 2–December 31 *Jeanie Moore (405) 622-6352*

Description (2): Take a 10K or 14K journey through natural beauty that first attracted early tribes, then settlers and now today's hikers and campers. Graveled trails and paved park roads will take you past fresh and sulphur springs and beaver dams, over stone bridges built by the WPA, through forests, and across prairies.

Hours: Daily, 8 A.M.–5 P.M., Sept.–May; 8 A.M.–9 P.M., June-Aug.

☑ Pets not allowed on part of the path. Stay on trails to avoid poison ivy, chiggers, and snakes.

See and Stay: Explore this beautiful area. Campers should call the center for information or write to Chickasaw National Recreation Area, P.O. Box 201, Sulphur, OK 73086.

Where Is It? Start at the Travertine Nature Center, (405) 622-3165. **From I-35:** From the north, take Exit 55 (Sulphur/Davis/Duncan). Go east on 7 through Davis and 8 mi. to Sulphur. From the south, take Exit 51 (Turner Falls/Davis). Go north on 77 to Davis. Turn east on 7 and go to Sulphur. In Sulphur, continue on 7 to the four-way stop, the main entrance to the Chickasaw National Recreation Area. Turn south into the park. At the first park road, turn left and go about 2 mi. to center.

Sponsor: Wandergruppe of Oklahoma City, P.O. Box 26282, Oklahoma City, OK 73126

In the Travertine Nature Center, water falls into a natural pool that is 50° to 65° year round. Photo courtesy of Al Heberlein.

OKLAHOMA

TULSA ♦ Keystone Lake Walk

Dates: January 1–December 31 *Bob Pugh (918) 446-7924*

Description (2): Walk along Keystone Lake and through scenic fields, camping areas and woods. Watch for wildlife—eagles, deer and squirrel.

See and Stay: Enjoy Keystone, which offers fishing, boating, a full-service marina, boat rentals, RV campsites, and unimproved campsites. Fully equipped, reasonably priced, year-round cabins—most with fireplaces—also are available. Call Keystone State Park direct, (918) 865-4991, to find out about rates and available dates, or contact the Oklahoma Tourism and Recreation Dept., Literature Distribution Center, P.O. Box 60000, Oklahoma City, OK 73146, for information and brochures. Call (800) 652-6552 daily.

Hours: Finish by 5 P.M. daily.

Where Is It? Start at the store near the dam at the entrance to Keystone State Park, between Hwy 51 and I-64. **From I-64:** Take the exit for Hwy 51A and go across the dam to the store.

TULSA ♦ Scenic City Walk

Dates: January 1–December 31 *Bob Pugh (918) 446-7924*

Description (1+): Find out how lovely Tulsa is on this sidewalk tour of beautiful neighborhoods, parks, historic sites such as the Philbrook Museum of Art, and the stylish Utica Square shopping area.

See and Stay: Stop and smell the roses in the Tulsa Rose Gardens, one of the finest municipal rose gardens in the nation.

Hours: Finish by 5 P.M. daily.

🚲 The club also sponsors a 25K bike path along the Arkansas River. Start at the Wheel Bicycle and Emporium Store, 815 Riverside Dr. Bike rentals available. Call Pugh for details and store hours.

Where Is It? Start at the Quik Trip Store #80, 2006 E. 21st St., between S. Utica and S. Lewis on East 21st. **From I-44:** Follow I-44/Hwy 66 into town. Take Lewis St. (Exit 92) and go north on Lewis to 21st, or take Exit 99 and go to 21st and then west to Lewis. Please don't park right in front of the store.

Sponsor: Green Country Wander-Freunde, P.O. Box 701856, Tulsa, OK 74170-1856, sponsors both walks.

OREGON

ALBANY ◆ Historical Downtown Walk
◆ City Walk

Dates: January 1–December 31   *Chuck Boeder (503) 967-9162*

Description (1+) (2): Albany has 500 of its early buildings still standing. The downtown walk will take you past many historical sites, across the Willamette River and along the river bike path to Montieth Park. The city walk goes along city streets and bike paths, through Heritage Mall (when open) and past duck-filled lakes and streams. (Please do not feed the ducks.) An additional 2K option is possible. The walk's sponsor suggests you not push strollers on the city walk.

See & Stay: Tour the area's covered bridges—Oregon has the most covered bridges outside New England. For information on bridges, lodging, attractions, and restaurants, contact the Albany Visitors Assoc., 300 Second Ave. SW, Albany, OR 97321, 1-800-526-2256.

☑ If you want a walking partner, call Boeder ahead of time. No restrooms at the start, but several along the route. Rain likely Oct.-April.

🚲 The club sponsors a 25K bike path that crosses the river and some railroad tracks.

Where Are They? Start at Pop's Branding Iron Restaurant, 901 Pacific Blvd. SE. **From the north on I-5:** Take Exit 234B, Hwy 99E/Pacific Blvd. **From the south on I-5:** Take Exit 233, Hwy 20/Santiam Hwy. Turn right (west) on 20, which joins Hwy 99E on Pacific Blvd.

Sponsor: The Albany Fitwalkers, P.O. Box 1218, Albany, OR 97321

Hundreds of Albany's original Victorian homes continue to delight visitors. Photo by Sharon Gleason, courtesy of the Albany Visitors Association.

OREGON

ASHLAND ♦ Hillside Walk

Dates: January 2–December 31 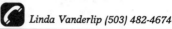 Linda Vanderlip (503) 482-4674

Description (3): This hilly walk rambles through neighborhoods and past quaint B&Bs, Southern Oregon State College, and the site of one of the oldest Shakespeare festivals. You'll climb for a scenic city view and then walk through 99-acre Lithia Park.

See and Stay: Culture and the outdoors combine in this area. Nearby Rogue River National Forest offers camping, whitewater rafting, and hiking. Mt. Ashland is a popular skiing area through April. From Feb.-Oct. take in a Shakespearean play.

Hours: Start no earlier than 9 A.M.; finish by dusk. Allow 3 hrs.

Where Is It? Start at Ashland Rexall Drug, 275 E. Main St., (503) 482-3366. **From I-5 southbound:** Take Ashland Exit 19, and follow signs into town. At old Hwy 99, turn left and go to the store. **From I-5 northbound:** Take the first Ashland exit, #11, onto old Hwy 99 south. Go several miles. (The street will change names.) Turn left at First St. and go 1 blk. to E. Main. Turn left; the drugstore is on your left in the middle of the block.

Sponsor: Ashland Hillclimbers, 305 Liberty St., Ashland, OR 97520

ASTORIA ♦ Scenic City Walk

Dates: January 1–December 31 Doris Larremore (503) 325-4734

Description (2 +): This scenic walk, mostly on city streets and sidewalks, goes past the old ferry landing and the spot where Lewis and Clark spent a winter at Fort Clatsop. You'll see filming sights of popular movies and museums, shops, and restaurants along a trail that includes some moderate hills and a small stretch along a railroad track.

Food and Fun: Gobble up seafood, shop on Pier 11, and visit the Columbia River Maritime Museum and the lightship *Columbia*.

Where Is It? Look for the self-start walk box in the lobby of Astoria's Columbia Memorial Hospital, 211 Exchange. Follow signs to Astoria from Hwy 101 or Hwy 30. **From the west:** Follow West Marine Dr. to Eighth St. Turn left onto Commercial and continue to 16th St. Turn right on 16th to Exchange. Turn left on Exchange and go to the hospital. **From the east:** Stay on Hwy 30 to 16th. Turn left on 16th. Then turn left on Exchange. Do not park in the hospital lot—it's often used for life-flight helicopter landings.

Sponsor: Turnaround Trekkers Volkssport Club, P.O. Box 975, Seaside, OR 97138-0975

OREGON

BEND ◆ *Neighborhood Walk*
◆ *Climber's Walk*

Dates: April 1–December 31 (seasonal) *Romona Greeno (503) 389-5036*

Description (1+) (4+): This sidewalk tour goes along city streets, through parks and the downtown, and along the Deschutes River. Two short, unpaved sections will be hard on strollers, but manageable. Climbers will love the walk that goes to the top of Pilot Butte for a panoramic view of central Oregon, including views of the Cascade Range, Mt. Hood, and Mt. Bachelor. At the start, you'll have a 500-ft. elevation gain in one continuous climb and then spiral upwards to the top, mostly on a paved path.

See and Stay: Recreation areas surround Bend: Tumalo State Park to the north, LaPine State Park to the south, and Drake Park along the Deschutes River, where you'll see flocks of waterfowl. Go to the High Desert Museum to the south and watch the otter feedings and birds of prey demonstrations.

This walking club also sponsors a seasonal 25K bike path along country roads with mountain views. Helmets required.

Where Is It? Start at a private home at 905 N.E. Franklin and look for the self-registration box in the carport. **From US 97:** Go into Bend and turn east on N.E. Franklin. Go to N.E. Tenth St. and turn right. Turn right again on N.E. Larch. Park behind the last house on the right on Larch (a cream-colored house with a blue metal roof). Walk around to carport.

Sponsor: Ponderosa Pathfinders, 905 N.E. Franklin, Bend, OR 97701

CANNON BEACH ◆ *Coastal Walk*

Dates: January 1–December 31 *Raymonda Dane (503) 738-7767*

Description (2+): This walk will take you past scenic coastal areas, beach homes, and Haystack Rock, the world's largest monolith. If the tide is out, explore the tidepools. Part of this walk is on the beach. An alternative is available for those who can't walk on dry sand.

See and Stay: Explore the stained glass, craft, and clothing shops on Hemlock. Visit Ecola State Park, 2 mi. up the coast, and observe sea lion and bird rookeries and a deer herd.

Hours: 10 A.M.–5 P.M., Jan.–late May and after Labor Day to Dec. 31; 10 A.M.–8 P.M. in season.

Where Is It? In Cannon Beach, start at Catch the Wind Kite Shop in Ecola Square at 1st and Hemlock. Follow the signs from Hwy 101 or Hwy 26 to Cannon Beach. Take the first Cannon Beach exit and follow Hemlock to the first street.

Sponsor: Turnaround Trekkers Volkssport Club, P.O. Box 975, Seaside, OR 97138-0975

CAPE PERPETUA ♦ *Three Climbers' Walks*

Dates: January 1–December 31 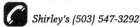 Shirley's (503) 547-3292

Description (3 or 3+): These walks each include a chance for walkers either to climb through spectacular old-growth forest or to get an expansive coastal view from the highest spot on the Oregon coast.

Walk No.1: This 10K walk goes near the ocean and the visitor center. An optional 4K walk will reward you with great views. The 4K walk climbs 600 ft. during 2K and increases the walk's difficulty rating to 4. Path might be weedy and windy.

Walk No. 2: This walk will climb about 4K through forest and into a meadow, then return through the forest to Gwynn Creek and the Oregon Coast Trail.

Walk No. 3: This 15K walk covers part of No. 2, but climbs an additional 400 ft. through forest into a meadow area, then returns via Cummins Creek and the Oregon Coast Trail.

See and Stay: Linger in Cape Perpetua and find an ancient rain forest, volcanic rock, tidepools and wildlife. See the sitka spruce that was a mere sapling when Columbus sailed. The visitor center offers *Discovery at the Edge,* a 15-min. movie describing the natural forces that created the Oregon coast. Siuslaw National Forest offers beachcombing and crabbing along 46 mi. of public beach, plus camping, boating, hunting, and picnicking.

Hours: **Cape Perpetua Visitor Center:** From Oct.-April, you can register from 10 A.M.–4 P.M. on weekends only and daily from May to Oct., from 9 A.M.–5 P.M. Park year-round at the center or at Devil's Churn Wayside, .25 mi. north of the Cape. **Shirley's:** Register daily from 9 A.M.–5 P.M. Please park on the street. Do not park in Clark's Market parking lot.

Where Is It? Register and pick up your maps and directions at either of two locations—the Cape Perpetua Visitor Center, (503) 547-3289, or Shirley's, next to the bakery in downtown Yachats. The season and times vary for each. The visitor center and Shirley's can be reached via coastal Hwy 101. Follow the signs for Yachats or the Cape Perpetua Visitor Center.

Sponsor: Yachats Coastal Gems, P.O. Box 896, Yachats, OR 97498

OREGON

COOS BAY ◆ 'Round Town Walk

Dates: February 1–December 31 Ann Warner (503) 269-4523/888-9809

Description (1+): This walk will take you along city streets to the bay, the Coos Bay Avenue of Flags, and to Mingus Park, which includes the Choshi Japanese Gardens.

See and Stay: Explore the largest city on Oregon's coast and one of the world's largest ports for forest products. Shop in the specialty stores at Mo's Golden Storehouse; visit the Coos Art Museum; tour the House of Myrtlewood, which manufactures various hardwood products; or visit Golden and Silver Falls State Park, with its two 200-ft. waterfalls.

Where Is It? Start at McKay's Market at the corner of Seventh and Central. Take coastal Hwy 101 to Coos Bay. Turn west at the First Interstate Bank (Commercial St.) and follow signs to ocean beaches.

Sponsor: South Coast Wavewalkers, Coos County ESD, 1350 Teakwood, Coos Bay, OR 97420

CROWN POINT STATE PARK ◆ Scenic Views Walk

Dates: April 15–Sept. 30 (seasonal) Ida Lieb (503) 663-9222

Description (5): This walk has some steep cliffs and dropoffs and may not be suitable for people afraid of heights or traveling with small children. Walkers are rewarded with spectacular views of the Columbia River Gorge.

See and Stay: The Vista House, built in 1917 for people traveling the then new Columbia River Highway, has a visitor information center. This is a day-use park, but you can camp overnight in nearby state campgrounds. For camping information, call (503) 695-2230, or call the Oregon State Parks and Recreation Department, (503) 378-6305.

☑ Stay on the trails and carry water. Restrooms and water can be found only near the start.

Hours: Daily, 9 A.M.–5 P.M.

Where Is It? Start at the Vista House/Gift Shop at Crown Point. **From I-84:** Take Corbett Exit 22. Go to top of the hill and turn left (east) on the Columbia River Scenic Highway to Vista House.

Sponsor: East County Windwalkers, P.O. Box 854, Gresham, OR 97030

OREGON

DESCHUTES RIVER ♦ Recreation Area Walk

Dates: January 1–December 31   *Cathie Bittler (503) 845-9499*

Description (4+): This walk on crushed gravel and semi-improved dirt trails has a 750-ft. elevation gain and offers magnificent views of the Deschutes and Columbia rivers.
See and Stay: Linger in the park to fish or whitewater raft. Camping is available. For information, call (503) 739-2322, or the Oregon State Parks and Recreation Department, (503) 378-6305. Nearby visit The Dalles, located on the trading crossroads Lewis and Clark named "the great Indian mart." This historic town, with 19th-century homes and churches and museums, offers self-guided tours.
☑ No water on the trail. Pit toilet at the 2K point.
Hours: Start no earlier than 8 A.M.; finish by 6 P.M. or dusk.
Where Is It? Start at Dinty's Cafe in the southeast quadrant of the road intersection. **From I-84:** Take Exit 104. Turn south about .25 mi. to the flashing traffic light.
Sponsor: Why B Normal Adventurers, 812 N. Meridian, Newberg, OR 97132

EAGLE CREEK ♦ Philip Foster Farm Walk

Dates: May 15–September 30 (seasonal)   *Marge Lusby (503) 252-7605*

Description (2+): Entirely on the shoulders of paved country roads, this 11K walk with one steep and one moderate hill goes along the Oregon/Barlow Trail. Foster Farm was a wagon stopover. You'll see livestock in this country setting and in the Eagle Creek park site. Watch for the colorful parachutes of the nearby jumping school.
See and Stay: Tour the farm or visit the recreational areas of nearby Mt. Hood. Several motel chains are located off I-205. Near Estacada and Carver you'll find camping facilities in several state parks.
☑ This walk will not be offered in 1994. Watch for poison oak along the roadways. Carry water and bring sun protection. Leashed dogs are welcome, but use caution around farm dogs and livestock.
Hours: Daily, 10 A.M.–6 P.M.
Where Is It? Start at Foster Farm General Store at the junction of Hwy 211 and Eagle Creek Rd. **From I-205:** Take Exit 12A at Clackamas to Hwys 212/224. Go 3.5 mi. Keep right at junction on Hwy 224 at Carver. Follow 224 left from Carver through Barton to junction of Hwy 211. Turn left at the flashing yellow. Go .25 mi. on Hwy 211, then 10 mi. at Eagle Creek. The farm is on the right. Do not park in front of the general store.
Sponsor: Columbia River Volkssport Club, 3333 NE 135th Ave., Portland, OR 97230

OREGON

EUGENE/SPRINGFIELD ♦ *Parks Walk*

Dates: *January 4–December 31*  Frank W. Ross (503) 726-7169

Description (2 +): Mostly on sidewalks and paved paths, the walk passes four parks and goes through the historic district and to two viewpoints. You'll climb a few short but significant hills, plus some stairs.

See and Stay: Explore Antique Peddlers I & II for such things as glass, primitives, pottery, books, quilts, and jewelry. Picnic on Island Park on the Willamette River or in Willamalane Park. Weyerhaeuser conducts early-morning tours of its pulp and paper facility.

🚲 The club sponsors a 31K bike path that goes for miles along beautiful McKenzie River. Bike/helmet rentals at Hutch's Bicycles, 2100 Main, (503) 741-2453.

Hours: Mon.-Sat., 10 A.M.–5:30 P.M.; Sun., noon–5:30 P.M.

Where Is It? In Springfield, start at the Antique Peddlers, 488 Main St., (503) 747-1259. **From I-5:** Take Exit 194A (I-105) at Eugene/Springfield and drive east to the first Springfield City Center exit. Turn right, go to north "A" St. Turn left to Fifth St., then turn right to Main, then right to Antique Peddlers. Off-street parking is available in city lots in the City Hall area.

Sponsor: Mossback Volkssport Club, c/o The Riverhouse, 301 N. Adams, Eugene, OR 97402

☑ The Mossback Volkssport Club also sponsors a walk and bike that start at Run Pro, 525 High St., in Eugene, (503) 343-1842. Call Frank W. Ross, (503) 726-7169, for more details and directions.

If you love walking near the ocean, then follow the walks south along Hwy 101 from Astoria to Gold Beach. There are 17 AVA-sponsored walks in 12 seaside communities beginning with Astoria and continuing south to Seaside, Cannon Beach, Lincoln City, Newport, Waldport, Yachats, Cape Perpetua, Florence, North Bend, Coos Bay, and Gold Beach. Come prepared for your ocean walks. Winter gusts can reach 80 m.p.h. and summer winds can gust to 60. Jan.-Mar. is the rainiest time and July-Sept. is the driest.

FLORENCE ♦ 'Round Town Walk

Dates: January 1–December 31 *Shirley's (503) 547-3292*

Description (1 +): The rhododendrons grow wild along the roadsides of this walk that will take you on city streets, sidewalks, and bike paths. You'll visit the old town area and have good views of the Siuslaw River.

See and Stay: The rhododendrons bloom in late spring and the town celebrates with a festival the third weekend in May. Visit the Sea Lion Caves, 11 mi. north on Hwy 101, the only year-round home for wild Steller sea lions on the mainland. A flight of stairs or elevator will take you to the 1,500-ft.-long viewing cavern. You'll also enjoy the sand dunes that lie between the town and the ocean. View the area from the observation deck in nearby Harbor Vista County Park. Catch a good bowl of clam chowder at Mo's.

Hours: From Oct. 1-April 30, 9 A.M.–7 P.M., Mon.-Sat.; 10 A.M.–5 P.M., Sun. From May 1-Sept. 30, 9 A.M.–9 P.M. Mon.-Sat.; 10 A.M.–6 P.M., Sun.

☑ Water and restrooms north of The Sportsman at the Chevron Station or other spots along the walk.

Where Is It? Start at The Sportsman, 249 N. Coast Highway. Take coastal Hwy 101 to Florence. Park on side streets near the store, but please do not park in The Sportsman's lot.

Sponsor: Yachats Coastal Gems, P.O. Box 896, Yachats, OR 97498

FOREST GROVE ♦ University Walk

Dates: January 1–December 31 *Wendy White (503) 357-3702*

Description (1 +): Surrounded by white oak and fir forests, Forest Grove is home to Pacific University, which the trail passes. Primarily on sidewalks, this route has a few uncut curbs.

See and Stay: Tualatin Vineyards, west on Hwy 26, offers tours and tastings and picnic facilities overlooking the Willamette River.

Where Is It? Start at the registration desk of Tuality Hospital, 1809 Maple St. **From I-5:** Take Exit 292, Hwy 217. Follow ocean beaches signs to Hwy 26 (Sunset Hwy). Following the ocean beaches signs, go about 9 mi. to the North Plains/Hillsboro exit. Go left on Glencoe Rd. Take Glencoe/First Ave. into Hillsboro. At Baseline Rd. (Hwy 8) turn right. Baseline Rd. changes names, becoming Pacific Ave. in Forest Grove. Maple is about 1 mi. past the city limits sign. Turn left on Maple to hospital. Park in lot.

Sponsor: Webfoot Walkers, P.O. Box 813, Forest Grove, OR 97116

OREGON

FORT STEVENS STATE PARK ♦ Beach Walk

Dates: January 1–December 31      Raymonda Dane (503) 738-7767

Description (2): You'll walk on soft sand dunes, crushed rock, or blacktop and descend steep stairs on this trail. This historical area on the Columbia River features a military museum, shipwreck remains, beach access, and a freshwater lake.

Food and Fun: The park offers fishing, boating, picnicking, and wildlife viewing. Call (503) 861-1671 to reserve a campsite or call the Oregon State Parks and Recreation Dept., (503) 378-6305, for park information. Visit Seaside, Oregon's largest and oldest ocean resort. Stop in nearby Astoria and explore the specialty shops at Pier 11 at the foot of 11th St., or sample the local seafood.

Hours: Start no earlier than 8 A.M.

 The club sponsors a 25K bike path through a scenic forest, and with views of the river.

Where Is It? Start in the main building of the KOA Campground across from the park's main entrance. **On Hwy 101:** Go north from Seaside or south from Astoria. At the traffic light between Young's Bay Plaza and the Shilo Inn, turn west on East Harbor Dr. toward Warrenton. Go 4.5 mi. to the four-way light at Pacific Hwy.

Sponsor: Turnaround Trekkers Volkssport Club, P.O. Box 975, Seaside, OR 97138-0975

GOLD BEACH ♦ 'Round Town Walk

Dates: March 1– December 31   Ann Warner (503) 269-4523/888-9809

Description (1 +): This walk goes along city streets and across a bridge at the mouth of the Rogue River. You have the option of walking along the beaches at low tide. The walk's sponsor says the walk, without the beach option, may be suitable for wheelchairs with some difficulty at the curbs.

See and Stay: Gold Beach is the gateway to the wild and scenic Rogue River. Take an exciting boat trip with any one of several companies and explore the whitewater of the Rogue and nearby wild river areas. Visit Cape Sebastian State Park, which offers scenic views, wildflowers, and hiking. Look for eagles, osprey, and deer.

Hours: Start no earlier than 8 A.M.

Where Is It? Start at McKay's Market on Hwy 101 in the middle of Gold Beach, on the west side of the street. **From I-5:** Take Hwy 38/42 to Hwy 101 and go south to Gold Beach.

Sponsor: South Coast Wavewalkers, c/o Coos County ESD, 1350 Teakwood, Coos Bay, OR 97420

OREGON

GOVERNMENT CAMP ♦ Laurel Hill Walk

Dates: May 1–October 31 (seasonal)   Jo Brooks (503) 648-8339

Description (3): This walk through older, second-growth forest follows a portion of the road cut for the pioneers taking the Barlow and Bennet Passes. You'll come to a grotto and waterfall halfway through the walk. In the spring, watch for blooming rhododendrons, and look for huckleberries in late summer.

See and Stay: Why not linger in Mount Hood National Forest and enjoy the views of Mt. Hood, the highest point in Oregon? This 1.1 million-acre forest has 115 campgrounds and 1,200 miles of trails. Timothy Lake, 13 mi. southwest of Hwy 26 on Skyline Rd., has a 1,400-acre lake and five camping and picnicking areas.

☑ No pets or smoking on the trail. Water and restrooms at start point, but none on the trail.

Where Is It? In Government Camp, go to the Val-U Inn Motel, 87450 E. Government Camp Rd., to pick up directions to the start point. **From I-5:** Take the I-84 eastbound exit and get off I-84 at Exit 16-A. You will be on 238th St., which becomes Hogan Ave. At 2.7 mi. from the exit, turn left on Burnside. At 3.5 mi. Burnside becomes Hwy 26. At 41.3 mi. turn left at the sign for Ski Bowl East and Government Camp. The motel is just a few blocks down.

Sponsor: The Tough Trail Trompers, P.O. Box 1422, Tualatin, OR 97062-1422

GRANTS PASS ♦ City Walk

Dates: January 1–December 31   Shirley O'Hare (503) 479-7989

Description (2): This 11K, moderately easy trail goes along city streets, through the center of town, and past historic homes and buildings. In some spots you'll have to walk along the shoulder of the road.

See and Stay: You're at the departure point for many of the Rogue River raft trips. The Grants Pass Chamber of Commerce, at 1501 N.E. Sixth St., Grants Pass, OR 97526, (800) 547-5927, has complete information on Rogue River trips and other attractions.

Where Is It? Start in the lobby of the Southern Oregon Medical Center, 1505 N.W. Washington Blvd. **From I-5:** Exit at north Grants Pass exit and go down Sixth St. to Midland St. (Pizza Hut is on the corner.) Turn right onto Midland and go to the cross street, which is Washington. Park on the street. Enter through Emergency Room admitting entrance off the parking lot.

Sponsor: Rogue Valley Walkers, 3395 W. Evans Creek Rd., Rogue River, OR 97537

OREGON

HILLSBORO ♦ *Refuge Walk*

Dates: March 1–December 31   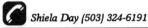 Shiela Day (503) 324-6191

Description (1): This 11K walk will go through the downtown section and residential areas and out to a waterfowl refuge. You'll pass historic homes and buildings, on a route the sponsor says is wheelchair accessible.

See and Stay: You're in wine country, and several of the wineries that produce gallons of fruit and berry wines offer tours and tastings.

Hours: Start after 8 A.M.

Where Is It? Hillsboro is about 15 mi. west of Portland. Start at the volunteer's desk in the main lobby of Hillsboro Tuality Community Hospital, 335 S.E. Eighth Ave., (503) 681-1111. **From I-405:** Take US 26 (Sunset Highway) to Cornelius Pass Rd. to N.E. Cornell. Go right on Cornell to Baseline Rd. and right on Baseline to parking at Eighth Ave.

Sponsor: Webfoot Walkers, P.O. Box 813, Forest Grove, OR 97116-0813

JOSEPH STEWART STATE PARK ♦ *Reservoir Walk*

Dates: January 1–December 31   Sharon Cripe (503) 773-7806

Description (1+) (1): This fairly easy walk offers an alternate route for physically challenged walkers.

See and Stay: The park offers first-come, first-served camping, a marina, store and cafe, swimming, bike trails, boating, and fishing. Call (503) 560-3334 for park information. Or call the Oregon State Parks & Recreation Dept., (503) 378-6305. Visit nearby Crater Lake National Park and gaze at the brilliant blue lake encircled by lava cliffs, or take a boat ride during the summer. Medford, a few miles to the south, is known nationwide for its pears.

Hours: Start after 8 A.M.

Where Is It? Start at the park marina office at Lost Creek Reservoir. **South on I-5:** Take Exit 101. Turn east and follow OR 227 to its intersection with OR 62. Turn left and go 10 mi. to the park's entrance. **North on I-5:** Take Exit 30 and go north on OR 62 for 33 mi. to park entrance.

Sponsor: Oregon Telephone Pioneers, 421 S.W. Oak Room 1N1, Portland, OR 97204

OREGON

KLAMATH FALLS ♦ Scenic Walk

Dates: January 1–December 31    *Pat Eck (503) 882-6511*

Description (3): This residential walk, primarily on sidewalks and asphalt roads, will give you panoramic views of Upper Klamath Lake and mountain ranges to the west. On a clear day, you'll even catch sight of Mt. Shasta.

See and Stay: In the summer, take a trolley through the downtown and pop in to one of the museums housing artifacts from Indian and pioneer days. The area has several wildlife refuges, so watch for white pelicans, snow geese, bald eagles, and trumpeter swans. The Best Western, Travelodge, and Comfort Inn all offer a 10% discount to walkers.

Where Is It? Start in the lobby of the Merle West Medical Center, 2865 Daggett. **From US Hwy 97 north:** Turn east off 97 at the intersection with the Oregon Institute of Technology and continue toward the McDonald's restaurant on Campus Dr. Continue toward the top of the hill, and turn right on Daggett. Watch for the Institute of Technology or hospital signs. Park in the visitor lot.

Sponsor: Pelican Pacers Volkssport Club, P.O. Box 7599, Klamath Falls, OR 97602

LAKE OSWEGO ♦ Scenic City Walk

Dates: January 2–December 31   *Julia Ferreira (503) 636-5520*

Description (2): You'll walk mostly on streets and bike paths on this walk that winds through downtown Lake Oswego, parts of Tryon Creek State Park, lake shore neighborhoods, a city park, and a view of the remnants of Oregon's first iron smelter. About 2K of this walk is on gravelled, all-weather paths. Watch for songbirds and waterfowl.

See and Stay: Picnic in George Rogers Park and then sightsee in nearby Portland, where you'll find lots to do and many other walks. See the Portland entry in this book.

Hours: Between 10 A.M.–7 P.M. on weekdays, and until 5 P.M. on weekends.

Where Is It? Start at the Phidippides Fitness Center, Lake Place Shopping Center, 333 S. State St., 8 mi. south of Portland and 6 mi. north of West Linn on Hwy 43. The center sits between Leonard and Wilbur Sts. on the east side of the road, at the south end of the business district, across from the Lakewood Center for the Arts. Please do not park directly in front of the stores.

Sponsor: Columbia River Volkssport Club, 3333 N.W. 135th Ave., Portland, OR 97230

OREGON

LAPINE RECREATION AREA ♦ Lava Walk

Dates: April 1–September 30 (seasonal)   Harry Saukants (503) 923-7313

Description (2): This 12K walk on the eastern slopes of the Cascades goes among ponderosa pine and lava lands. You'll follow earthen trails and some paved and crushed rock surfaces.

See and Stay: Explore the Deschutes National Forest, the state's second largest national forest, with 1.6 million acres of heavily forested land, volcanic landscapes, more than 200 lakes, and miles of streams. LaPine, located in the forest, offers fishing, boating, and first-come, first-served campsites. Call (503) 388-6055 for park information or the Oregon State Parks & Recreation Dept., (503) 378-6305.

Where Is It? Follow the signs to the camping area and check in with park host in camp loop F, site F-1. **From US 97:** About 7 mi. north of LaPine or 21 mi. south of Bend, turn west at the road to LaPine State Recreation Area.

Sponsor: Ponderosa Pathfinders, 905 N.E. Franklin, Bend, OR 97701

LEBANON ♦ City Walk

Dates: January 1–December 31   Chuck Boeder (503) 967-9162

Description (1 +): This city walk goes through parks and crosses the Santiam River. You might catch glimpses of the mountains surrounding the valley area.

Food and Fun: Feast on strawberry shortcake at the June strawberry festival, or ride through the countryside of this agricultural area and admire the many covered bridges. Visit the Willamette National Forest with more than 1,400 miles of trails and over 80 campgrounds.

This club sponsors a 27K bike path through farmland with mountain views.

Where Is It? Start at the Lebanon Community Hospital, 525 Santiam Hwy. **From the north on I-5:** Take Exit 233, Hwy 20/Santiam Hwy. Turn right on 20 and go about 11 mi. to the hospital. **From the south on I-5:** Take Exit 228, Hwy 34. Turn right on 34 and go about 7 mi. to Lebanon. At the junction of Hwy 20 and Santiam, turn left and go to the hospital.

Sponsor: The Albany Fitwalkers, P.O. Box 1218, Albany, OR 97321

OREGON

LINCOLN CITY ♦ Three D River Walks

Dates: January 1–December 31  Lucille Fenske (503) 994-5998

Description (2) (3): Each walk includes a stretch of this ocean community's 7.5 miles of public beach and a view of the D River, the world's shortest river.

Walk No. 1: This walk goes through the town, past shops and the bakery. Walkers then have the option to return via paved streets along the ocean or by way of the sandy beach.

Walk No. 2: Goes on the sandy and sometimes rocky beach from the river to Road's End Wayside and back.

Walk No. 3: Goes on the sandy, rocky beach from the river to Siletz Bay, which is being preserved as a coastal wetlands wildlife refuge. This walk is the most isolated of the three.

See and Stay: Visit or camp at Devil's Lake State Park, favored by those who enjoy sailing and other water sports. Anglers can fish for salmon and steelhead. Shoppers will enjoy Quality Factory Village with its 50 discount stores, or the specialty shops lining the miles of beach. Local winery tours, kite flying, and beachcombing also are popular with visitors.

☑ Check the tide tables before heading out on the two beach walks. These walks are cancelled during severe weather, wind, or tide conditions. Be cautious when walking the beach and never turn your back on the ocean. Watch for sneaker waves and logs rolling in with a wave. The wind can be strong.

Where Is It? Self-register for these walks in the motel lobby of the Sea Gypsy Motel, 145 NW Inlet Ave. **From Hwy 101:** Go to the D River Wayside off Hwy 101. Park in the middle of town at S.W. First St. Walk the D River bridge to N.W. Second St. and go left to the motel. Please park at the D River Wayside or the other side of Hwy 101—do not park at the Sea Gypsy. The Chamber asks that you park away from the building.

Sponsor: Lincoln Fogchasers, P.O. Box 151, Neotsu, OR 97364

Oregon's state park campgrounds include three types of campsites: full hook-ups with sewer, water, and electricity; electrical hook-ups with water and electricity; and improved tent sites, with water nearby. All have paved parking areas, tables, and camp stoves. Most are near restrooms with flush toilets and showers. Call (503) 378-6305 for camping information.

MCMINNVILLE ♦ *Quaint Town Walk*

Dates: January 1–December 31 *Roberta Van Dybe (503) 472-7168*

Description (2): This walk in the heart of wine country follows city streets and sidewalks through a quaint town, residential areas, and parks, and past historic homes. The gravel road and three small hills may make it hard to push a stroller.

See and Stay: Explore the wineries or the 100-acre campus of Linfield College, established in 1857, or take a peek at the 1930s steamboat locks in Lafayette Locks County Park in Lafayette.

Where Is It? Start at the McMinnville Community Hospital, 603 S. Baker St. **From Portland:** Take US Hwy 99 west. This highway becomes Adams St. as it passes through town. Follow the hospital signs. **From Salem:** Take Hwy 22 west to Rickreall and turn right onto Hwy 99 West and go into town. Park in the Mini Mart lot north of the hospital. Do not park in the hospital's lot.

Sponsor: Mac Trackers, 1330 Century Ct., McMinnville, OR 97128

MADRAS ♦ *Canyon Trail*

Dates: April 1–December 31 *Romona Greeno (503) 389-5036*

Description (3): The highlight of this 13K walk is the stretch of the Willow Creek Canyon that is part of the Oregon Trail system. From the rim, you'll enjoy panoramic views of the Cascades. The elevation change is 200 ft. You'll encounter some rough surfaces.

See and Stay: You're in high desert terrain and surrounded by the Mount Jefferson Wilderness Area. Enjoy some whitewater rafting on the Deschutes River. Oregon River Experiences offers one to five day river trips. Call or write them at 18800 N.E. Trunk Rd., Dundee, OR 97115-9031, (503) 538-3358, for information. Go rockhounding for thunder eggs, the state rock. The Chamber of Commerce has a list of good rockhounding locations, (503) 475-2350.

Where Is It? Start at the Mountain View Hospital, 470 N.E. A St. **From US 26 or US 97:** Turn east on B St. and go about 7 blks. to 12th St. Turn left on 12th and go 1 blk. to A St., then right on A for 2 blks. to the hospital entrance. Use the east (emergency) entrance and check in at the admissions desk. Please be patient if the attendant is busy.

Sponsor: Ponderosa Pathfinders, 905 N.E. Franklin, Bend, OR 97701

MT. ANGEL ♦ Abbey Walk

Dates: January 1–December 31   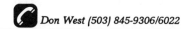 Don West (503) 845-9306/6022

Description (2): Visit Mount Angel Abbey on this walk that will take you through this lovely city and past the Benedictine Sisters convent before making your climb up to the abbey.

See and Stay: In July the abbey hosts a three-day Bach festival in the gardens. Oktoberfest, complete with German music, food, and street dancing, happens the third weekend in September. Call the Chamber of Commerce, (503) 845-9440, for information.

☑ During Oktoberfest weekend, the start point moves to City Hall, 1 Garfield St.

Hours: Begin as early as 7 A.M. Mon.-Sat., but no earlier than 9 A.M. on Sun. Finish by dark.

Where Is It? Start at Burger Time, 450 N. Main St. **From the north on I-5:** Take Woodburn Exit 271, and follow Hwy 214 to Mt. Angel, about 10 mi. **From the south on I-5:** Take Market St. Exit 256 at Salem and follow the signs and Hwy 213 east through Silverton. In Silverton, follow signs for Mt. Angel. Burger Time is a few blks. north of downtown. Do not park in its lot.

Sponsor: Angel Trekkers, P.O. Box 66, Mt. Angel, OR 97362

NEWBERG ♦ Country Walk
♦ City Walk

Dates: January 1–December 31   Nancy Dorey (503) 538-3993

Description (2): This city walk on streets and sidewalks has one short, semi-steep hill down to the Willamette River. The country walk on streets, sidewalks, and country roads has one .5-mile uphill grade with several flat sections.

See and Stay: Visit scenic Champoeg State Park, with several visitor spots plus camping and picnicking. Newberg was the first Oregon community to permit Quaker services, and it was the childhood home of Herbert Hoover. The Hoover-Minthorn House Museum contains Hoover mementos. Some old and large wineries are in the area.

Where Is It? Start at a private home at 812 N. Meridian, where you will find registration materials and directions. **From I-5:** Take Newberg-Tigard Exit 294. Go west on 99W for about 18 mi. In Newberg, highway will make a sharp right and become one-way (at the light). Continue the on highway, going 3 blks. on the one-way street, and turn right on Meridian. Go about 7 blks. House is on the right just before railroad tracks.

Sponsor: Newberg Healthnuts, 1715 Elderberry Ct., Newberg, OR 97132

OREGON

NEWPORT ♦ South Beach State Park Walk

Dates: February 1–December 31    Lucille Fenske (503) 994-5998

Description (2): The Marine Science Center estuary trail, views of the bay and ocean, and the South Beach State Park day trail are included on this walk. You'll also pass the entrance to the new Oregon Coast Aquarium.

See and Stay: Return to explore the aquarium or visit one of Newport's many attractions, such as the Yaquina Head Lighthouse, Devil's Punch Bowl State Park, or the Newport Visual Arts Center. In the spring and winter, go on a university-sponsored whale watch.

Where Is It? Start at the Oregon State University/Hatfield Marine Science Center, 2030 Marine Science Dr. Take Hwy 101 to South Beach, on the south side of the Yaquina Bay bridge from Newport. Exit Hwy 101 following the signs to the science center. The self-start box is outside to the right of the center's entrance. Please park away from the entrance.

Sponsor: Lincoln Fogchasers, P.O. Box 151, Neotsu, OR 97364

NORTH BEND ♦ 'Round Town Walk

Dates: March 1–December 31   Ann Warner (503) 269-4523/ 888-9809

Description (1 +): This walk on city streets goes past many points of interest in this commercial fishing town with a history that goes back to logging and shipbuilding.

☑ When you pass the Museum in Simpson Park, stop in and pick up a copy of the guided walking tour of North Bend, which describes many of the spots you will pass on the walk.

See and Stay: This commercial fishing town started as a lumbering center and contains many points of interest. North Bend also is the gateway to the Oregon Dunes National Recreation Area in the Siuslaw National Forest. At Pacific Coast Recreation, 5 mi. north on Hwy 101, take a narrated dune excursion in a World War II military vehicle.

Hours: Start no earlier than 8 A.M.

Where Is It? Start at the McDonald's restaurant at the corner of Newmark and Broadway. Follow coastal Hwy 101 to North Bend. Follow the signs to the ocean beaches, turning west on Virginia St., past Pony Village Mall. Turn left (south) at Broadway and go about 1 mi.

Sponsor: South Coast Wavewalkers, c/o Coos County ESD, 1350 Teakwood, Coos Bay, OR 97420

OREGON CITY ♦ *City Walk*

Dates: January 1–December 31 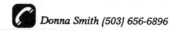 Donna Smith (503) 656-6896

Description (3): This walk takes you down along the Willamette River and then 90 ft. up in a municipal elevator, known as the city's vertical street. At the top you'll walk along the promenade, past homes and businesses, check in at the Clackamas County Museum, and then walk up a moderate hill to the finish. If the elevator's not working, you may have to climb some stairs.

See and Stay: Explore this end point of the Oregon Trail and the state's first capital. Willamette Falls, Mount St. Helens on a clear day, and the city's observation deck offer scenic beauty. The Oregon Trail Interpretive Center recalls the difficult journey made by 300,000 pioneers. Watch wildlife in the ponds and creeks at The John Inskeep Environmental Learning Center.

Where Is It? Start at the Willamette Falls Hospital, 1500 Division St. Go to the left of the reception desk and turn left just before the gift shop. Registration is in a cubbyhole just past the shop. **From I-205:** Take Oregon City Exit 9. Go left (south) on McLoughlin Blvd. (Hwy 99E). Turn left on 14th Ave. At the signal light turn left on Washington. Turn right on 15th and go up the hill until you come to the hospital at the flashing light. Hospital parking is limited, so please park on the street.

Sponsor: Valley Volkswalkers, P.O. Box 230698, Tigard, OR 97223

In addition to Oregon's many year-round and seasonal walks, walkers can join in the many weekend walking events held statewide. The Oregon Trail State Volkssport Association's walking information hotline gives information on these weekend walks. Callers will hear a listing of upcoming walks, including the start point addresses and the club's contact phone number. The message runs for about 3 min. If what you want to know isn't included in the recorded message, leave your name and number and club volunteers will respond by phone or by mail to your requests. Call (503) 243-5725.

OREGON

PORTLAND

Portland is a walker's paradise—at least 10 volkssport trails wind through this scenic city, and many of the city's outdoor areas include walking paths. With more than 150 parks, an interesting mix of historic and modern buildings, rose gardens, and views of the majestic Cascade Mountains, Portland certainly has outgrown its 1800s nickname, "Stumptown," named for the tree stumps that covered the town site. The weather is mild—the average mean temperature is 61° F in the summer and 44 ° in the winter, when there's normally little to no snow.

When you've finished your walks, you won't have any trouble finding fun things to do. If you're with children (and even if you're not), visit the Metro Washington Park Zoo, 3 mi. west on US 26, which specializes in breeding rare species and in creating exhibits that recreate natural environments.

Visit Pittock Mansion, 3229 N.W. Pittock Dr. Included in one of the Northwest District of Portland's walks, this 16,000-square-ft. residence provides expansive lawns for picnicking and viewing the mountains. Or have lunch or afternoon tea at the Gate Lodge, a quaint caretaker's cottage. Call (503) 823-3627 for reservations.

If you're in Portland between February and June, visit the Crystal Springs Rhododendron Gardens next to the Eastmoreland Golf Course. More than 4,000 rhododendron and azaleas put on a spectacular show. Call (503) 771-8386 for times.

Great dining, theater, shopping and antiquing, cruises, museums, sports activities and events—the choices are too numerous. You'll just have to contact the Portland Oregon Visitors Association, (503) 222-2223, so you can get the most from this incredible city.

OREGON

PORTLAND ◆ Two Columbia River Walks

Dates: January 1–December 31   Marge Lusby (503) 252-7605

Description (1): One walk on paved bike paths and sidewalks will give you mountain views and a stroll along the Columbia River. On a clear day, Mt. Hood looms in front of you. The second walk on city streets and sidewalks, with one short hill, will take you through the Grotto of the Sanctuary of Our Sorrowful Mother. For $1, the 10-story elevator will take you up to the wooded area. The rest room at the start point is not wheelchair accessible.

Lodging: There are several reasonably priced motels on or near the route. Camp in Abernathy State Park, about 30 mi. away.

Hours: Daily 10 A.M.–6 P.M., or dusk. Store is open until 10 P.M.

☑ Dogs are not allowed in the grotto.

🚲 The club also sponsors a 25K bike route that goes along the Columbia River with scenic views of the Cascades and Columbia River Gorge.

Where Is It? Start at Videoland, 10302 N.E. Sandy Blvd. **From I-205:** Take Sandy Blvd. Exit 23A. Continue east on Sandy to N.E. 103rd, about 8 blks. **From I-84:** Exit north on I-205 and continue as above. Park on the street; do not use the Videoland lot.

Sponsor: Columbia River Volkssport Club, 3333 N.W. 135th Ave., Portland, OR 97230

PORTLAND ◆ Two Downtown Walks

Dates: January 1–December 31   Lena Davis (503) 287-2284

Description (1+) (2+): One 10K walk has a 14K extension if you want to keep walking. City streets with gradual inclines will take you along the river for almost half the walk and then head to the downtown area. The 14K addition goes out and back to Terwilliger Blvd. The second 10K walk is along city streets with one long uphill and some steps. You'll head down to the waterfront area and through downtown.

☑ You'll find urban and street people along the busy waterfront.

Where Are They? Go to the switchboard area adjacent to the main lobby information desk of the Good Samaritan Hospital, 1015 N.W. 22nd at Lovejoy. **North on I-5:** Take Exit 299B to I-405. Exit at Everett St., Exit 2B, onto N.W. 14th. Continue north for 2 blks. to Glisan St. Turn left and stay on Glisan to 21st. Turn right on 21st to Marshall St., at the flashing light. Turn left on Marshall and go to hospital parking building 2 or 3. **South on I-5:** Take Exit 302B to I-405. Cross Fremont Bridge and take Exit 2B toward Everett. Follow directions on road signs to get on Glisan. Follow as above.

Sponsor: Rose City Roamers, 14320 S.E. Cedar, Milwaukie, OR 97267

145

OREGON

PORTLAND ◆ *Hollywood Neighborhood Walk*
◆ *Laurelhurst Neighborhood Walk*

Dates: January 1–December 31   Donald Hull (503) 234-0106

Description (1 +): These two walks take you through historic, picturesque neighborhoods. The Laurelhurst walk goes through that neighborhood and park and the Belmont neighborhood. The 11K Hollywood walk goes through the historic Hollywood District, Grant Park, and the Irvington and Aladema neighborhoods.

Where Are They? Start at the securities desk in Providence Hall at Providence Medical Center at 49th Ave. **Eastbound I-84:** Take Exit 3, 58th Ave. Turn right at the signal (Glisan St.) and proceed to 49th. Turn right to lower level of parking garage. **Westbound I-84:** Take Exit 2, 43rd Ave. Turn right at signal (Halsey St.) to 47th Ave. Turn right on 47th and continue to Glisan. Turn left and go to 49th. Turn left into lower level of parking garage. Parking is free. I-84 is reached from I-5 Exit 301 or I-205 Exit 21B.

Sponsor: Rose City Roamers, 14320 S.E. Cedar, Milwaukie, OR 97267

PORTLAND ◆ *Two Northwest Portland Walks*

Dates: January 2– December 31    Bob Parsons (503) 620-4467

Description (1 +),(2 + or 3 +): One walk is along city streets, with gradual inclines, and features downtown Portland and Portland State College. The second walk gives you two 10K alternatives. One option goes along parks and city streets then up to Lower Macleay trail and back through the historic Northwest District. The second alternative goes to the Pittock Mansion by way of about 6K of nature trails with an elevation gain of almost 1,000 ft.

Hours: Daily, 9 A.M.–9 P.M.

Where Are They? Start at the Food Front Co-op Grocery, 2375 N.W. Thurman St., (503) 222-5658. **Northbound I-5:** Take Exit 299B to I-405. Take Exit 3 (St. Helens, West 30). Take Vaughn St. ramp. Turn left at signal at N.W. 23rd to Thurman and go right on Thurman for 1 blk. **Southbound I-5:** Take Exit 302B to I-405. Cross Fremont Bridge and take Exit 3 (N.W. Industrial Area/Vaughn). Take Vaughn ramp and continue as above. Please do not park in the grocery's lot.

Sponsor: Rose City Roamers, 14320 S.E. Cedar, Milwaukie, OR 97267

OREGON

PORTLAND ◆ *Tyron Creek Walk*

Dates: January 1–December 31  *Cathie Bittler (503) 845-9499*

Description (3+): This 11K walk takes you through a 644-acre park within Portland. Logged in the 1880s, the forest has naturally regrown into a mixed stand of red alder, Douglas fir, big leaf maple, and western red-cedar. Over 80 species of birds and small mammals, including beaver, live here.

☑ Carry water. Water and restrooms only at the start point. Dogs must be kept on a 6-ft. leash.

Where Is It? Start at the Nature House nature center. **From I-5:** Take Exit 297. Go south on Terwilliger Blvd. and follow state park sign about 3 mi. Follow signs to the Nature House.

Sponsor: Why B Normal Adventurers, 812 N. Meridian, Newberg, OR 97132

Dense vegetation surrounds walkers in Tryon Creek Park, a secluded oasis within the city. Photo courtesy of the Oregon State Parks and Recreation Department.

OREGON

PORTLAND ◆ Willamette River Walk

Dates: January 1–December 31   *Marge Lusby (503) 252-7605*

Description (1): This walk on paved paths and sidewalks will take you across Sellwood Bridge and then along the Willamette River, with views of downtown, Mt. Hood and Mt. St. Helens in the background. You'll pass the Sellwood Antique Row, with about 50 quaint antique and crafts shops, and restaurants and stores in the Johns Landing area. The walk's sponsor says the walk is wheelchair accessible, for the most part, with some deviation.

☑ No public rest rooms at the start, but they are available in the area and on the route.

Hours: Daily, 10 A.M.–6 P.M.

Where Is It? Start at the Columbia Sportswear Outlet, 8128 S.E. 13th. **Northbound I-5:** Take Corbett St., Exit 298. Turn right on Corbett to S.W. Nebraska, about 1 mi. Turn left to S.W. Macadam, about 3 blks. Turn right onto Macadam to Sellwood Bridge. Turn left onto Sellwood Bridge to S.E. 13th and Tacoma. Turn right to outlet. **Southbound I-5:** Take Exit 299, the Lake Oswego-Johns Landing-Macadam exit south on Macadam to the Sellwood Bridge. Turn left onto bridge and proceed as above. Please do not call the outlet for information or directions. Park on the street only.

Sponsor: Columbia River Volkssport Club, 3333 N.W. 135th Ave., Portland, OR 97230

PORTLAND ◆ Gateway District Walk

Dates: January 1–December 31   *Phil Alberts (503) 255-0918*

Description (2) (1): This walk through Portland's Gateway District near the center of the city goes through the Glendoveer Golf Course. Here you'll encounter 2K of a bark dust path with a gradual hill and will visit the grave marker of an Oregon pioneer girl. This part of the route is not suitable for wheeled vehicles and walkers with pets. But the walk's sponsor has provided an alternate option that is wheelchair accessible and open to pets.

Where Is It? Start at the Woodland Park Hospital, 10300 N.E. Hancock. **From I-205:** Take Exit 21A (Glisan St.). Go east to 102nd Ave., then north about 5 blks. past four stop lights to Hancock St. Turn right (east) to hospital entrance. Park in the lots around the hospital or office building.

Sponsor: East County Windwalkers, P.O. Box 854, Gresham, OR 97030

OREGON

ROSEBURG ♦ *Downtown Walk*
♦ *Veterans Walk*

Dates: March 1–December 31   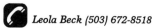 Leola Beck (503) 672-8518

Description (1) (1+): The paved downtown route with two small hills will take you through a bike path system, across the South Umpqua River, and past historic homes. The walk's sponsor says this path is wheelchair friendly. The walk through the grounds of the Veterans Administration goes through an older neighborhood, along part of a bike route, and through the VA Medical Center and cemetery. Part of this path is not on sidewalks. An alternate route is provided for people in wheelchairs.

See and Stay: This popular recreation area is sandwiched between the ocean and mountains. Follow scenic Hwy 138 to Crater Lake or Diamond Lake. Just south off I-5, you'll find Wildlife Safari, a 600-acre, drive-through zoo. Sample wine in nearby vineyards.

☑ Dogs are not allowed in the administration building, but there is an alternate route.

Where Is It? Start at self-start box in the main lobby of the Douglas Community Hospital, 748 W. Harvard. **From I-5 south:** Take Exit 124. The hospital is across from the exit ramp on your left. **From I-5 north:** Take Exit 124. Turn left on Harvard. Go 1 blk. to the light. The hospital is on the right. Parking is limited.

Sponsor: Umpqua Valley Walkers, 1354 N.E. Beulah, Roseburg, OR 97470

ST. PAUL ♦ *Champoeg State Park Walk*

Dates: January 1–December 31   Gary Ston (503) 538-7462

Description (2): This walk through scenic Champoeg State Park on the Willamette River includes some natural trails and gentle hills.

See and Stay: The park houses the Pioneer Mothers' Memorial Chapel, furnished with pioneer artifacts, and the Robert Newell House, with antique quilts and Indian artifacts.

Hours: Mon.-Fri., 8 A.M.–4 P.M.; weekends Jan.-May, 1 P.M.–4 P.M.; Memorial Day to Labor Day, 9:30 A.M.–5 P.M.

Where Is It? Start at the visitor center of Champoeg State Park. **From I-5:** Take Exit 278 (Aurora/Donald) and go west for 3.6 mi. on Ehlen Rd., which becomes Yergen Rd. Turn right on Case Rd. and go 1.4 mi., then left on W. Champoeg Rd. and go 3.5 mi. to the park.

Sponsor: The Walking Connection, 812 N. Meridian, Newberg, OR 97132

OREGON

SALEM ◆ Capital Walk

Dates: July 1–December 31  *Linda Baller (503) 588-5122*

Description (1+): Tour the state capital. You'll pass the government complexes, the Capitol Mall, Willamette and Tokyo International universities and the notable Bush House and Deepwood Estate. Not all the sidewalks have cutouts.

See and Stay: Go back to explore Bush's Pasture Park, a 100-acre city park where you can picnic and wander through the gardens. In mid-July catch the Great State Art Fair and Festival, or the West Salem Waterfront Festival in mid-August. Local wineries offer tours and tasting. Hunt for antiques and specialty gifts at the Mission Mill Village.

Where Is It? Start at the Execu*Lodge, 200 Commercial St., (800) 452-7879. **South on I-5:** Take Exit 260A (Salem Pkwy) and stay on the parkway. At the bridges downtown, the parkway merges with Commercial St. Ignore this and bear right and stay on the parkway. You'll pass through town and merge with Commercial at the Execu*Lodge. **North on I-5:** Take Exit 253 (Hwy 22) and turn left on 22. Go straight on toward the city until you're on Mission St. Go until you reach Liberty St. and turn right. Go north on Liberty for 5 blks.

Sponsor: Willamette Wanderers, P.O. Box 17994, Salem, OR 97305

SEASIDE ◆ River/Ocean Walk

Dates: January 1–December 31   *Pauline Vincent (503) 738-5960*

Description (1): This walk on city streets and sidewalks will take you along the Necanicum River and the famous Seaside Promenade along the ocean and into a new housing area.

See and Stay: This year-round resort offers the Seaside Aquarium, where you can feed the seals and touch marine life. Browse in the craft, kite, and clothing shops on Broadway, or visit Tillamook Head and its lighthouse. Amble along the 1.5-mile beach promenade.

☑ Rent bikes or skates at the Prom Bike Shop at 622 12th Ave., from 10 A.M.–6 P.M.

Hours: Jan. 1–Apr. 30 and Nov. 1–Dec. 31, Mon.-Fri. 9 A.M.–5 P.M.; Sat. 10 A.M.–4 P.M.; Sun. noon to 4 P.M.; May 1–Sept. 30, Mon.-Sat. 8 A.M.–6 P.M.; Sun. 9 A.M.–5 P.M.; October, Mon.-Sat. 8 A.M.–5 P.M.; Sun. 9 A.M.–5 P.M.

Where Is It? Start at the Seaside Chamber of Commerce, 7 N. Roosevelt Dr. Stay on Hwy 101 to the stoplight at the junction of Hwy 101, called Roosevelt as it goes through town. Turn east off Hwy 101 and then left off Broadway into the chamber parking lot. The chamber asks that you park away from the building.

Sponsor: Turnaround Trekkers Volkssport Club, P.O. Box 975, Seaside, OR 97138-0975

OREGON

SHORE ACRES STATE PARK ♦ *Garden Walk*

Dates: *January 1–December 31* Ann Warner *(503) 269-4523/888-9809*

Description (4+): This walk will take you through the forest and along ocean cliffs in a park that was once a coastal estate known for its exotic gardens.

Food and Fun: Linger in the park and enjoy the azaleas, rhododendron, and other plants. Spot whales from the glass-walled shelter overlooking the ocean. Or visit nearby Charleston and sample the fresh-caught salmon, tuna, halibut, snapper, crabs, clams, and other ocean delicacies. Charters there will take you fishing or whalewatching or for scenic bay cruises.

☑ Dogs are not allowed in the park. An entry fee is charged on summer weekends and holidays.

Hours: Daily 9 A.M.–5 P.M.

Where Is It? Start at Davy Jones Locker Grocery. **From I-5:** From the north, take Exit 162 to OR 38, and from the south take Exit 116 to OR 42. Go west to US 101. Follow the signs to Coos Bay/North Bend and then signs to Charleston. After crossing the bridge into Charleston go to the grocery on the right side of the road.

Sponsor: South Coast Wavewalkers, 1350 Teakwood Ave., Coos Bay, OR 97420

SILVER FALLS STATE PARK ♦ *Forest Walk*

Dates: *April 15–October 31 (seasonal)* Cathie Bittler *(503) 845-9499*

Description (3+): The 11K walk in this 8,700-acre park will take you through old-growth and second-growth Douglas fir and western hemlock and past or behind six waterfalls; several are over 100 ft. high. Walkers must climb steep stairs when leaving the canyon.

See and Stay: Silver Falls, Oregon's largest state park, offers swimming, fishing, and wildlife viewing, a 4-mi. bike trail, and first-come, first-served campsites, Memorial Day through Labor Day. For park information, call (503) 873-8681, or call the Oregon State Parks and Recreation Dept., (503) 378-6305.

Hours: Start any time after 8 A.M.

☑ Dogs are not allowed on the trails.

Where Is It? Start at Roth's IGA Foodliner, 918 N. First. **North on I-5:** Take Woodburn exit 271. Go East to US 99, turn south to OR 214, turn left. The park is 15 mi. southeast of Silverton on OR 214. **South on I-5:** Take Exit 256, and follow signs to Silverton on OR 213; in Silverton follow signs to Silver Falls (Hwy 214).

Sponsor: Silverton Walk Abouts, P.O. Box 297, Mt. Angel, OR 97362

OREGON

SILVERTON ◆ *Town 'n Country Walk*

Dates: January 1–December 31   Dorothy Hettwer (503) 634-2498

Description (2): This walk, mostly on paved paths, will take you through wooded areas and the downtown. One substantial hill will give you a view from the top that will make the climb worthwhile. A short patch of gravel may make the going temporarily rough for those pushing baby strollers. On a clear day you'll see the mountains and Mt. Hood and Mt. St. Helens. Watch for deer and numerous birds, and note the town's hanging flower baskets.

See & Stay: Visit nearby Mt. Hood National Forest, with its 1.1 million-acre forest. Alpine meadows, waterfalls, glaciers, hot springs, streams, and lakes await you, along with 115 campgrounds and 1,200 mi. of trails. Or stop at Silver Falls State Park, Oregon's largest, and take another walk.

☑ The route has little shade.

Where Is It? Start in the lobby of Silverton Hospital, 342 Fairview St., (503) 873-6336. **From the north on I-5:** Take Woodburn/Silverton Exit 271. Go toward Silverton on Hwy 214. Turn right on "C" St. and follow to second stop sign. Continue up the hill, when the street becomes Westfield. Follow blue hospital signs. Turn left on West Center St. and then left on Fairview to the hospital's gravel lot. **From the south on I-5:** Take Salem Market St. Exit 256. Follow signs to Silverton on Hwy 213. As you enter city, there is a stop sign. Turn right there onto Westfield. Go 1 blk. and turn left on West Center, then left again on Fairview. Do not park in the main hospital lot, as this is often cleared for a Life Flight helicopter landing.

Sponsor: Silverton Walk Abouts, P.O. Box 33, Silverton, OR 97381

From the first Monday in March through Labor Day weekend, the Oregon State Parks Campsite Information Center gives up-to-the-minute information on campsite availability. Out-of-state or Portland callers should call (503) 238-7488; in-state callers, call (800) 452-5687, Mon.-Fri., 8 A.M.–4:30 P.M. Staff can tell you about campsite vacancies and give you recreation information. You cannot make reservations by telephone, but you can cancel reservations.

OREGON

TROUTDALE ♦ *Sandy River Walk*

Dates: April 1–October 31 (seasonal) Ida Lieb (503) 663-9222

Description (1 +): Your trail will take you through the historic parts of Troutdale and along the scenic Sandy River.

See and Stay: Head a few miles west and explore Portland. Take in another walk at Crown Point State Park and catch great views of the Columbia River Gorge. In Troutdale's Lewis and Clark State Park you can picnic, hike, boat, and fish.

Where Is It? Start near the water fountain in the Burger King at 366 N.W. Frontage Rd. **From westbound I-84:** Take Exit 17 (Troutdale) and turn left at the stop sign. Turn right at the second stop sign. The Burger King is on your left. **From eastbound I-84:** Take Exit 17 to the frontage road. The restaurant is on the right, .5 mi. down.

Sponsor: East County Windwalkers, P.O. Box 20998, Portland, OR 97220

WALDPORT ♦ *Old Town Walk*
♦ *Alsea Bridge Walk*

Dates: January 1–December 31   Shirley's (503) 547-3292

Description (1) (1 +): The town walk includes a tour of Old Town, the Highlands subdivision, and the Alsea Bay Bridge. The bridge walk includes parts of Old Town and tours this popular fishing town's southern section, providing outstanding views of Alsea Bridge. May be difficult for strollers.

See and Stay: Visit any one of a dozen state parks lining the ocean north and south of Waldport. The timbered slopes of the 630,000-acre Siuslaw National Forest meet the ocean and offer 46 mi. of crabbing, beachcombing, and fishing along the public beach.

☑ Food is available along the route, but bring a picnic for one of the pretty spots on the path.

Hours: Apr. 15-Oct. 1, 9 A.M.–4 P.M. daily; Oct. 1-Apr. 14, 10 A.M.–3 P.M., Wed.-Sun.

Where Are They? Start at the Waldport Interpretive/Visitor Center, at the south end of the bridge just west of Hwy 101, (503) 563-2133. Park along the seawall about 100 yds. south of the center. Take the coastal highway north or south (Hwy 101) to Waldport.

Sponsor: Yachats Coastal Gems, P.O. Box 896, Yachats, OR 97498

OREGON

WALLOWA LAKE STATE PARK ◆ Lake Walk

Dates: May 1–September 30 (seasonal) Joanna Brooks (503) 648-8339

Description (3): You'll walk in the "Switzerland of America" among the massive Wallowa Mountains. This walk at the south end of Wallowa Lake follows paved paths and roads, plus gravel-based trails.

See and Stay: Explore the park and climb into the rugged peaks and alpine meadows of the Eagle Cap Wilderness Area. Visit Chief Joseph's grave near the north end of Wallowa Lake or take one of the country's longest and steepest tram rides. Call (503) 432-5331 for the tram's seasonal schedule. The area also offers fishing, boating, and swimming, plus reservable campsites, a marina, and wildlife viewing. Call (503) 432-4185 for park information, or call the Oregon State Parks & Recreation Dept., (503) 378-6305.

Where Is It? Start at the Wallowa Lake Lodge. **From I-84:** Take LaGrande Exit 261. Turn northeast on OR 82 and go about 76 mi. Wallowa Lake is at the end of the highway.

Sponsor: Tough Trail Trompers, P.O. Box 1422, Tualatin, OR 97062-1422

YACHATS ◆ 'Round Town Walk

Dates: January 1–December 31   Shirley's (503) 547-3292

Description (1): This easy walk ambles through this village-like town, along a public use trail, and past Yachats State Park, two modern sculptures, and the Little Log Church by the sea.

Food and Fun: Yachats's shore is one of the few places in the world where smelt—sardine-like fish—come to spawn, so from April to October smelt fishermen come to Yachats, and non-fisherman enjoy eating this delicacy. Beachcombing, rockhounding, and birding are popular pastimes, or visit Cape Perpetua, the highest point on the Oregon coast. The walking club also sponsors three walks there. You can register for these walks at Shirley's.

Where Is It? Start at Shirley's, next to the bakery, in the Town Center. Yachats is on coastal Hwy 101. Please park on the street. Do not park in Clark's Market parking lot.

Sponsor: Yachats Coastal Gems, P.O. Box 896, Yachats, OR 97498

OREGON

☑ If you want to walk in **Warrenton** in Oregon's northwest tip, go to the KOA Campground on Pacific St. The Turnaround Trekkers Volkssport Club sponsors this year-round walk. You can get more information by contacting Raymonda Dane, (503) 738-7767, P.O. Box 975, Seaside, OR 97138.

☑ **West Linn**, just south of Portland, has a seasonal walk from April through Oct., that starts at Zupan Food Pavilion, 19133 Willamette Dr. For directions and information contact Carmela Parsons of the Valley Volkswalkers, 5433 S.W. Red Leaf, Lake Oswego, OR 97035, (503) 620-4467.

☑ If you'd like to walk in **Beaverton**, near Portland, you might check with the Cedar Milers, who have sponsored a seasonal walk there in the past. Contact Shirley Corey, (503) 224-2323, or write her at 12075 N.W. Vallevue Ct., Portland, OR 97229.

Call the Oregon State Parks & Recreation Dept., (503) 378-6305, for information on special camping facilities for hikers, bicyclists, horseback riders, and group campers. The department also has information on special state programs: Scenic Waterways, the Willamette River Greenway, the Recreational Trail System, the State Historic Preservation Office, and Oregon's ocean shores.

PENNSYLVANIA

KLEINFELTERSVILLE ♦ *Wildlife Walk*

Dates: March 2–October 24 (seasonal)   *Brian Grumbling (717) 626-0256*

Description (1): You'll be entirely on paved roads as you enjoy the beauty and wildlife of this natural setting. The path includes some gently rolling hills, but the sponsor says the route is suitable for wheeled vehicles.

See and Stay: You're in beautiful country. Plan to explore towns like Lancaster, Ephrata, Lebanon, and Reading.

🚲 The walking club also sponsors a 28K bike path on paved roads over gently rolling hills. Helmets suggested.

☑ Please don't pick the vegetation. Local law requires that pets be leashed and that owners clean up all stool.

Hours: Tues.-Sat., 9 A.M.–3 P.M.; Sun., noon–3 P.M. Closed Mondays and holidays.

Where Is It? Start at the Visitors Center of the Middle Creek Wildlife Management Area, on Museum Rd., (717) 949-2099. **From Baltimore and south:** Take I-83 north to the Pennsylvania Turnpike. Go east on the turnpike to Exit 20 (Lebanon/Lancaster). Turn left on Rt 72, and follow it north 1.7 mi. to Rt 322 east. Take 322 east for 8 mi. to Rt 501 north to Brickerville. Go left on 501 north for 5.8 mi. to Schaefferstown. Turn right onto Rt 897 south and go 2.5 mi. to Kleinfeltersville. Turn right onto Hopeland Rd. and go 2.5 mi. to the Visitors Center on Museum Rd. **From Harrisburg and points west:** Take the turnpike east to Exit 20 and proceed as above.

Sponsor: The Penn-Dutch Pacers Volksmarch Club, P.O. Box 7445, Lancaster, PA 17604-7445

If you're in **Chambersburg**, in the south-central region of the state, catch the year-round walk that starts at the Olympia Ice Cream Parlor, 43 S. Main. This walk is sponsored by the Cumberland Valley Lead Foot Club, and you can get details on this walk from James Humelsine, P.O. Box 371, Shippensburg, PA 17257-0371, (717) 263-8633.

PENNSYLVANIA

LANCASTER ♦ *Amish City Walk*

Dates: January 1–December 31 *Jim McLaughlin (717) 656-6929*

Description (1 +): This 11K trail will give you a wonderful look at this city known for its Amish community and quaint charm. You'll get a sidewalk view of historic buildings, unique monuments in the cemetery, the Franklin and Marshall College campus, parks, old churches, and interesting shops.

See and Stay: Thousands flock each year to the Lancaster area to observe the Amish, enjoy the countryside, and attend the many seasonal events. If you're walking on a Tuesday, Friday, or Saturday, drop in at Lancaster's Central Farmer's Market, between 6 A.M.–4:30 P.M. weekdays and 6 A.M.–1 P.M. Saturday. Sample funeral pie, sausages, relishes, apple butter, and scrapple. Visit the historical society or go next door to Wheatland, the home of President James Buchanan. Drop by the Lancaster City Tourist Information Center in the Southern Markethouse for information about things to do in the area. The Your Place Country Inn offers walkers a $10 discount.

☑ If you bring your camera, please remember not to take facial shots of the Amish.

🚲 This club also sponsors a 25K bike path on asphalt surface through Amish countryside. The bike's start/finish point is Your Place Country Inn.

Hours: Start no earlier than 8 A.M.

Where Is It? Register at Your Place Country Inn, 2133 Lincoln Hwy East, (717) 393-3413. From here you will get directions to the Lancaster County Historical Society, where the walk starts. **From the PA Turnpike:** Take Exit 21 (Lancaster/Reading). Follow Rt 222 south to US 30 east and go to the end of this limited access highway. Continue east past the traffic light at East Towne Mall for about 2 blks. The inn is on the left side of the road.

Sponsor: The Penn-Dutch Pacers Volksmarch Club, P.O. Box 7445, Lancaster, PA 17604-7445

PENNSYLVANIA

NEWPORT ◆ *State Park Walk*

Dates: January 1–December 31  Louise Clouser (717) 567-9537

Description (3+): Little Buffalo State Park, with its 830 acres and 88-acre lake offers walkers the chance to experience woods and grasslands and take in views of the lake. Mostly you'll be on nature and fitness trails, with two sections of moderate-to-difficult hills. A walking stick might help in wet weather. Watch for deer, bluebirds, and wild turkey.

See and Stay: You can't camp in the park, but you can boat, swim, fish, and picnic in summer and ice skate, ice fish, and cross-country ski in winter. Explore the park's attractions: Shoaff's Mill, Rudolph's Cemetery, Clay's Covered Bridge, the Blue Ball Tavern, which is the library and museum, and the Little Buffalo Game Farm just outside the park. If you'd like information on the area's three B&Bs or on restaurants and other lodging and campgrounds, stop at the start point or write to the club sponsor. Campers can use the new Campground of Truth, located next to the park. Call (717) 567-7370.

☑ Depending on the season, there may be only one open bathroom in the park. Carry water. Protect against ticks.

Hours: Mon.-Sat., start no earlier than 8 A.M., or 9 A.M. on Sunday.

Where Is It? Register at Sharar's Grocery, 19 S. Second St. **From US 322:** Take Rt 34 into Newport. Turn left in the square (Second St.), and the grocery will be on the left. At the grocery you will get directions to the start point. **From I-83 or I-81S:** Exit for US 322 and follow directions above.

Sponsor: The Susquehanna Rovers Volksmarch Club, R.D. 4, Box 461, Newport, PA 17074

PENNSYLVANIA

OHIOPYLE ♦ State Park Walk

Dates: January 2–December 31 Sandra Zimmerman (814) 266-1854

Description (3): Hillsides shrouded in wildflowers and rhododendron, picture-postcard waterfalls, and the foaming water of the Youghiogheny River await you. About half of this tree-shaded walk is in Ferncliff Peninsula, a National Natural Landmark. A walking stick may be helpful. Watch for deer.

See and Stay: Explore the 18,700-acre Ohiopyle State Park, gateway to the Laurel Mountains. You can arrange guided raft trips and whitewater excursions at the start point. The park has AYH hostel accommodations. The dramatic home, Fallingwater, one of architect Frank Lloyd Wright's most acclaimed works, is nearby in Mill Run to the north. Call to reserve a tour date, (412) 329-8501.

🚲 This club also sponsors a seasonal 25K bike ride, March-Nov.
Hours: Daily 9 A.M.–4 P.M. Closed weekends in Jan., Feb., and Dec.
Where Is It? Start at the Laurel Highland Outdoor Center, (800) 4-RAFTIN, on Rt 381 in the center of town. **From Pennsylvania Turnpike West:** Take Exit 9 at Donegal. Go east on 31/711 to south on 381/711. Follow 381 to Ohiopyle. From the railroad tracks at Ohiopyle, it is .2 mi. to the outdoor center. Parking may be a problem between March and Oct.
Sponsor: Summit Striders of Johnstown, P.O. Box 966, Johnstown, PA 15907

PHILADELPHIA ♦ Liberty Bell Walk

Dates: January 7–December 31 Virginia Rohr (215) 357-8358

Description (1 +): You'll see the historic sites as you walk through old and new parts of downtown Philadelphia: the Betsy Ross House, Independence Hall, Elfreths's Alley, and, of course, the Liberty Bell.

See and Stay: To make the most of your visit, contact the Philadelphia Visitor Center, 1525 John F. Kennedy Blvd., Philadelphia, PA 19102, (215) 636-1666 or (800) 523-2004, and ask for the visitors guide.

Where Is It? Start at the Holiday Inn, Independence Mall, Fourth and Arch Sts., (215) 923-8660. **From the Pennsylvania Turnpike:** Take Exit 24 (Valley Forge) to Rt 76 east. Follow 76E to Rt 676 east exit. Take 676E to Eighth St. (Independence Mall) exit. Take the off ramp to the right and go to the first light at Race St. Take a left and go 4 blks. to Fourth. Take a right and go 1.5 blks. to the hotel entrance. For a fee you can park in the hotel garage, or look for street parking.
Sponsor: Liberty Bell Wanderers, 1504 Poplar Rd., Feasterville, PA 19053

PENNSYLVANIA

VALLEY FORGE ◆ Historic Park Walk

Dates: January 1–December 31   *Jim Simons (215) 275-7336*

Description (1): In the winter of 1777-78, George Washington and his soldiers camped on the ground you'll cover. The 11K multi-use trail, mostly on blacktop, will take you through the park's most historic sections. The sponsor says the path has only one 12-degree slope.

See and Stay: At the visitor center be sure to see the 15-min. film that describes the Revolutionary War encampment and sparks your imagination for the walk. The center also features an extensive collection of weapons and accessories from the period. Stop at the travel desk and pick up information about lodging, restaurants, and area attractions.

Hours: Daily, 9 A.M.–4:30 P.M.

Where Is It? Start at the Valley Forge National Historical Park Visitors Center book store. **From the northeast extension of the turnpike:** Exit turnpike at Valley Forge Interchange 24. Take 202 south (Exit 26A) to 422 west and go to Valley Forge Rt 23 west exit. Go right on 23 west and cross the intersection into the park. Go to the visitor center.

Sponsor: Valley Forge Troopers, 561 Hamilton St., Norristown, PA 19401

Park visitors can tour the Isaac Potts house, which Washington used as his headquarters. Photo courtesy of the National Park Service, Valley Forge National Historical Park.

160

RHODE ISLAND

BRISTOL ♦ *Blithewold Estate Walk*

Dates: April 1-October 31 *(seasonal)* Beryl Wolf (518) 383-2880

Description (1 +): The Blithewold Estate, gardens, Narragansett Bay and a quaint, historic, port village await you on this walk. You'll walk mostly on level sidewalks with some grass and gravel. People in wheelchairs may need just a little help on this route.

Food and Fun: Linger in the Blithewold Gardens and Arboretum or walk through the 45-room mansion between April and October. Visit Linden Place, the 1810 mansion featured in *The Great Gatsby* movie. Explore the Waterfront Historic District or the museums, including Coggeshall Farm Museum, a working farm showing life on a 1790s marsh. Stop at Colt State Park for spectacular sunsets or catch a delicious seafood dinner at one of the many restaurants. If you're a biker, try the 14-mile, bikes-only path along the water, with bike rentals at Bay Path Cycles, 13 State St., (401) 254-1277. The Rhode Island Tourism Division, (800) 556-2484, will send information on camping, lodging, attractions, and other tourist information.

Hours: Daily 10 A.M.-4 P.M. Closed Mondays.

☑ Dogs are not allowed at Blithewold. There is an entrance fee to the grounds, which are part of the walk: $3 for adults and $.50 for children. In 1993, Blithewold offers $1 off the admission to walkers and $3 off a Blithewold T-shirt. Guided mansion tours are available April 1-Oct. 31, from 10 A.M.-4 P.M., except Mondays and holidays.

Where Is It? Start your walk at Blithewold Gardens, 101 Ferry Rd. (Rt 114), (401) 253-2707. **From Providence:** Take Exit 2 in Massachusetts off Rt 195. Follow Rt 136S for 8.5 mi. Turn right onto Griswold Ave., and follow to the end. Take left onto Ferry Rd. Blithewold is .25 mi. on right. **From Boston:** On Rt 24, take the Mt. Hope Bridge exit. Cross the bridge and bear left at fork onto Ferry Rd. (Rt 114). Blithewold is on the left. **From Newport:** Take Rt 114N. Cross the Mt. Hope Bridge and bear left at the fork onto Ferry Rd. (Rt 114). Blithewold is on the left.

Sponsor: Empire State Capital Volkssporters, P.O. Box 6995, Albany, NY 12206-6995

RHODE ISLAND

Blithewold Mansion offers a peek into the gracious summer living of the early 1900s. Photo by Dr. Stanley Summer.

SOUTH DAKOTA

BROOKINGS ◆ Park Walk

Dates: April 1–December 31 (seasonal)   *Fayne Bell (605) 692-5352*

Description (1+): You'll go through two parks on this walk—one with a playground, the other with a swimming pool. Plan to take a picnic lunch and stop in the park. Sidewalks and streets will take you past museums, historic sites, and shopping areas. Not all the sidewalks have curb cuts.

See and Stay: On the campus of South Dakota State University, you'll find McCrory Gardens featuring 1,000 rose varieties, a rock garden, a maze, and 12,000 flowering annuals and perennials. The South Dakota Art Museum includes Sioux tribal art.

☑ Be careful at busy street crossings. In the summer, try to start early to avoid the sun.

 The walking club also sponsors a bike path that leaves from the same start point.

Hours: Start no earlier than 7 A.M.

Where Is It? Start at the main desk of the Brookings Hospital, 300 22nd Ave., (605) 692-6351. **From I-29:** Take Exit 132 on Hwy 14 (Sixth St.). Turn west to first stop light on 22nd Ave. Turn south. The Pamida Discount Center is on your left, Rotary Park on your right. The hospital is 3 blks. south on the left side of 22nd Ave. Park in the lot in front of the hospital, not on 22nd St. Enter under the portico on the west side.

Sponsor: Prairie Wanderers Volkssport Assoc., 415 11th Ave., Brookings, SD 57006

CORONA ◆ Hartford Beach Walk

Dates: Mid-June–mid-September (seasonal)   *Jeff Nodsle (605) 432-6374*

Description (3): Gravel and asphalt roads, plus dirt trails and mowed grass, will take you through this state park near the Minnesota border.

See and Stay: Looking for lunch? Try the cafe at the start/finish point. The park offers camping, hiking, boating, and fishing. Call the park, (605) 432-6374, for information.

Hours: Daily no earlier than 8 A.M.

Where Is It? Start at the cafe at Hartford Beach Resort. **From I-29:** Take Exit 213 on Hwy 12 and go 17 mi. to the resort. The state park and the resort share the same access road. Pay for your park license at the entrance station.

Sponsor: SDPRA Volkssport Assoc., R.R. 2, Box 2495, Brandon, SD 57005

SOUTH DAKOTA

CUSTER ◆ *State Park Walk*

Dates: May 15–September 30 (seasonal) Todd Gagne (605) 255-4464

Description (3): This state park covers 73,000 acres in the Black Hills. Your trail will take you through varied terrain, from hard-packed dirt trails to grassy meadows with mowed pathways. Part of the trail passes through forest, so be sure to walk when you have enough light to read the trail markers. You're sure to see large wildlife—buffalo, bighorn sheep, antelope, mountain goats, deer, and wild donkey are common and visible. The donkeys have been known to stick their heads in car windows!

See and Stay: After your walk, explore the park by car. Three scenic drives cut through the park. Return to the visitor center and find out about the summer theater, trail rides, naturalist programs for children, and patio talks. Of course you won't want to miss Mount Rushmore National Memorial. If you can, go the amphitheater at 9 P.M., when floodlights bring these granite wonders dramatically to life. You'll also want to visit the Crazy Horse Memorial. When completed, this statue will be the largest in the world. You can camp in the park for $10 a night. For reservations, call (605) 255-4000. Plan to spend a night in the historic Custer State Game Lodge, where presidents once summered and where the simple, rustic decor makes you feel at home.

Where Is It: In Custer State Park, start at the Peter Norbeck Visitor Center on Hwy 16A, (605) 255-4464. **From Rapid City:** Take Hwy 79 south to Hermosa, then go west on Hwy 36 for about 9 mi. to the park entrance. Follow the signs to the park. Once in the park, follow the signs to the Visitor Center.

Sponsor: SDPRA Volkssport Assoc., R.R. 2, Box 2495, Brandon, SD 57005

Custer State Park is home to one of the world's largest free-roaming bison herds. Photo by Cindy West.

SOUTH DAKOTA

DELL RAPIDS ◆ Dells Walk

Dates: April 1–December 31 (seasonal)      *Eunice McGee (605) 446-3484*

Description (2): You'll enjoy views of the dells, which were formed when a glacier passed through about one million years ago. This walk will take you along the Big Sioux River and past many of the town's historic homes and buildings, including a stone water tower, the stone bathhouse and amphitheater, and the graceful home of author Lucile F. Fargo. You'll walk mostly on blacktop with some grass and gravel surfaces.

See and Stay: Linger in this little city with 19-century charm. Picnic in the park along the river and enjoy the flower beds. The Rose Stone Inn, on the National Register of Historic Places, has reasonably priced rooms. Camp for free in shady spots along the Sioux River.

Hours: Start no earlier than 7:30 A.M.

Where Is It? Start at the Rose Stone Inn, 504 E. Fourth St., (605) 428-3698. **From I-29:** Going north of Sioux Falls, take the exit for Dell Rapids (Hwy 115) and go east into town.

Sponsor: Prairie Wanderers Volkssport Association, 415 11th Ave., Brookings, SD 57006

FLANDREAU ◆ City Walk

Dates: April 1–December 31 (seasonal)   *Connie Hove (605) 997-2595*

Description (2): Walk in a community that blends the traditions of the Santee Sioux and the white settlers. From the bridge, take in views of the Big Sioux River and dam and then follow the river to the well-groomed city park. Watch for many birds and maybe deer. The trail includes about 3 mi. where you'll walk along the highway, possibly in single file.

See and Stay: Explore Flandreau. The Moody County Museum Complex features antiques and collectibles. See the murals on the Courthouse walls. Stop in the First Presbyterian Church, the state's oldest operating church, and while there visit the grave of Santee Sioux Chief Little Crow. Picnic in the park or camp along the Big Sioux.

Where Is It? Start at the Trading Post, 510 E. Pipestone, (605) 997-2738. From there you will go to the city park to start your walk. **From I-29:** Take exit for Hwy 32. Follow 32 east to Flandreau. Hwy 32 merges with and becomes Pipestone within the city.

Sponsor: Prairie Wanderers Volkssport Association, 415 11th Ave., Brookings, SD 57006

SOUTH DAKOTA

MADISON ♦ Lake Herman Walk

Dates: First weekend in June–last weekend in August (seasonal)  *Laurie Schumacher*
(605) 256-3613

Description (2): Asphalt roads and mowed hiking trails will take you along the edge of Lake Herman. An exercise trail is thrown in just for the fun and fitness of it. Watch for birds and small wildlife and pack a lunch to eat at one of the many picnic tables.

See and Stay: This state park offers a modern campground, with electrical sites and a pump station. You'll find lodging and a variety of restaurants in Madison, which takes its name from Wisconsin's capital. The Smith-Zimmermann State Museum on the Dakota State University campus features a covered wagon and 19th-century period rooms.

☑ You must purchase a park entrance license. Protect against ticks.
Hours: Weekdays start no earlier than noon; 10 A.M. on weekends.
Where Is It? Register at the entrance booth to Lake Herman State Park, (605) 256-3613. From there you'll park in the lot for picnic shelter #1, and begin your walk. **From I-29:** Take the exit for Hwy 34 and Madison. Go west on 34. The park is 1 mi. south and 2 mi. west of Madison.
Sponsor: SDPRA Volkssport Association, R.R. 2, Box 2495, Brandon, SD 57005

MITCHELL ♦ Town Walk

Dates: April 1–December 31 (seasonal) *Carol Swisher (605) 996-4798 (evenings)*

Description (2): You'll walk through open, unshaded areas of the city's perimeters on hard surfaces and unimproved roads, and through parts of town, where you'll pass the Corn Palace and the balloon and doll museums.

See and Stay: Make sure you get a good look at the Corn Palace. Each year about 3,000 bushels of corn and grass are used to decorate this Moorish-looking building. Revisit the Enchanted World Doll Museum with more than 4,000 antique and modern dolls. Take a guided tour of the 900 A.D. Indian village, just 1 mi. north of town.

☑ There's always a breeze, but it can be hot. Carry water.
Where Is It? Start at the registration desk of Queen of Peace Hospital, Fifth and Foster, (605) 995-2000. **From I-90:** Take Exit 332, Mitchell-Parkston (Burr St.). Turn north on Burr to Fifth Ave. Go right on 5th to the hospital. Park in the lot south of the hospital. Enter through the main entrance on the south side.
Sponsor: Prairie Wanderers Volkssport Association, 415 11th Ave., Brookings, SD 57006

SOUTH DAKOTA

RAPID CITY ♦ *Downtown Walk*

Dates: January 1–December 31   Doug Kapaun (605) 348-5191

Description (1+): You'll be on city sidewalks and bicycle paths in this city that serves as the entrance to the Black Hills recreation area. Your path will take you past downtown sites and parks, Rapid Creek, flower gardens, and the Executive Golf Course.

See and Stay: Don't miss Custer State Park and see bison, deer, bighorn sheep, and antelope in the wild. The Black Hills area is crammed with interesting things to see and do. Contact the Rapid City Convention and Visitors Bureau, Box 747, Rapid City, SD 57709, (605) 343-1744, for information on attractions and accommodations. If you're heading east on I-90, don't miss Wall Drug. This flamboyant retail complex is much more than a drug store and has to be seen to be believed. The hot donuts are great!

Where Is It? Start downtown at the historic Hotel Alex Johnson, 523 Sixth St., at the corner of Sixth and St. Joseph, (605) 342-1210. **From I-90:** Take Exit 57 onto I-190 southbound. You will be on West Blvd. Go left on St. Joseph (St. Joe) to Sixth and the hotel.

Sponsor: Black Hills Volkssport Association, 3020 Sunny Hill Circle, Rapid City, SD 57702

SPEARFISH ♦ *Town Walk*

Dates: January 1–December 31   Cliff Hanson (605) 642-3232

Description (1): Walk in a small town that's tucked in a northern valley of the Black Hills. You'll get a sidewalk view of parks, homes, and a university campus. As you follow the bike path along Spearfish Creek, imagine the Sioux who came to these waters to spear fish—hence the town's name.

See and Stay: Enter or leave town via scenic highway US 14, which goes through Spearfish Canyon, one of the film locations for *Dances With Wolves*. From June-August, see the Black Hills Passion Play performed in an outdoor setting with mountains as the distant backdrop. Camp on the banks of the creek near the fish hatchery.

☑ Carry water on hot days.

Where Is It? Start at the BIG D Texaco Station, 305 W. Jackson Blvd., (605) 642-5151. **From I-90:** Take Exit 12 onto Jackson Blvd. Continue on Jackson to the Texaco station on the left side of the street, 2 blks. past the traffic light.

Sponsor: Black Hills Volkssport Assoc., 3020 Sunny Hill Circle, Rapid City, SD 57702

SOUTH DAKOTA

SIOUX FALLS ◆ *Falls Walk*

Dates: April 1–December 31 (seasonal)    *Gwen Pickett (605) 692-5495*

Description (1+): See the magnificent falls that gave this city its name. This route through the historic area includes the downtown shopping district, playgrounds, and two museums.

See and Stay: Enjoy the lovely biking and walking trails, with views of the rivers that surround the town. Visit the Great Plains Zoo, with 300 regional animals. Shop in the revitalized downtown or go back to Falls Park for a picnic.

 This club also sponsors a bike route from the walk's start point.

Where Is It? Start at the Town House Motel (Best Western), 400 S. Main St., (605) 336-2740. **From I-29:** Take the 12th St. exit and go east on 12th. It will jog over to 11th St. At 11th and Main, turn right and go 1 blk. The motel is between Main and Phillips. **From the east on I-90:** Take I-229 (south). Take the 10th St. exit and turn right. Follow 10th to Main, which is one-way. Get into left-turn lane, and turn left. Go south 2 blks. to 12th. Park in the adjacent lot.

Sponsor: Prairie Wanderers Volkssport Association, 415 11th Ave., Brookings, SD 57006

WATERTOWN ◆ *City Walk*

Dates: April 1–December 31 (seasonal)    *Eunice Solem (605) 874-2437*

Description (1+): You'll walk along several parks, including the Bramble Park Zoo; get acquainted with the downtown; and view several lovely buildings, including the Mellette House, home of the state's first governor.

See and Stay: Pack a picnic and visit the zoo, featuring animals from around the world. Camp in Memorial Park or Sandy Shores State Park, both near Watertown on Lake Kampeska.

Where Is It? Start at the Prairie Lakes Hospital West, 400 10th Ave. NW, (605) 882-7000. **From I-29:** Take the Watertown exit and go west.

Sponsor: Prairie Wanderers Volkssport Association, 415 11th Ave., Brookings, SD 57006

YANKTON ♦ *State Park Walk*

Dates: April 1–December 31 (seasonal)   Eileen Neubauer (605) 665-3105

Description (1): You'll catch wonderful views as you walk along the mighty Missouri River and through a state park. The asphalt path is flat, and the sponsor says it's wheelchair accessible.

See and Stay: This area has several Army Corps of Engineer lakes with opportunities to camp, boat, fish, and picnic. Return to the fish hatchery to learn about indigenous aquatic life and about fish management. Visit the Dakota Territorial Museum in the West Side Park and see restored pioneer buildings, including a train depot and a fully outfitted blacksmith shop.

Where Is It? Start at Rick's Lake Area Convenience Store, Hwy 52 West, (605) 665-1631. **From I-29:** Take Yankton-Vermillion exit and go west on Hwy 50 about 32 mi. to Yankton. Go through town, past Sacred Heart Hospital around the curve. You are now on Hwy 52. Drive a few miles west and on the north side of the highway you will see the convenience store. Park in the fringe area of the fish hatchery.

Sponsor: Prairie Wanderers Volkssport Association, 415 11th Ave., Brookings, SD 57006

TENNESSEE

CLARKSVILLE ♦ City Walk

Dates: January 1–December 31 *Dayton Herrington (615) 648-8122*

Description (2): See the historic sights and travel along the new river walk in this old 1784 Cumberland River port. All on sidewalks or streets, the walk includes two steep hills.

See and Stay: Explore this old 1780 town overlooking the Cumberland and Red rivers. In the early spring, listen in at the state's Old-Time Fiddlers' Championships; in early July watch horse people from 15 states compete in the Annual Walking Horse Show; and the first weekend in October, enjoy Oktoberfest, which may include a 10K walk. Catch the 10K walk in nearby Fort Campbell. The Clarksville/Montgomery County Tourist Commission, (615) 648-0001, 180 Holiday Road, Clarksville, TN 37043, can help you plan your visit.

☑ Watch out for chiggers, ticks, or poison ivy if you stray off the path.

Where Is It? The walks starts at the Ramada Riverview Inn, the tallest building in town, 50 College St., (615) 552-3331. **From I-24:** take the exit for Hwy 41A and go into Clarksville.

Sponsor: Clarksville Volksmarchers, 174 Taft Drive, Clarksville, TN 37042

☑ This walking club also plans two additional year-round walks in this community. If you'd like information on those walks, call Herrington or write the club and request a brochure. Be sure to enclose an SASE.

Volunteers Make These Walks Happen

Volunteers make the more than 3,000 miles of walking trails in the U.S. volkssport network possible. They map out the paths, write the directions and brochures, design the awards and keep track of who walks. Local businesses volunteer their time at the start and at the checkpoints. You also can help make these walking trails possible.

- Register even if you walk for free. Clubs need to know how many people use their trails.
- Be patient at the start/finish and checkpoints while workers take care of customers.
- Thank them for their time and patronize their businesses if you can.
- Tell a club if you've particularly enjoyed the walk, and be sure to tell them if you had problems. Your feedback will make the walk even better.

TEXAS

ABILENE ♦ *City Walk*

Dates: January 1–December 31  Chris Scott (915) 698-5616

Description (2): You'll see the downtown and Oscar Rose Park and pass a playground, the Grace Cultural Center, historic buildings, and shops on this 11K walk. An optional elevator ride will give you a 20-story-high view of the city.

See and Stay: Go north and visit the remains of Fort Phantom Hill. At the start point, be sure to get the list of shops and restaurants along the route that offer walker discounts. For campers, the local KOA has lots of shade, propane, and a camp store, (915) 672-3681. The Abilene Convention and Visitors Council, (800) 727-7704, P.O. Box 2281, Abilene, TX 79604, can provide you with tourist information.

Where Is It: Start at the Quality Inn, 505 Pine St., (800) 221-2222. **From I-20:** Take Exit 286A. If you're coming from the east, you'll curve right and stay on Pine going south to the inn. If you're coming from the west, you'll stay on the frontage road and curve right at Colonial Inn onto Pine. Go south to the inn. Park along the streets.

Sponsors: Shoeleather Express, 3117 Meander St., Abilene, TX 79602

The sun's out year-round in Texas, so protect yourself against those warm rays in any season. Heat, wind, and perspiration can drain moisture from your body, so carry water on every walk.

With at least 40 year-round and seasonal walks and 44 AVA walking clubs, Texas is among the most active states in the volkssport network. Contact Kendella Baker of the Texas Volkssport Association, 4509 Manzanillo Dr., Austin, TX 78749, (512) 467-0222, if you'd like more information about volkssporting in Texas.

TEXAS

AUSTIN ◆ *Historical Walk*
◆ *Town Lake Walk*

Dates: January 1–December 31  *Lolita Slagle (512) 837-6547*

Description (1 +): Explore the Texas capital on the historical walk, which will take you to the beautiful grounds of the capitol, the Lyndon B. Johnson Presidential Library, and the University of Texas campus, as well as the city's lovely oldest sections. You can avoid some steep steps with an alternate route, and will encounter many mild hills. The Town Lake walk follows the granite-gravel hike and bike trails along the beautifully landscaped lake.

See and Stay: You'll find plenty to do in Austin, but outdoor enthusiasts will particularly enjoy Zilker Park. This 349-acre park, the city's largest, borders Town Lake and features a 1,000-foot-long, spring-fed swimming pool. A 15-acre botanical garden and an 80-acre nature center composed of wildlife, plant, and dinosaur exhibits adds to your enjoyment, as does a large natural area with ponds, creeks, and waterfalls.

The Austin Children's Museum gives preschool and grade-school children hands-on fun. The Sixth Street Historic District, with its renovated 19th-century buildings filled with shops, galleries, and restaurants, has been favorably compared with New Orleans's Bourbon St. For more information on places to stay and things to do, contact the Austin Convention and Visitors Bureau Information Center, 300 Bouldin Ave., P.O. Box 1088, Austin, TX 78767, (512) 478-0098 or (800) 888-8AUS.

☑ The historical walk has little to no shade. Some parts of the lake walk are isolated.

🚲 The club also sponsors a 25K bike route along hike and bike trails and through neighborhoods.

Where Is It? Start at the Hyatt Regency Austin Hotel, 208 Barton Springs Rd., (512) 477-1234. **From I-35:** Take the Riverside exit just south of the river. Go west on Riverside to Barton Springs Rd. Turn right; the hotel is on the left. Park on the hotel's south side.

Sponsor: Colorado River Walkers, P.O. Box 13051, Austin, TX 78711-3051

TEXAS

BOERNE ♦ *Town Walk*
♦ *Country Walk*

Dates: *January 1–December 31*   *Barbara Hill (210) 537-4172, evenings*

Description (1) (1 +): Enjoy this German-heritage town designed to resemble the European communities the early settlers had known. The town walk includes the serene atmosphere of the Benedictine Convent and beautiful views of the surrounding area. Quaint shops, friendly neighborhoods, and a park with ducks add to the pleasure. Bring some food for the ducks! This walk includes stairs, but an alternate path makes this walk wheelchair accessible. Look for wildlife—armadillo, deer, turkey, and roadrunners—on the country walk, which is flat and easy.

See and Stay: Explore this 1850s town, set in a small valley, within the Texas Hill Country. Visit the Agricultural Heritage Center, the Cibolo Wilderness Area, or Cascade Caverns, with a 100-ft. underground waterfall.

☑ No bathrooms or water on the country walk.

 The walking club also sponsors a 26K bike route over Boerne's paved country roads. Carry water on the route.

Where Is It? Start in the lobby of the Key to the Hills Motel, 1228 S. Main, (210) 249-3562. Go to the table to the left of the front door and open the three drawers. **From I-10:** Take Exit 540 (Hwy 46) and turn east. Go to next intersection (Hwy 87 or Main St.) and turn left at the traffic light, by Wendy's. The motel is on the left, next door to the Dutch Boy Restaurant. Park in the back lot behind the Dutch Boy.

Sponsor: Hill Country Hikers, P.O. Box 1252, Boerne, TX 78006

CORPUS CHRISTI ♦ *Bayfront Walk*

Dates: *January 1–December 31* *Margaret Schindler (512) 852-3844*

Description (1 +): You'll walk along the bay in the heart of this resort community. This easy walk on paved surfaces, with some ramps, goes past the Art Museum of South Texas and Heritage Park.

See and Stay: Visit the Texas State Aquarium, at 2710 Shoreline Blvd. Nearby Padre Island National Seashore offers picnicking, camping, hiking. The Corpus Christi Area Convention and Tourist Bureau, 1201 N. Shoreline, P.O. Box 2664, Corpus Christi, TX 78403, (512) 882-5063 or (800) 678-6232, has more information.

Where Is It? Start at the Sand and Sea Budget Inn, 1013 N. Shoreline Dr., (512) 882-6518. **From I-37:** Follow I-37 into Corpus until it dead-ends into Shoreline.

Sponsor: The Sparkling City Strollers, P.O. Box 6805, Corpus Christi, TX 78411

TEXAS

DALLAS ♦ Downtown Walk

Dates: January 1–December 31    Earl Anderson (214) 341-8654

Description (2): You'll see Dallas's downtown and prominent points of interest on this walk on busy city streets. The architecture alone, designed by some of the country's leading architects, should delight you. The walk's sponsor discourages strollers because of the heavy traffic rather than any hills or curbs.

See and Stay: While you're in Union Station, ask the folks at the Dallas Visitors Information Center about everything there is to do in this dynamic city. You'll probably get information about the arboretum and botanical garden, Six Flags Over Texas, the zoo, the museum of art, the Dollhouse Museum of the Southwest, the John Fitzgerald Kennedy Memorial, the observation desk at the Reunion Tower of Dallas, and The Sixth Floor, an exhibit about JFK in the building and floor from which the shots that killed him are believed to have been fired. You'll have only one problem—deciding what to do first.

Hours: Daily 9 A.M.–5 P.M.

Where Is It? Start at the Visitor Center Information Desk at Union Station, 400 S. Houston St., on Dallas's west end. See the security guard if there is no one at the desk. **From I:35:** Take the exit for Houston St. and go north on Houston to the station.

DALLAS ♦ White Rock Lake Walk

Dates: January 1–December 31   Earl Anderson (214) 341-8654

Description (1): During this 15K walk, you'll circle the lake, a picturesque recreation area in northeast Dallas. The easy path is on well-marked, paved hike and bike trails.

Hours: Start no earlier than 9 A.M.; finish by 7 P.M.

This club also sponsors a 25K bike route from this start point.

Where Is It? Start at the Jack Johnston Bicycle Shop, 7820 Garland Rd., at Winsted St. **From I-30:** Take the East Grand exit and go northeast on Grand until it intersects Winsted. Grand becomes Garland Rd.

Sponsor: The Dallas Trekkers, 11460 Audelia, #187, Dallas, TX 75243, sponsor both walks.

TEXAS

DESOTO ◆ Town Walk

Dates: January 1–December 31 *Earl Anderson (214) 341-8654*

Description (1 +): You'll walk mostly on pavement, except for a short patch of grass. The walk has some slight hills, and strollers may have a little trouble with a few curbs and a street without sidewalks.

See and Stay: You're just south of Dallas, and will probably want to explore some of the sights there.

Hours: You can start as early as 6 A.M.—great in the hot summers.

Where Is It? Start at the customer service desk in Albertson's supermarket, 901 Polk St., at the northwest corner of Pleasant Run and Polk. DeSoto is 14 mi. south of Dallas. **From I-35:** Take Exit 415, and go west on Pleasant Run Rd. to the third traffic light at Polk. Albertson's is on the corner.

Sponsor: The Dallas Trekkers, 11460 Audelia, #187, Dallas, TX 75243

EL PASO ◆ Fort Bliss Walk

Dates: January 1–December 31 *Dorina Hobbs (915) 568-7506*

Description: The only walk near Texas's far west border, this path on Fort Bliss will take you on the grounds of the U.S. Army Air Defense Center.

See and Stay: Within El Paso you'll find some of the oldest settlements in Texas. This city reflects the cultural and architectural mix of its Spanish, Indian, and more modern influences. Contact the El Paso Convention and Visitors Bureau at 1 Civic Center Plaza, El Paso, TX 79901, (800) 592-6001, for information on all this city has to offer. Visit Ciudad Juarez, the fourth largest city in Mexico. Bus tours leave daily; contact the El Paso office of AAA Texas/New Mexico/Oklahoma for details.

Where Is It? Fort Bliss is located off I-10. Contact Hobbs for directions to the walk's start point and for details about the walk's route.

Sponsor: Fort Bliss Wanderers, 4301 Loma de Brisas, El Paso, TX 79934

FORT WORTH ◆ Nature Center Walk

Dates: January 1–December 31 *Bill Weikert (817) 457-6720*

Description (3): This 3,500-acre refuge harbors a variety of plant and animal life. You'll walk 12K almost entirely in fields and woods and along the river on dirt trails and will encounter some uphill and sandy areas. The wildlife, such as deer, bison, prairie dogs, and birds are plentiful.

See and Stay: Look over the exhibits in the interpretive center. You might want to head out on another nature trail.

☑ Dogs not allowed.

Hours: Tues.-Sat., 9:30 A.M.–4 P.M.; Sun., 12:30–4 P.M. Gates locked at 5 P.M.

Where Is It? Start at the Hardwicke Interpretive Center (headquarters and visitor center), in the Fort Worth Nature Center, (817) 237-1111, located in northwest Fort Worth just off Hwy 199, between Lake Worth and Eagle Mountain Lake. **From Hwy 199:** Go northwest and exit at Buffalo Rd., located 2.1 mi. northwest of the bridge over Lake Worth. Turn right and go to the first intersection, and take the left fork. Follow this to next intersection. Turn right to center's parking lot. The center is 100 yds. up the walk from the end of the lot.

FORT WORTH ◆ Downtown Walk

Dates: January 1–December 31 *Bill Weikert (817) 457-6720*

Description (1 +): This 11K walk along park trails and city streets will go by or near many of the city's attractions, including the Botanic Garden, the Cattlemen's Museum, and the Sid Richardson Collection of Western Art in Sundance Square.

See and Stay: Return to the Botanic Garden or wander through Forest Park, which offers a miniature railroad and zoo. If you love flea markets, don't miss Traders Village in Grand Prairie just east of Fort Worth, where more than 1,600 vendors gather at this weekend bazaar in open, covered, and enclosed market spaces. The kids will love nearby Six Flags Over Texas, a 205-acre amusement park with over 100 rides, shows, and attractions.

Where Is It? Start at the Ramada Inn, 1700 Commerce St., (817) 335-7000, across from the Water Gardens and south of the Convention Center. **From I-35W:** Exit to I-30 West and go to Commerce. Exit at Commerce and go north to the inn.

Sponsor: Tarrant County Walkers, P.O. Box 602, Arlington, TX 76010, sponsors both walks.

FREDERICKSBURG ◆ *Three Pilgrimage Walks*

Dates: January 1–December 31   Becky Lindig (210) 997-8056

Description: Welcome to the U.S. home of volkswalking! Volkssporting began in Fredericksburg in 1976, and the Pilgrimage Walk, the first year-round walking event, opened in 1980. This walk consists of three separate, sanctioned routes.

Cemetery Walk (1): This 10K walk passes two historical cemeteries on paved roads, and charming old houses. The walk does not include wandering through the cemeteries, but walkers may want to return to find the graves of the town's pioneers.

Town and Country Walk (1 +): This 11K walk will give you a nice sense of the town. You'll have one stretch of dirt path, which may be troublesome for strollers. From a hillside view you can look down at the numerous churches, which gave the town its nickname of "City of Steeples."

Historical Walk (1): This 13K walk originated as the chamber of commerce's self-guided tour of the Fredericksburg Historic District. You'll walk totally on paved roads.

See and Stay: Linger in this town that's considered one of Texas's most attractive small towns. You'll see several 19th-century Sunday Houses, occupied by ranchers when they came to town on the weekends for church services. Residents are lovingly restoring original homes. A reproduction of the first church, the eight-sided Vereins Kirche, holds a local history collection. The Toy Museum, open Wed.-Mon., has a 2,000-piece collection. The Pioneer Museum Complex at 309 W. Main, includes a stone house with eight furnished rooms and wine cellar, a log cabin, barn, smokehouse, and a Sunday House.

Where Is It? All three walks start at the Comfort Inn, 908 S. Adams, Hwy 16, .5 mi. south of Main St., Hwy 290. The town is located 22 mi. north of I-10 on Hwy 16 (from Kerrville) or Hwy 87 (from Comfort). Park in the inn's lot only if you are staying there.

Sponsor: Volkssportverein Friedrichsburg, P.O. Box 503, Fredericksburg, TX 78624

TEXAS

GALVESTON ♦ *Grand Homes Walk*

Dates: January 1–December 31 *Raz Hopkins (713) 996-5735*

Description (2): You'll go along the Seawall east to the East End Historic District and around the Strand past many historic buildings and beautiful homes. The walk, mostly on sidewalks or paved streets, can be bumpy with patches of grass. Strollers will have trouble with some curbing.

Food and Fun: Soak in the atmosphere of this seacoast town, once home of the famous pirate Jean Lafitte. Gaslights, restored Victorian buildings, and the clip-clop of horse-drawn carriages along the Strand will carry you back to the turn of the century. The Galveston Flyer, a handcrafted trolley, runs between all points of interest. Seafood is a specialty in this town, so enjoy!

Hours: From Memorial Day to Labor Day, 9 A.M.–5:30 P.M. From Labor Day to Memorial Day, finish by 5 P.M.

Where Is It? Start at the Galveston Island Convention and Visitors Bureau, 2106 Seawall Blvd., (800) 351-4237 outside of Texas or (800) 351-4263 inside Texas. **From I-45:** Go south from Houston to Galveston. Continue on I-45 (Broadway) to 21st and go right to the visitors bureau (Moody Center) and Seawall.

Sponsor: Friendswood Fun Walkers, 911 Mary's Court, Friendswood, TX 77546

GARLAND ♦ *Duck Creek Walk*

Dates: January 1–December 31 *Earl Anderson (214) 341-8654*

Description (1 +): Walk along the Duck Creek greenbelt and through Audubon Park on paved hike and bike trails. You'll encounter some city streets and a few curbs on your way to and from the park.

See and Stay: Explore Dallas or zip down Garland Rd. to the 15K walk at White Rock Lake.

Where Is It? Start at the Express Way Convenience Store, 3925 Broadway. Ask for the volkssport box. Garland is northeast of Dallas. **From I-635:** Take the exit for Hwy 78/Garland Rd. and go to Garland. Pass just to the east side of Garland and look for Broadway Blvd. Go south on Broadway to the store. **From I-30:** Look for the Beltline Rd./Broadway Blvd. exit. Go north on Broadway to the store. Park on the north side of the lot.

Sponsor: The Dallas Trekkers, 11460 Audelia, #187, Dallas, TX 75243

GRANBURY ◆ Historic Walk

Dates: January 1–December 31  Ardyce Pfanstiel (817) 326-2164

Description (2): This route includes historic landmarks, turn-of-the-century homes, the Historic Square, the Granbury Opera House, plus shops and restaurants.

See and Stay: Explore this town with a 19th-century feel brought on by the restoration of such buildings as the courthouse, jail, opera house, and bank. Catch a live performance most weekends at the opera house or take a sightseeing cruise on the *Granbury Queen*, departing from the landing at Lake Granbury. You'll have an excellent choice of quaint B&Bs and guest houses, RV parks and shops. The Convention and Visitors Bureau, (817) 573-5548 or (800) 950-2212, has gobs of information on what to see and do in this historic town.

Hours: Start no earlier than 8 A.M.

Where Is It? Start at The Lodge of Granbury, 400 E. Pearl St., one walking block from the downtown Square. **From Loop 820 (I-20) in Fort Worth:** Go southwest on Hwy 377 about 30 mi. to Granbury. In Granbury, take the Historic District exit (Hwy 377 Business) and cross over the new bridge. You are now on Pearl. The lodge will be on your left. Additional parking at the courthouse.

Sponsor: Hood County Hummers, 114 Fairway, DCBE, Granbury, TX 76049

HOUSTON ◆ University Walk
◆ Hermann Park Walk

Dates: January 1–December 31   Connie Bath (713) 665-2663

Description (1+): You'll get a great sidewalk view of Texas's largest city. The varied 11K university walk follows shaded, paved streets and sidewalks past the famous Medical Center, charming shops and eateries in the Village, the renowned art museums and sculpture gardens, scenic residential areas, and the beautiful campus of Rice University. The walk in Hermann Park passes many things you should return to afterwards: the zoo, golf course, museums, and theaters. Enjoy the shady hike and bike trails on this walk.

See and Stay: Don't rush out of this seaport town 50 mi. from the Gulf of Mexico. You'll find much to explore. Space Center Houston, to the southeast, offers tram tours of the Johnson Space Center, live demonstrations, and hands-on experiences. Take a boat tour of Port Houston. Return to Hermann Park to visit the Houston Museum of Natural Science and its Burke Baker Planetarium, the zoo, and the aquarium. Amble through the 155-acre forest at the Houston Arboretum and Nature Center, or let the kids explore the Children's Museum of Houston. Ask the Holiday Inn about its walker's discount.

TEXAS

Where Is It? Start at Houston's Holiday Inn Medical Center, 6701 S. Main St. **From the 610 South Loop:** Take Main north to the inn entrance. **From US 59:** Take Greenbriar south to University, then left on University to Fannin and right on Fannin to the inn's entrance. The inn is just northeast of the Main/Holcombe intersection. Parking is free, but you must obtain and display a parking permit on your vehicle.

Sponsor: Houston Happy Hikers, 2502 Watts, Houston, TX 77030

The Museum of Fine Arts Houston includes the world famous Cullen Sculpture Gardens. Photo by Peg Sampson.

IRVING ♦ Heritage Walk

Dates: January 1–December 31

 Gary Whitford (214) 579-7384

Description (1+): You'll walk through Old Irving, which contains the homes of the early settlers. Strollers will have some difficulty in spots.

See and Stay: Part of the greater Fort Worth/Dallas area, Irving has several interesting attractions. The 12,000-acre Las Colinas development includes a movie studio complex (scheduled to offer tours), communications museum, and equestrian center. The Mustangs of Las Colinas is believed to be the largest equestrian sculpture in the world. An exhibit in the lobby of the West Tower at Williams Square explains the creation of this sculpture. Tour Texas Stadium, home of the Dallas Cowboys. The Irving Convention and Visitors Bureau, (214) 252-7476 or (800) 247-8464, can send information.

Where Is It? Start at the McDonald's restaurant, 302 W. Irving Blvd. **From the north on I-35:** Pick up Loop 12 (South) past Texas Stadium to Irving Blvd (Hwy 356); turn right and continue to McDonald's. **From I-30:** Take Loop 12 (Walton Walker Blvd.) north to Irving Blvd. Turn left and proceed to McDonald's.

IRVING ♦ Las Colinas Walk

Dates: January 1–December 31

 Dick Snyder (214) 717-4189

Description (2): This 11K walk goes through an area of lovely homes, around Williams Square, the Mustangs Sculptures, the Irving Convention Center, and along the canals. Mostly on city sidewalks with some grass, the path includes some hills.

Hours: Mon.-Fri., 7 A.M.–5 P.M.; Sat., 8:30 A.M.–5 P.M.; Sun., noon–5 P.M.

Where Is It? Start at Velma-Ultimate Chocolate Cookie, 5205 O'Connor, 100 Williams Square, on the south side of the plaza. **From the north on I-35:** Take the Northwest Hwy (Loop 12) exit and go west on Spur 348 to O'Connor and left to Williams Square. **From the South on I-35E:** Stay on until road splits; stay on left side. This is Carpenter Fwy. Get off at O'Connor and go right to Williams Square.

Sponsor: Irving Star Trekkers, 1518 McHam, Irving, TX 75062, sponsors both walks.

KERRVILLE ◆ *Historical Walk*
◆ *Residential Walk*

Dates: January 1–December 31  Phil Latham (512) 782-3361

Description (1 +): You'll get the feel of a small Texas town on these walks. The historic walk includes buildings from the late 1800s and early 1900s and a view of the Guadalupe River. The residential walk takes you through beautifully landscaped sections of this town nestled in the rugged Hill Country.

See and Stay: Visit the Cowboy Artists of America Museum, featuring the works of living Western American artists. Ask the inn about its special walker's rates. Campers might want to reserve space in Kerrville-Schreiner State Park, 2385 Bandera Hwy, (512) 257-5392.

Where Is It? Start at Inn of the Hills, 1001 Junction Hwy, (800) 292-5690. **From I-10:** Take Exit 505. Turn left at intersection of Harper Rd. and Junction Hwy (signal light). The inn will be on your right and can be seen from the intersection.

Sponsor: Kerrville Trailblazers, P.O. Box 2097, Kerrville, TX 78029

MCKINNEY ◆ *Victorian Homes Walk*

Dates: January 1–December 31 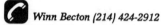 Winn Becton (214) 424-2912

Description (1 +): Grand Victorian homes and distinctive turn-of-the-century buildings on the National Register of Historic Places grace this walk.

See and Stay: Visit the Heard Natural Science Museum and Wildlife Sanctuary, 4 mi. south on SR 5, then 1 mi. east on FM 1378. This 274-acre museum is dedicated to the natural history of north Texas.

Where Is It? Start at the Holiday Inn, Central Expressway at White Ave. **From US 75:** Take Exit 40B (White Ave.). The inn is at the intersection of 75 and White.

Sponsor: Plano Plodders Walking Club, 2012 E. Park Blvd., Plano, TX 75074-5128

TEXAS

PLANO ◆ Creek Walk

Dates: January 1–December 31　　　Winn Becton (214) 424-2912

Description (1 +): You'll walk along the Chisholm Hike and Bike Trail, an 8-ft.-wide concrete trail that runs along a creek.

See and Stay: Visit the Heritage Farmstead, just off US 75, a four-acre example of an early Texas farm. You'll see a late Victorian farmhouse, 12 outbuildings, gardens, and a country store. Costumed guides give tours. You're only 20 mi. from Dallas, and might want to explore that city.

Where Is It? Go to the office at the Brookshire's Food Store, 2060 Spring Creek Pkwy, and ask for the volkssport lock box. **From US 75:** Take Exit 31, Spring Creek Pkwy, and go west to Custer Rd. The store is on the southeast corner of Spring Creek.

Sponsor: Plano Plodders Walking Club, 2012 E. Park Blvd., Plano, TX 75074-5128

SALADO ◆ Historical Walk

Dates: January 1–December 31　　　Karl or Beverly Kittinger (817) 547-1403, evenings

Description (1 +): This 11K trail will take you through historical areas and past quaint shops and residences. The path is paved and has some rolling hills.

Food and Fun: Treat yourself to a meal in the Stagecoach Inn, a restored 1860s stage stop. The inn, nestled among giant oak trees, offers a pool, a mineral spa, and tennis.

Where Is It? Start at the Stagecoach Inn (817) 947-5111. **From the north on I-35:** Take Exit 284 and cross over I-35 and continue to Main St. Go right on Main and cross Salado Creek. Take the first right to the inn and go into the parking lot. **From the south on I-35:** Take Exit 284 and turn right at the Exxon station, then go 1 blk. to Main.

Sponsor: Trotting Texas Turtles, 712 Ridge St., Copperas Cove, TX 76522-3137

183

TEXAS

SAN ANTONIO ♦ *Fort Sam Houston*

Dates: *January 1–December 31*   *Lyn Ward (210) 651-6536*

Description (1): This walk on Fort Sam Houston, one of the oldest forts in the country and a National Historic Landmark, offers an outstanding opportunity to view historic structures and sites. You'll also see free roaming deer, fowl, and rabbits inside the Quadrangle. The trail is flat and easy.

See and Stay: Don't hurry your walk. Take time to enjoy Fort Sam Houston, which has one of the largest collections of historic buildings—more than 900—representing each of the major styles of Army architecture. This post has almost nine times as many historic buildings as Colonial Williamsburg. The Quadrangle, where Apache Chief Geronimo once was held prisoner, is second only to the Alamo as a state historic structure.

☑ Leashed dogs are permitted on the fort, but cannot enter the Quadrangle.

Where Is It? Start at Post Headquarters, Bldg. 300, at Stanley Rd., (210) 221-2810. Look for the flag pole and two cannons in front of the building. Park at the side or rear of the building. From the rear, go to Room 7, marked "Staff Duty Officer." **From I-35:** Take Exit 159A. Turn north on N. New Braunfels Ave. and go to Stanley. Turn right on Stanley and go to Bldg. 300.

Sponsor: Texas Wanderers, 9355 Blazing Star Trail, Garden Ridge, TX 78266

The Quadrangle, dating back to 1876, is home to free-roaming deer, descendant from frontier times. Photo courtesy of the Department of the Army, Fort Sam Houston.

SAN ANTONIO ♦ Sea World Walk

Dates: March 13–October 31 (seasonal)   Lyn Ward (210) 651-6536

Description (1): This walk through San Antonio's biggest attraction is entirely within the 250-acre park and passes all the shows and exhibits.

☑ Tickets for Sea World cost $23.95, plus tax, for adults; $15.95, plus tax, for children 3-11; children 2 or under are free. If you present your walking record books at the Will Call window, you'll receive a 15% discount. Limit six discounts per person.

☑ No dogs allowed. Texas law prohibits leaving pets unattended in vehicles. The park offers free, self-service, covered and open-air dog shelters at the south end of the parking lot.

Hours: Sea World opens at 10 A.M. and closes between 6 P.M. and 10 P.M., depending on the season. It's open daily from June-August. From March to October, it opens primarily on weekends, with exceptions during spring break and several three-day weekends. It's best to confirm days and closing times with the park, (512) 523-3611 or (800) 422-7989.

Where Is It? Start at the Guest Relations Window located just inside Sea World's main gate. Identify yourself as a volkswalker and you'll be given the box with your registration cards and map. Sea World is located 16 mi. northwest of downtown San Antonio, just off SH 151, between Loop 410 and Loop 1604. It is at the intersection of Ellison Dr. and Westover Hills Blvd., off 151. Parking costs $3, or $8 for a season's pass.

Sponsor: Texas Volkssport Association, 9355 Blazing Star Trail, Garden Ridge, TX 78266

TEXAS

SAN ANTONIO ♦ *Mission Trail Walks*

Dates: *February 1–December 31*   *Phyllis Eagan (210) 496-1402*

Description: Together these walks take you to three of the four Spanish missions that make up the San Antonio Missions National Historical Park. These 18th-century missions were outposts of Spain's northern frontier.

Walk Route 1 (1+): This 12K walk along a hike and bike trail follows along the San Antonio River and goes from Mission San José to Mission Concepción and then returns along the same route.

Walk Route 2 (1): This 11K is along a hike and bike trail and a rural road and goes from Mission San José to Mission San Juan and returns along the same route.

See and Stay: Take time to explore the missions. San José Mission, founded in 1720, has the Rosa window, one of the finest examples of stone carving in America. The barracks, granary, and Indian quarters appear as they did in the 1700s. Before leaving the area, don't miss the Alamo, the oldest of San Antonio's missions. You can see the Alamo on the San Antonio 11K River Walk.

☑ Most of the routes are not shaded. Leashed pets are allowed on the trails, but not in the mission grounds.

Hours: 8 A.M.–5 P.M., Feb.-April 3 and Oct. 31-Dec. 31; 9 A.M.–6 P.M., April 4-Oct. 30.

🚴 The club also sponsors a 30K bike route that includes Mission Espada, with one of the last Spanish aqueducts in the U.S.

Where Are They? Start at the ranger station inside Mission San José, located at the corner of South Roosevelt and San José Dr. **From US 281:** Exit at Southwest Military Dr. and go west past Brooks Air Force Base to Roosevelt, about 1 mi. Turn right (north), and on the right (east) side of the street a National Parks sign will direct you to the mission.

Sponsor: Selma Pathfinders, 17314 Springhill, San Antonio, TX 78232

SAN ANTONIO ♦ River Walk

Dates: January 1–December 31 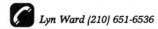 Lyn Ward (210) 651-6536

Description (1+): You'll experience the romance and charm of San Antonio when you take this 11K walk along the San Antonio River and through the historic downtown, including a look at The Alamo.

See and Stay: Simply enjoy San Antonio, especially the specialty shops and restaurants along the *Paseo del Rio* (Riverwalk). Return to the Alamo to see the video presentation and the two museums that record Texas history. Kids really will enjoy Brackenridge Park, which covers 343 acres and includes a zoo and a miniature railroad. Its Kiddie Park, the oldest amusement park in Texas, has 10 rides, including a 1918 carousel. Paddleboats, unguided horseback riding, and golf also are available. For tourist information call (800) 447-3372.

☑ No dogs allowed on walk.

Hours: Start after 8 A.M.

Where Is It? Start at the Holiday Inn Riverwalk North, 110 Lexington Ave., (210) 223-9461. From any highway into the city, get on US 81, north of downtown. Take Exit 157B "Downtown" and turn south on Lexington. Ten-hour metered parking is available on Baltimore and around the square between Baltimore and Lexington.

Sponsor: Texas Volkssport Association, 9355 Blazing Star Trail, Garden Ridge, TX 78266

SAN MARCOS ♦ University Walk

Dates: January 4–December 31 Barbara Piersol (512) 396-4463

Description (2): This trail goes along the popular Aquarena Springs, through the Southwest Texas State University campus, historic neighborhoods, and along the San Marcos River. You'll be on streets and sidewalks and encounter some hills and steps. Watch for birds.

See and Stay: Have fun in Aquarena Springs at the headwaters of the San Marcos River. Underwater shows, glass-bottom boat rides, the Texana Village, a candle factory, and a skyride to the Hillside Gardens will more than entertain you. Walkers can get a coupon for a $2 discount on the "All Adventure Pass." For tourist information, call (800) 782-7653, ext. 177.

Where Is It? Start at Aquarena Springs Inn, 1 Aquarena Springs Dr., located at the headwaters of the San Marcos River. Be sure to go to the inn, not to the park—the two are near each other. **From north I-35:** Take Exit 206 (Aquarena Springs Dr.) and turn right. Follow Aquarena Springs Dr. to Aquarena Springs Resort. The inn, a two-story, beige building, is behind the swimming pool. **From south I-35:** Take Exit 206 and follow Aquarena Springs Dr. to Aquarena Springs Resort.

Sponsor: San Marcos River Walkers, 100 E. Laurel Ln., San Marcos, TX 78666

TEXAS

SHINER ♦ Historical Walk
♦ Park Walk

Dates: January 1–December 31   Virginia Helweg (512) 594-3304

Description (1) (1 +): This historical walk through residential areas and the downtown include several historical markers and a short loop on the outskirts of town. You'll walk entirely on pavement. The park walk is through Green-Dickson Park, with a creek, playground, picnic tables, and residential areas. You'll encounter some gravel roads and will have to walk through a small pasture.

See and Stay: Tour Spoetzl Brewery, Mon.-Thurs. at 11 a.m., and see one of the smallest commercial brew kettles in the U.S. Visit the Wolters Museum and learn about the town's history. RV hook-ups are at Green-Dickson Park. Contact the Chamber of Commerce, P.O. Box 221, Shiner, TX 77984, (512) 594-4180 and ask for a visitors' guide.

Where Are They? Start at Howard's Diamond Shamrock, 1701 N. Avenue E, (512) 594-4200, outside of town at the corner of Boehm Dr. and Hwy 90A West. **From the east on I-10:** Exit at Flatonia. From Flatonia take Hwy 95 to Shiner, about 20 mi. **From the west on I-10:** Exit at Luling and take Hwy 183 to Gonzales and then Hwy 90A East to Shiner.

Sponsor: Shiner Half Moon Walkers, P.O. Box 294, Shiner, TX 77984

UNIVERSAL CITY ♦ Main Street Walk

Dates: January 1–December 31   Dick Toth (512) 659-3913

Description (1): You'll go through residential areas, an undeveloped industrial park, a city park, and along the city's main street on this 11K walk. The walk's sponsor says you'll encounter about 100 yds. of dirt trail, but the path is wheelchair accessible.

See and Stay: While you're in Universal City, don't miss your chance to visit the national headquarters of the American Volkssport Association at 1001 Pat Booker Rd. This is the place to pick up walking pins, state bars, patches, fanny packs, and walking memorabilia. The Comfort Inn offers a walker's discount.

🚴 This club also sponsors a 28K and a 32K bike route that start from the inn.

Where Is It? Start at the Comfort Inn, 200 Palisades Dr., (512) 659-5851. **From I-35:** Exit at Loop 1604 South (the 172-mile marker). Loop 1604 crosses over Pat Booker Rd. The first left is Palisades Dr.

Sponsor: Randolph Roadrunners, P.O. Box 44, Randolph A.F.B., TX 78108-0044

188

TEXAS

VANDERPOOL ◆ Lost Maples Walk

Dates: February 1–December 31   Phyllis Eagan (210) 496-1402

Description (2): You'll follow park roads and somewhat rocky, but level, nature trails. An optional trail (4+) over hilly land has a significant grade change, but rewards you with a beautiful overlook of the valley. Those with walking sticks should bring them.

See and Stay: Enjoy the natural beauty: rugged limestone canyons, grasslands, wooded slopes, and clear streams. Eagles are seen in the winter. The maples put on a colorful show in early November. Campsites are available at the park. Call (210) 966-3413.

Hours: Lost Maples State Natural Area is open weekends year-round and weekdays except for January and the first three weeks of December; during the winter, 8 A.M.–5 P.M., and until 8 P.M. the rest of the year. Check with the park to confirm times, (210) 966-3413.

☑ Smoking forbidden in the wooded areas.

Where Is It? Check in at the ranger station inside the gates of Lost Maples State Natural Area and drive to the picnic area to begin your walk. The park is on FM 187 north of Vanderpool. **From San Antonio:** Go northwest on Hwy 16 to Bandera and Medina, then west on FM 337 to FM 187. Turn right and go north 5 mi. to the park.

Sponsor: Selma Pathfinders, 17314 Springhill, San Antonio, TX 78232

WICHITA FALLS ◆ Lucy Park Trail
◆ Museum Trail

Dates: January 1–December 31   Chuck Samus (817) 691-0584, evenings

Description (1+): The park walk goes along paths near the Wichita River and the falls. You'll cross a swinging bridge over the red-colored river. On the museum walk, you'll travel through the country club section of town. Enjoy the lovely homes and large shade trees. The early settlers planted many of the trees still seen around town.

See and Stay: Be sure to appreciate the falls. The originals were about 5 ft. tall. The settlers were so impressed with the modest falls in this flat land that they named the town after them, only to have the falls wash away in 1882. In 1987, the city reestablished the falls by building a 54-ft. high cascade downstream from the original waterfall.

Where Are They? Start at the Econo Lodge, 1700 Fifth St., (817) 761-1889. **From the north:** Follow 287/281 and take the off ramp to Abilene. **From the south:** Follow 287/281 to the Broad St. off ramp at Eighth. At the third light, turn left on Fifth and go to the lodge.

Sponsor: Buffalo Chip Kickers, P.O. Box 8523, Wichita Falls, TX 76307

189

UTAH

OGDEN ◆ Two City Walks

Dates: January 1–December 31 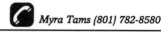 Myra Tams (801) 782-8580

Description (1 +): You'll have your choice of two 10K routes on your tour of this city nestled between the Wasatch Mountains and the Great Salt Lake. The "A" route goes through the business and residential areas and out along the Ogden River. The "B" path goes along a boulevard through the eastern side of Ogden.

See and Stay: Visit Union Station, an original railroad depot that's now a civic center. The station houses several museums and exhibits: a gem and mineral exhibit, museums of firearms and cars, the Myra Powell Gallery, a railroad museum, and the M. S. Browning Theater. Stop in at the visitor center of the Latter-day Saints Temple.

🚲 This club also sponsors a 75K bike route broken up into three 25K paths.

Where Is It? Start at Kar Kwik, 1918 Washington Blvd., near the Ogden River, (801) 392-2104. **From I-15:** Take Exit 346 at 21st St. near the Flying J Plaza. Go east toward the mountains to Washington Blvd. Turn left at the light and drive to 19th. Watch for the "Welcome to Ogden" sign that spans Washington over the Ogden River. The store is on the east side.

Sponsor: Golden Spike Striders, 3897 N. 1050 W., Ogden, UT 84414

PROVO ◆ City Walk

Dates: January 2–December 30   Joyce Ottens (801) 225-7007

Description (2 +) (1): This 11K route goes through business and residential areas and includes a small portion of the Brigham Young University campus. You'll be on sidewalks and paved streets, but will encounter a steep area and stairs on the BYU campus that is not suitable for wheeled vehicles. An alternate section included with your walking map will take wheeled vehicles along an accessible path that avoids the campus.

Hours: 8 A.M.–5 P.M. weekdays; 10 A.M.–6 P.M. weekends.

Where Is It? Start at the Utah County Travel Council, in the historic County Courthouse, 51 S. University, (801) 370-8393. **From the north on I-15:** Take Exit 268 (Provo). Go east on Center to University Ave., and turn right. The courthouse is on the southeast corner of University and Center. **From the south on I-15:** Take University to the courthouse on the right. The travel office is at the south entrance.

Sponsor: Gadabout, 75 E. 350 N., Orem, UT 84057

SALT LAKE CITY ♦ Three City Walks

Dates: January 1–December 31   Marianne Ausseresses (801) 943-8146

Description (1) (2): You'll have your choice of three routes. Route 1 follows a flat path on paved streets and sidewalks past historic homes and buildings. Route 2 is an 11K walk that includes one steep hill and also passes historic homes and buildings. Route 3 includes a steep hill up to the Capitol and another to Brigham Young's grave. You'll also pass through Kimball Cemetery where Kimball and his 33 wives and Whitney and his 13 wives are buried. The walk's sponsor says Routes 2 and 3 are good for wagons, strollers, and wheelchairs, but Route 1, which includes steps going down to Memory Grove, is not.

See and Stay: Go back to Temple Square where you'll find six free, 15-min. tours on various aspects of the square. Nearby major Mormon structures such as Brigham Young's Beehive House and the Family History Library also offer guided tours. For information about other things to do and places to stay in Salt Lake City, contact the Salt Lake Convention & Visitors Bureau, 180 S.W. Temple, Salt Lake City, UT 84101, (801) 521-2822. For information about travel in the state, contact the Utah Travel Council, Council Hall, Capitol Hill, Salt Lake City, UT 84114, (800) 538-1030. The Shilo Inn gives volkswalkers a $10 discount.

Where Are They? Start at the Shilo Inn, 206 S.W. Temple. **From I-15:** Take the Sixth South Exit and go to west Temple. Turn left and go to Second South. The inn is on the southwest corner of Second South and West Temple.

Sponsor: The Footloose Volkssport Club, 3525 Summer Hill Dr., Salt Lake City, UT 84121

TOOELE ♦ Downtown Walk
♦ Scenic Walk

Dates: January 1–December 31   Carolyn Lai (801) 250-2755

Description (1+) (3): The downtown walk gives you a tour of Tooele and passes several historic homes and buildings. The more difficult scenic walk goes up a steep hill in limited shade, but you'll be rewarded with views of the countryside and the Great Salt Lake. Watch for wildlife. The scenic walk has no water or restrooms on the trail.

Where Are They? Start at the customer service desk in Albertson's Food Store, 250 N. Main. **From I-80 west:** Take Exit 99 and drive 12 mi. down Rt 36 to Tooele. Rt 36 becomes Main. The store is on the left (east) side.

Sponsor: The Footloose Volkssport Club, 3525 Summer Hill Dr., Salt Lake City, UT 84121

VERMONT

WHITE RIVER JUNCTION ♦ Town Walk

Dates: April 1–December 1 (seasonal) *Pat Stark (802) 296-2192*

Description (2): This walk through town and residential areas includes one long, steep hill and several small ones. The hills are paved and may not stop a hearty stroller pusher. The route includes historic buildings and a mill site, and crosses the White River, with a short detour to the Wilder Dam and Visitors' Center on the Connecticut River.

See and Stay: Explore the town's historic points or take a tour of the brewery, just 1 blk. from the start point. The historic Hotel Coolidge offers a 10% discount to walkers. Camp in Pine Valley, 3 mi. out on Rt 4 west.

Where Is It? This walk starts at the Hotel Coolidge, 17 S. Main St., (800) 622-1124. **From I-91:** Take Exit 11 (White River Jct.) and continue on Rt 5 North about 1 mi. to the second stop light. Continue straight for 3 blks. Park in the town lot near antique locomotive No. 494.

Sponsor: Twin State Volkssport Association, P.O. Box 184, Wilder, VT 05088

Fashionable Volkswalking

The only fashions that count on the volkswalking trails are the ones that are comfortable. The only style that matters is the one that's friendly. Walkers don't need to buy any special gear—helmets, goggles, color-coordinated shorts and sweatbands, or spandex britches. You will need some simple equipment, however, and a little clothes sense.

- Invest in a good pair of shoes and buy those shoes from someone who knows shoes, measures feet, and takes the time to fit you properly.
- Buy good socks. Wear soft, absorbent, snug-fitting socks that won't bunch up or down.
- Wear natural fibers (cotton, wool, silk) so your skin can breathe and stay dry.
- Layer up so you can peel it off. You'll be surprised how quickly you heat up.
- Get a fanny pack that has an attached plastic water bottle.
- Protect your head and any exposed skin from the sun.
- Get a walking stick to use on slippery slopes or uneven paths.

VIRGINIA

ALEXANDRIA ◆ Two Old Town Walks

Dates: January 2–December 31 Bob McLean (703) 455-1878

Description (1 +): Both walks travel through the streets and parks of this old (1749) tobacco port and offer great views of the Potomac River. You'll see the homes of Robert E. Lee and George Washington and other historic sites and buildings.

See and Stay: Lose yourself in early American history and visit historic spots such as Gadsby's Tavern where George Washington attended birthday balls and meetings, or walk Prince St., known as Captain's Row because the homes were built by sea captains. Numerous quaint shops, eateries, and lodgings will tempt you.

Hours: Tues.-Sat., 10 A.M.-6 P.M.; Sun. 12-5 P.M. Closed Mondays.

Where Are They? Start at the Bavarian Alps, at 924 King St., (703) 683-3994. **From D.C.:** Take the subway to King St. stop, which is 8 blks. from the shop. **From I-95/I-495 (Beltway):** Take Exit 2 and go north on Telegraph Rd. Turn right (east) on Duke St. (Rt 236), left on Callahan Dr. and right on King (Rt 7) to Bavarian Alps. Free 2- or 3-hr. parking is available on Prince and Cameron streets. Metered spots and commercial lot are also available.

Sponsor: Northern Virginia Volksmarchers, P.O. Box 7096, Fairfax Station, VA 22039-7096

FREDERICKSBURG ◆ Historic City Walk

Dates: January 7–December 31 Peter Sniffin (703) 373-0773

Description (1 +): This walk takes you on a historic tour of this Civil War battle site. The path goes into the Fredericksburg National Cemetery, with the graves of 15,000 Union soldiers, and past the Fredericksburg Battlefield Visitor Center.

See and Stay: History buffs will enjoy seeing the homes associated with George Washington's mother and sister, and viewing the James Monroe Museum and Memorial Library, which houses many of this former president's personal possessions.

Hours: Daily 9:30 A.M.-4:45 P.M.

Where Is It? Start at the Fredericksburg Visitor Center, 706 Caroline St., (703) 373-1776. **From I-95:** Take Exit 45A (Rt 3 East), which becomes Williams St. within the city limits. Follow the blue signs with the city logo about 3 mi. to the town's center.

Sponsor: Germanna Volkssport Association, P.O. Box 7674, Fredericksburg, VA 22404-7674

VIRGINIA

JAMESTOWN ♦ *Historic Park Walk*

Dates: January 1–December 31   *Annette Tollett (804) 766-3065*

Description (1 +): Follow in the footsteps of the 17th-century English on this 11K walk through the New World's first permanent English-speaking colony. The trail is along the shoulder of the road and along the dirt paths where the town was located.

See and Stay: This historic park gives a feel for what this early settlement must have been like. The Memorial Cross marks the graves of the 300 settlers who died during the severe winter of 1609. Glass-blowers demonstrate their craft at the Glasshouse.

Hours: Daily 9 A.M.; finish by 5-6 P.M., depending on the season.

🚲 The club also sponsors a bike path. Call Tollett for information.

Where Is It? Start in the Visitors Center gift shop in the Colonial National Historic Park. **From I-64:** Go to Exit 242A, Rt 199 West. Go 3.4 mi. to the second light, and turn right onto S. Henry St. (Rt 132). Immediately turn right again; at the bottom of the ramp turn right onto Colonial Parkway toward Jamestown. Follow the parkway for 7.4 mi. to the entrance for the Jamestown portion of the Colonial National Historical Park. Pay your fee and follow the signs to the center.

Sponsor: Peninsula Pathfinders, Box 7100, Hampton, VA 23666

MANASSAS ♦ *Historic Walk*

Dates: January 2–December 31   *Dick or Evelyn Reichert (703) 335-1428*

Description (1 +): This 11K walk will take you through a Civil War town. You'll see grand old homes that were standing when this town was an important railroad junction for both North and South.

See and Stay: Go just north of town to visit the famous Civil War battlefields of Bull Run. The Manassas Museum in Baldwin Park displays Civil War memorabilia.

✔ This is a self-service walk with directions in the walk box.

Hours: Mon.-Sat., 10 A.M.–4:30 P.M. Closed Sundays.

Where Is It? Start at Two Days Gifts, 9249 Center St. in Historic Old Town, (703) 368-9858. **From I-95:** Take Exit 152 (Rt 234) west toward Manassas. Route 234 becomes Grant Ave. as you come in to town. Take Grant to Church St. Turn left at Church and go 1 blk. to Peabody. Turn left on Peabody and go 1 blk. to Center. Turn left. The shop is 1 blk. down on the right.

Sponsor: Wood & Dale Wanderers, P.O. Box 2422, Woodbridge, VA 22193-2422

VIRGINIA

NORFOLK ◆ MacArthur Walk

Dates: January 2–December 31   Charlie Hornsby (804) 464-6881

Description (1): This 11K walk features the MacArthur Memorial and a tour of this port city's historic buildings. You'll also find interesting shops and restaurants along this level, easy sidewalk tour.

See and Stay: Take time to explore the MacArthur Memorial. Hop on a boat and tour one of the world's finest harbors. The *Spirit of Norfolk* offers daily lunch and dinner cruises, (804) 627-7771, for reservations; and the *Carrie B*, a 19th-century riverboat replica, leaves daily from 333 Waterside Dr. for a 1.5-hr. narrated cruise. Stop in at the Virginia Zoological Park or the Norfolk Botanical Garden, where you can picnic near a lake. Contact the Norfolk Convention and Visitors Bureau, (804) 441-1852, for information on the many points of interest.

Hours: Mon.-Sat., 10 A.M.–4.30 P.M.; Sun., 11 A.M.–4:30 P.M.

Where Is It? Start at the MacArthur Memorial Theatre building, at Bank St. and City Hall Ave., (804) 441-2965. **From I-64:** At Norfolk, take Exit 284A (I-264 west) to downtown Norfolk. Leave I-264 west at Exit 10 (City Hall Ave.) and go to the memorial.

Sponsor: The Gator Volksmarsch Club, P.O. Box 14025, Norfolk, VA 23518

VIRGINIA BEACH ◆ Seashore Walk

Dates: January 2–December 31   Becky Baronet (804) 486-0664

Description (2): This walk will take you from paved sidewalks to a maintained and marked trail in Seashore State Park. You'll find some uphill climbs, a dirt trail, and some beach.

Food and Fun: This resort with a 29-mi. coast is noted for its seafood. Hop a trackless trolley and explore the beachfront. Stop by the Life-Saving Museum of Virginia, 24th St. and Atlantic Ave., for displays of shipwrecks and maritime memorabilia. Kids will love the Ocean Breeze Fun Park, which includes four parks in one. Contact the visitors bureau for more information, (800) 425-7511.

Where Is It? Virginia Beach Resort Hotel & Conference Center, 2800 Shore Dr., (804) 481-9000. The hotel is 3.5 mi. east of the Chesapeake Bay Bridge-Tunnel on Rt 60 (Shore Dr.). **From the north:** Use the Bridge-Tunnel to Rt 60 east. **From the northwest, south and southwest:** Use I-64 to Rt 13 North (Northampton Blvd.) to Rt 60 east.

Sponsor: The Gator Volksmarsch Club, P.O. Box 14025, Norfolk, VA 23518

VIRGINIA

WILLIAMSBURG ♦ *Colonial Walk*

Dates: January 1–December 31 *Annette Tollett (804) 766-3065*

Description (2): This walk goes through the historical area of Colonial Williamsburg and the William and Mary campus. You'll walk along the shoulder of the roads and on a dirt trail.

See and Stay: With more than 500 preserved, restored, or rebuilt houses, shops, taverns and buildings, this popular tourist attraction offers a wealth of sights and an array of restaurants and lodging. The craft shops are particularly delightful.

Hours: Mon.-Fri., 6 A.M.-8 P.M.; Sat., 8 A.M.-7 P.M.; Sun., 11 A.M.-5 P.M.

🚲 The club also sponsors a bike and a swim. Ask in the sports shop or call Tollett.

Where Is It? Start at the sport shop in the Tazewell Fitness Center in the Williamsburg Lodge. **From I-64:** Follow the signs for Williamsburg and then signs to the historic area. Turn left onto South England St. You will see a sign for the Conference Center. The lodge is at this corner. Park in the lot to the left and in front of the lodge. Take the covered walkway to the fitness center.

Sponsor: Peninsula Pathfinders, 3 Delmont Ct., Hampton, VA 23666

This brick shop is one of many restored areas that demonstrate the early trade crafts in Williamsburg. Photo by Ralph Lauterwasser.

YORKTOWN ♦ *Battlefield Walks*

Dates: January 1–December 31 *Annette Tollett (804) 766-3065*

Description (2): An 11K or a 15K trail takes you through this Revolutionary War battlefield area. The walks go along the shoulder of the roads, through the battlefield area and the historic town where George Washington accepted the surrender of Lord Cornwallis.

See and Stay: The National Park Visitors Center gives a short film and offers exhibits and a special overlook of the battlefield. You'll see the site of Washington's headquarters, siege lines, redoubts and the Moore House where officers drafted the terms of surrender.

Hours: Daily 8 A.M.; finish by 5–6 P.M., depending on the season.

The walking club also offers a bike trail. Ask at the gift shop or call Tollett.

Where Is It? Start the walk at the gift shop in the visitors center of the Colonial National Historic Park. **From I-64:** Take one of the Yorktown exits (258B or 242B) and follow the signs to Yorktown and the Colonial National Historic Park and battlefield. Once in the park, follow the signs to the visitors center. Park there.

Sponsor: Peninsula Pathfinders, 3 Delmont Ct., Hampton, VA 23666

WASHINGTON

ANACORTES ♦ Waterfront Walk

Dates: January 1–December 31 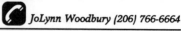 JoLynn Woodbury (206) 766-6664

Description (1 +): You'll see the marina waterfront area, Guemes Channel (the salt-water shipping channel), an interesting rocky park, and the downtown on this walk at the tip of Fidalgo Island. The path is fairly level, but does includes one uphill block that might challenge wheeled vehicles.

See and Stay: Visit the Anacortes Museum, which includes the *W. T. Preston*, the last snag boat to operate in Puget Sound. Drive to Mount Erie—the island's highest point—and see Mount Rainier, the Cascade and Olympic mountains, and the area's islands. Bridges and daily ferry service connect Anacortes to the mainland, to other spots in the San Juan Islands, and to Vancouver, British Columbia.

☑ Restrooms at the new chamber of commerce are closed Sundays; those at Guemes Ferry Dock are closed evenings.

Where Is It? Start at the Island Hospital, 1213 24th St., and go to the podium in the lobby where you will find the self-registration materials. You'll have to pay by check or exact change because no change is available. **From I-5:** Take Exit 230 west. Follow Hwy 20 to Anacortes. Turn left on 24th St. The hospital is on the left; use street parking.

Sponsor: Skagit Tulip Trekkers, P.O. Box 1084, Anacortes, WA 98221

The following state agencies can give you travel tips and help when you start planning your Washington vacation:

• For recreation information, contact the State Parks and Recreation Commission, 7150 Clearwater Ln., Olympia, WA 98504, (206) 753-2027.

• For information on national parks and forests, contact the Outdoor Recreation Information Office, 915 Second Ave., Room 442, Seattle, WA 98174, (206) 553-0170.

• For more visitor information, contact the Travel Development Division, Dept. of Commerce and Economic Development, General Administration Bldg., Olympia, WA 98504, (206) 586-2088.

WASHINGTON

BELLEVUE ♦ Greenbelt Trail Walks

Dates: January 2–December 31   Susan Eichner (206) 746-1160

Description (2 +): Both trails are mainly along gravel and asphalt trails through the Lake Hills Greenbelt. Both routes pass Larsen and Phantom lakes and the Robinswood Park area. One walk is 11K and the other is a 10K with an additional 2K option. The 10K walk includes the Boeing Jogging Trail and the Mormon Temple. The added 2K option takes you around Larsen Lake. Watch for waterfowl and wildlife. A ranger station adjacent to the trail can provide free information on winter weekends from noon–4 P.M. and in the summer Wed.-Sun., from noon–6 P.M.

Food and Fun: Visit Kelsey Creek Park with its playgrounds, hiking trails, barnyard zoo, and Japanese garden. Restored Old Bellevue features shops and galleries. If you love Greek food, visit Stamos, a family-run restaurant just 2 blks. away from the club.

Hours: Mon.-Fri., 8 A.M.–dusk; weekends, 10 A.M.–dusk.

Where Are They? Start at the Samena Swim & Recreation Club, 15231 Lake Hills Blvd., (206) 746-1160. No parking fee for volkswalk participants. **From the south:** Take I-405 north to I-90 east to Spokane. Take Exit 11B (148th SE) heading north past Bellevue Community College and the Mormon Temple. At the stop light on Lake Hills Blvd., turn right. Samena is on the right side, just past the little league field and across from the library. Park in the lot adjacent to the Greenbelt Trail.

Sponsor: Samena Striders, 2616 N.E. 20th, Renton, WA 98056

BED AND BREAKFAST ROUND LONG DISTANCE WALKS

Dates: July 1, 1992–December 31, 1993   Myrna Goddard (206) 863-8406

Description: The Round Long Distance Walk comprises a dozen 10K walks. In Washington, each walk starts at a different bed and breakfast inn that is a member of the Washington Bed and Breakfast Guild. Walkers have 18 months to complete all 12 walks.

The trails include beaches and mountains, city streets, and country lanes. To participate in this 120K event, walkers must purchase a $6 guidebook, good for all 12 walks. To get a list of the participating B&Bs, the guidebook, maps, and details, write to Myrna Goddard, 3326 119th Ave. E., Puyallup, WA 98372. In 1994, call Goddard to see if the program was renewed.

Sponsor: Washington Bed and Breakfast Volkssporting Club, 3326 119th Ave. E., Puyallup, WA 98372

WASHINGTON

CARLSBORG ♦ *Railroad Walk*

Dates: January 1–December 31   Dick Cable (206) 681-2504

Description (2): Travel along the old Milwaukee Railroad grade. You'll cross the rebuilt railroad bridge across the Dungeness River and the old mill town of Carlsborg and be hit with spectacular views of the Olympic Mountains. It's not unusual to see deer and eagles.

See and Stay: Enjoy the dry, sunny weather and the many outdoor activities. The Dungeness National Wildlife Refuge, 4.5 mi. west on Hwy 101, contains one of the longest U.S. natural sandpits—a rest stop for thousands of migratory waterfowl. You can clam, crab, and fish, but bikes, pets, camping, and fires are prohibited. At the nearby Olympic Game Farm you'll watch wild animals being trained for films and television, and can drive through roads to observe fields of bear, bison, zebra, elk, and other animals.

Where Is It? Start at the Carlsborg Store, Carlsborg Rd., (206) 683-4340. **From Hwy 101:** Carlsborg Rd. is just off Hwy 101, about 4 mi. west of Sequim and 11 mi. east of Port Angeles. There is a caution light at the intersection of 101 and Carlsborg Rd. Turn north at this intersection and go about 1 mi. to the store. Please do not park directly in front of the store.

Sponsor: Olympic Peninsula Explorers, P.O. Box 1706, Sequim, WA 98282

CLE ELUM ♦ *Yakima River Walk*

Dates: April 10–October 31 (seasonal)   Jane Butler (509) 965-1357

Description (2): Cle Elum, the Indian word for "swift water," is on the Yakima River. This walk along sidewalks, county roads, and some gravel areas, will take you along the river and return through the residential areas.

See and Stay: You're at the gateway to a vast recreation area. The Wenatchee National Forest and Mount Baker-Snoqualmie National Forest abound with opportunities for camping, hiking, fishing, and enjoying the varied wildlife and wilderness areas.

☑ Water and restrooms are only at the start/finish.

Where Is It? Start at the Stewart Lodge, 805 W. First St., (509) 674-4548. **From I-90:** Take Exit 84. From the west, follow the exit road directly to the lodge on your left, across from Safeway. From the east, you will exit on Oakes Ave. At the intersection with W. First St., turn left and follow the road to the lodge on your right at the top of the hill.

Sponsor: Yakima Valley Sun Striders, P.O. Box 10523, Yakima, WA 98909

WASHINGTON

DES MOINES ◆ Scenic Sound Walk

Dates: January 1–December 31 *Carolyn Dexheimer (206) 927-5185*

Description (3): You'll get wonderful views of Puget Sound on a walk that goes along the marina and through a park.

See and Stay: The Des Moines Marina on South 27th St. has a 670-ft. public fishing pier. The Des Moines Beach Park is a 20-acre reserve of meadows and woodlands. Picnic in this rustic area that until recently served as a church retreat. For more information, contact the Chamber of Commerce, P.O. Box 98672, Des Moines, WA 98198, (206) 878-7000.

Where Is It? Start at the Masonic Home of Washington, 23660 Marine View Dr. S. Your walking materials are in the bench on the left, just inside the first set of double doors. **From I-5:** Take Exit 149 (Kent-Des Moines) and follow signs to Des Moines. Cross Hwy 99 and continue west to the light at Marine View Dr. Turn left and go south on Marine View Dr. The home is a large Gothic-style building on the left. Park along the circular drive.

Sponsor: StarWalkers Volkssport Club, 29630 11th Place S., Federal Way, WA 98003

EDMONDS ◆ Waterfront Walk
◆ Woodway Walk

Dates: January 2-December 30 *Lorrie Pedersen (206) 542-8694*

Description (1 +): One walk will take you along the waterfront, through the picturesque downtown and residential areas. The other goes along a wildlife sanctuary, through the rural-feeling parts of Woodway, along portions of the waterfront, and onto Brackett's Landing and Jetty. Detailed directions will add to your walking enjoyment.

See and Stay: Picnic at the Marine Park and let the kids explore the playground. Wander along the marina and watch for the varied bird life. Take a ferry boat ride or visit the galleries, antique shops, and specialty stores in Old Mill Town, a 22-store complex.

☑ Several walkers have told the Puget Sound Sloshers they have one of the prettiest walks.

Hours: Weekdays you can start in daylight as early as 5:30 A.M., 7:30 A.M. weekends.

Where Are They? Start at the Harbor Square Athletic Club, 160 W. Dayton, (206) 778-3546. **From I-5:** Take Exit 177 and go west on SR 104 (Edmonds/Kingston Ferry). At the intersection of SR 104 and Dayton (at ferry ticket booth), turn left and go 1 blk. Turn left into the Harbor Square complex.

Sponsor: Puget Sound Sloshers Volkssport Club, P.O. Box 31, Lynnwood, WA 98046-0031

WASHINGTON

FEDERAL WAY ♦ Twin Lakes Walk

Dates: January 1–December 31   *Dorman Batson (206) 838-6981*

Description (1): Walk in Twin Lakes, a planned community in Federal Way, a large suburban community in the Seattle/Tacoma area. You'll walk on sidewalks through residential areas and get views of Puget Sound, the Olympic Mountains, and Mt. Rainer, if the weather is clear. You'll encounter some minor hills.

See and Stay: The kids will enjoy the Enchanted Village, a 50-acre family entertainment park with rides, a maze, bumper boats, picnic areas, and a toy and doll museum. Wild Waves Water Park, adjacent to the village, has a 24,000-sq. ft. pool and four waterslides.

Where Is It? In Federal Way, start at Jim's Market and Deli, 4612 S. 320th, at 320th and Hoyt Rd., (206) 952-4434. **From I-5:** Take Exit 143 onto S. 320th. From the north, turn right onto S. 320th. From the south, turn left heading west for 4.5 mi. until the road intersects with Hoyt. Jim's is on your right at the east end of the shopping center.

Sponsor: Evergreen State Volkssport Assoc., P.O. Box 5737, Vancouver, WA 98668

FEDERAL WAY ♦ Residential Walk

Dates: January 1–December 31   *Evelyn Wilton (206) 888-1345*

Description (1): This moderately easy walk along lovely residential streets and paved paths will give you a good view of this Puget Sound city.

Hours: The manor is open weekdays, 8 A.M.–8 P.M.; weekends, 10 A.M.–6 P.M.

Where Is It? Start at Hallmark Manor, 32300 First Ave. S., (206) 874-3580. **From I-5:** Take Exit 143. Go 1.5 mi. west on S. 320th St. to the traffic light at First Ave. S. Turn left and go .5 blk to the manor on the left.

Sponsor: Sea-Tac Volkssports Club, P.O. Box 7613, Federal Way, WA 98003-7613

> Most Washington communities have strict pooper-scooper laws that they enforce. If you bring your dog on a walk, put some plastic bread bags or sandwich bags in your pocket. With your hand in the bag, you can quickly make a sanitary "hand scoop."

WASHINGTON

KELSO ♦ Town Walk

Dates: January 1–December 31  Pete Hauser (206) 577-7435

Description (2+): You'll get a good view of this town known as the "Smelt Capital of the World." All-weather roads and maintained paths will take you through lovely residential areas and past some unique landmarks.

See and Stay: Visit the Kelso Volcano Tourist Information Center, near the start point, and learn about the 1980 eruption of Mount St. Helens from photographs, rock samples, and a scale model with narrative.

Where Is It? Start in the lobby of the Red Lion Inn, 510 Kelso Dr. **Southbound I-5:** Take Exit 39 (SR 4/Kelso). At the stop light, turn left. Go under the interstate and go two lights to Kelso Dr. Turn right on Kelso Dr., a frontage road, and go about 400 meters to the inn. Park in the side or rear parking areas. **Northbound I-5:** Take Exit 39 (SR 4/Kelso/Longview). At the stop light, turn right for one short block to Kelso Dr. Turn right on Kelso Dr.

Sponsor: Border Crossers, 2325 Nichols Blvd., Longview, WA 98632

KENNEWICK ♦ Panoramic Walk

Dates: January 1–December 31  Margaret Johnson (509) 783-7314

Description (2): You'll get excellent views of the Tri-Cities from the top of the hill in Panoramic Heights and sidewalk views of residential areas with names like Cherry Blossom Heights and Street of Dreams. You'll find some gravel and dirt areas and a short, steep hill.

See and Stay: Kennewick is the departure point for scenic and recreational cruises on the Columbia. Take a 3-hr. dinner train ride to Prosser through desert and farm country. Call (800) 876-7245 for time and details. Camp in the Columbia Park Recreation Area and take the kids to Oasis Waterworks.

☑ Water and restrooms only at start point. No shade on trail.

Where Is It? Start at the Sun Mart (Exxon), Hwy 395 and 27th Ave., at 4201 W. 27th. **From I-82:** Take Exit 113 toward Kennewick/Spokane. Park away from the entrances. **From Hwy 395:** Exit the highway at 27th Ave.

Sponsor: Eastern Washington Telephone Pioneers, 419 W. Loop Dr., Moses Lake, WA 98837

WASHINGTON

KIRKLAND ◆ Three Walks

Dates: January 1–December 31 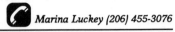 Marina Luckey (206) 455-3076

Description (1) (3): Old neighborhoods and parks, waterfront views of Lake Washington, overlooks of Seattle and the Olympic Mountains, or paths through a nature park are among your choices on these walks of varying length and difficulty. You can choose from a 10K, 11K, or 20K walk, but only the 10K is suitable for wheeled vehicles.

See and Stay: If you like water sports, you'll love Kirkland, which has more public waterfront areas than any other Washington city. This major boating center gives you beaches, plus the chance to sail, windsurf, swim, and fish. The deli gives walkers a complimentary coffee.

Where Is It? Start at Peter K's Deli, 215 Central Way, (206) 889-0711. **From I-405:** Take Exit 18 and head west toward Lake Washington on Central. The deli is across the street from Peter Kirk Park at Third and Central in the downtown. Park in the lot across from Third St., adjacent to the park.

Sponsor: Interlaken Trailblazers, P.O. Box 70068, Bellevue, WA 98007

LONGVIEW ◆ Lake Sacajewea Walk

Dates: January 1–December 31 Pete Hauser (206) 577-7435

Description (1+): Walk around the scenic Lake Sacajewea along an 11K path that is mostly flat. The all-weather, maintained trails also will take you to residential areas and past historic landmarks. Wheeled vehicles may have a little trouble on the park paths.

See and Stay: This planned city is a major industrial port. The Port of Longview on Port Way offers guided tours of the port, including ship-loading, cargo movement, and operations. Free, but reservations are required. Call (206) 425-3305.

Where Is It? Go to the Tel-Med desk at the St. John's Medical Center, 1614 E. Kessler Blvd. Enter the center from Delaware St. The start counter is inside the door, along the lower-level corridor, just before you reach the cafeteria. You'll find instructions at the counter. **Northbound I-5:** Take Exit 36. Follow this route 3.4 mi. to 15th Ave., the fifth stop light. Turn right on 15th. Go 2 blks. to Delaware; turn left. Go 1 blk.; the center's lot is on the left. **Southbound I-5:** Take Exit 40. At the stop sign, turn right. Follow SR 4 to the first light. Turn right. Go over the Cowlitz River Bridge along Washington Way to 15th Ave. Turn half-left on 15th. Go seven stop lights to Delaware; turn right. Go 1 blk.

Sponsor: Border Crossers, 2325 Nichols Blvd., Longview, WA 98632

WASHINGTON

MUKILTEO ♦ 'Round Town Walk

Dates: January 1–December 31   *Nelda Severin (206) 353-9483*

Description (2): The waterfront, historical sites, Mukilteo State Park, residential areas, and downtown will entertain you on this 11K walk with several moderate hills.

See and Stay: Take a ferry ride to Clinton on Whidbey Island and explore the island. Call (800) 542-7052 (in Wash.) for times.

Hours: Weekdays start as early as 6 A.M., 7 A.M. on weekends. In summer, the store closes at 8 P.M. weekdays, 5 P.M. weekends. In the winter, it closes at 6 P.M. and at 5 P.M. on weekends.

Where Is It? Start at the Mukilteo Coffee Company, 619 Fourth St. **North on I-5:** Take Exit 182. Follow Rt 525 (Mukilteo Speedway) to Mukilteo. Turn right on Third, then right on Lincoln. The coffee company is in the back facing the Speedway. **South on I-5:** Take Exit 192. Go west on 41st and Mukilteo Blvd. into Mukilteo. Turn right at the Speedway, then right on Third, and right on Lincoln. Please park on the street.

Sponsor: Seattle Strasse Striders, P.O. Box 27573, Seattle, WA 98125

OLYMPIA ♦ Capital Walk

Dates: January 1–December 31   *James Lance (206) 357-9898*

Description (2 +): Sidewalks, paved roads, trails, and steps will take you on your 11K tour of Olympia, the state capital.

See and Stay: Visit the Nisqually National Wildlife Refuge with its fresh- and salt-water marshes, forests, grasslands, and streams. Olympic National Forest and Olympic National Park offer scenic wilderness, from mountain glaciers to ocean waves. Watch for elk.

☑ No dogs.

🚲 This club also sponsors a 25K bike ride. Call Lance for details.

Hours: Start no earlier than 8 A.M.

Where Is It? Start at the Bayview Market Place Deli, 516 W. Fourth Ave., (206) 352-4901. **South on I-5:** Take Exit 105, then 105B, following signs to the port. You'll arrive at Plum St. Go on Plum to State Ave. and turn left. Stay in right lane. State turns left for 1 blk., then turns right on Fourth Ave. Two blocks after that, turn right on Simmons St., then left into the market parking lot. **North on I-5:** Take Exit 105 following signs to the port. Turn left at the stop sign on Plum and continue as above.

Sponsor: Capitol Volkssport Club, P.O. Box 977, Olympia, WA 98507

WASHINGTON

PORT ANGELES ♦ *Downtown Walk*

Dates: January 1–December 31 Dick Cable (206) 681-2504

Description (2 +): This scenic 11K walk goes through the downtown and parks and along the harbor. Plan to picnic or take a swim at the excellent beach area. Some streets are without sidewalks and there's one long, steep hill.

Food and Fun: Restaurants along the coast specialize in preparing tempting seafood dishes—so enjoy. From scenic Port Angeles take the passenger ferry to Victoria, British Columbia, 18 mi. across the strait. Call (800) 663-1589 for dates and times.

Hours: Mon.-Sat., 8 A.M.–5 P.M.; Sun., 9 A.M.–5 P.M.

Where Is It? In Port Angeles, start at the service counter in Swain's General Store, 601 E. First St., (206) 452-2357. **From Hwy 101:** Hwy 101 is called both E. First and Front St. through Port Angeles, both streets one-ways running in opposite directions. From the east, turn left on Albert St., cross First and go left on Second. From the west, follow First up the hill; Swain's is on your right.

PORT TOWNSEND ♦ *Scenic Walk*

Dates: January 1–December 31 Frances Johnson (206) 732-4623

Description (3): Stroll along the beach, walk under a rose arbor, explore the historic downtown and Fort Worden State Park, and enjoy the many impressive Victorian houses on this scenic trail through one of the state's oldest towns. You'll encounter several hills and some gates.

See and Stay: Welcome to ferry rides, picnics in waterfront parks, and bike rides through 19th-century neighborhoods. Call (800) 628-1826 for the ferry schedules to Seattle and the San Juan Islands. Free bikes are available at various points. Johnson says you should "look for the ugly green bikes in racks and ask inside."

☑ Bring a windbreaker. Port Townsend summers can be breezy. Bathrooms are not available at start, but are along the route.

🚲 If you like to bike, ask the Olympic Peninsula Explorers about the club's 32K bike route in the Dungeness Valley.

Hours: Mon.-Sat., 8 A.M.–5 P.M.; Sun., 9 A.M.–5 P.M.

Where Is It? Start at the front desk of the James G. Swan Hotel, corner of Water and Monroe Sts., (206) 385-1718 or (800) 776-1718. **From Hwy 101:** As you approach the northernmost point of Hwy 101, look for signs for Hwy 20 and take 20 into Port Townsend. The highway becomes Water St. in town. Go to Monroe. The hotel is on your right.

Sponsor: Olympic Peninsula Explorers, P.O. Box 1706, Sequim, WA 98282, sponsors both walks.

WASHINGTON

RENTON ◆ Town Walk

Dates: January 1–December 31 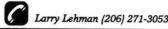 *Larry Lehman (206) 271-3053*

Description (2): Explore Renton at the southern tip of Lake Washington on this trail along residential areas, through parks and past "Stonehedge." You'll encounter some non-paved street shoulders.

Food and Fun: The Valley Medical Center has an excellent cafeteria. If you crave outdoor fun, go to the Gene L. Coulon Memorial Beach Park, 2 mi. north on Lake Washington Blvd., and fish, swim, boat, or walk the nature trail.

Where Is It? Start at the information desk in the Valley Medical Center, 400 S. 43rd, (206) 226-0718. **From I-405:** Take Exit 2 south to Auburn on Hwy 167. Exit about 1 mi. south on S.E. 43rd St. Turn left on East Valley Rd. and go to the left turn lane at 43rd and turn left. Go uphill to Talbot Rd. S. Go left on Talbot to the hospital parking lot. Park in rear of patient parking lots.

Sponsor: Global Adventurers Volkssport Club, 2023 Aberdeen Ave. SE, Renton, WA 98055

RENTON ◆ Top of the Hill Walk

Dates: January 1–December 31 *Larry Lehman (206) 271-3053*

Description (2): You'll walk along residential streets and on the right-of-way trails of the Seattle Water Dept., as well as some gravel roadways. You'll find water only at the start point.

Where Is It? Start at the Circle K Store, 2000 Benson Rd. S., (206) 226-0718. **From I-405:** Take Exit 2 (SR 167), Rainier Ave., and go to Grady Way. Turn right on Grady Way and go three lights. Turn right on Talbot Rd. S and go to S. Puget Dr. Turn left up the hill on S. Puget Dr. and go to Benson Rd. S. Turn left. The Circle K is in the East Benson Shopping Center. Please park away from the stores.

Sponsor: Global Adventurers Volkssport Club, 2023 Aberdeen Ave. SE, Renton, WA 98055

Puyallup, just south of Tacoma, has a 10K walk that starts at Happy Donut Shop, 305 Second St. NE. The town is known for its iris, tulip, and daffodil bulb industry. For information on the walk and directions to Happy's, contact Nancy Walen, (206) 863-0431, 7408 F 142nd Ave. W., Sumner, WA 98390.

WASHINGTON

RICHLAND ♦ *Historic Walk*

Dates: *January 1–December 31*   *Don Wicks (509) 943-5118*

Description (1): You'll pass Indian burial grounds and where Lewis and Clark and Sacajawea made camp. You'll also pass Hanford, a 560-sq. mi. nuclear power site and reminder of Richland's role in the Manhattan Project. The 3,600-ft. Rattlesnake Mountain, sacred to the Yakima Indians, is the highest mountain in the U.S. without trees. Watch for wildlife.

See and Stay: In 1944 Richland became one of four development sites for the atomic bomb, and has since grown into a technological center. Visit the Hanford Science Center, next to the Federal Building at 825 Jadwin. This U.S. Department of Energy public information center offers hands-on exhibits and computerized games that give an array of energy information. Ask to see one of the center's 40 films. You're also in wine country and within a few hours drive of scenic attractions such as Mounts Hood, St. Helens, and Rainier, and the Cascade Mountains.

☑ Be prepared for hot summers in this desert region and sandstorms in the spring and fall.

🚲 This club sponsors two bike paths—a 30K path and a 40K. Both have small hills and are on concrete trails. Tack weed or puncture weed can be a problem.

Where Is It? Go to the front desk of the Shilo Inn, 50 Comstock, (509) 946-4661 or (800) 222-2244. **From I-182:** Take the George Washington Way exit. Turn right at the first traffic light. Park in the inn's lot. Ask for the volkssport briefcase and sign in and get your directions.

Sponsor: Columbia Basin Windwalkers, 1813 Hunt Ave., Richland, WA 99352

WASHINGTON

ROSLYN ♦ *"Northern Exposure" Walk*

Dates: April 10–October 31 (seasonal) *Millie Haupt (509) 453-8710*

Description (3): Get ready, *Northern Exposure* fans, to take a trip to Cicely, Alaska, via Roslyn, the town where Maggie and Joel and the gang film their popular weekly television series. You'll walk on sidewalks and gravel/dirt trails, encounter a few hills, and wind your way through the town's 1875 cemetery.

See and Stay: When the club sponsored a one-day walking event in Roslyn in 1992, 1,200 walkers came to see "Cicely" and walk by the radio station, the Brick Tavern, and Ruth Ann's grocery store. Just enjoy the sights through this mid-1800s coal-mining town nestled in the heart of the Cascade Range. Be prepared for some delays on weekdays when the film crews shut down pedestrian and car traffic. The crew takes breaks to let traffic pass, but you may have to be patient. Maybe you'll get a chance to be an extra!

☑ Bathrooms are portable units along the route and public restrooms in the park. This walk may not be repeated in 1994, so check with Haupt before heading out.

Hours: Mon.-Sat., 8 A.M.–5:30 P.M.; Sun., 10 A.M.–5 P.M.

Where Is It? In Roslyn, start at Susie's Chocolates and Terri's Espresso store at 4 N. Second St. **From I-90:** Take Exit 80 (Roslyn/Salmon LaSac). Take exit road to the north and follow signs to Roslyn. At junction with First Ave. (Hwy 903), turn left to downtown, about 3 mi. Turn left on Pennsylvania, the main crossroad. Turn right on Second St. The store is on the right side. Park along the street.

Sponsor: Yakima Valley Sun Striders, P.O. Box 10523, Yakima, WA 98909

Some Yakima Valley Sun Striders pose by this now famous cafe sign. Photo by C. "Hoppy" Haupt.

WASHINGTON

SEATTLE ◆ Lake Union Walk

Dates: March 1–December 31 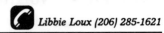 Libbie Loux (206) 285-1621

Description (2): This 11K path encircles Lake Union, an urban attraction featuring houseboats, unusual businesses, ships, museums, and parks. One section has no sidewalks and some traffic.

See and Stay: Near Lake Union, visit the Center for Wooden Boats and Gas Works Park. For a water view of Seattle, go to Pier 55 at the foot of Seneca St. and take the 1-hr. Seattle Harbor Tours. Or see Seattle from 520 ft. up in the air at the Space Needle, the city's most visible landmark. Visit the Woodland Park Zoo. For a free brochure of other Puget Sound attractions, write for the council brochure, 2200 Sixth Ave., #804, Seattle, WA 98121, (800) 426-1205.

Hours: Weekdays, dawn to dusk; weekends 8 A.M.–4 P.M.

Where Is It? Start at Benny Lyles Burgerworks, 1802 N. 34th St. **From I-5:** Take Exit 169 (N.E. 45th St.). Turn west onto 45th and at the top of the hill, turn left onto Wallingford Ave. N., heading south. The restaurant is on the southeast corner of Wallingford and N. 34th.

Sponsor: Seattle Strasse Striders, P.O. Box 27573, Seattle, WA 98125

SEATTLE ◆ Waterfront Walk
◆ Queen Anne Hill Walk

Dates: March 1–December 31 Frank or Anna Denton (206) 243-7367

Description (1 +): See most of Seattle's famous spots, from the harbor or a hilltop.

Waterfront Walk: On this 11K walk, you'll get the grand tour of Seattle's most popular sites: the site of the 1962 World's Fair; Myrtle Edwards and Elliot Bay parks; the revitalized waterfront; Pioneer Square; Klondike Gold Rush National Historic Park; the famed Pike Place Market; and more.

Queen Anne Hill Walk: You'll climb one long, gradual hill and several short, steep ones on this 11K walk that passes through Kinnear Park and the north end of Queen Anne. You'll be treated to great views of Lake Union.

☑ Allow 2.5 to 3 hrs. for these walks, more if you sightsee.

Where Are They? Start at The Park Inn, 225 Aurora N. between John and Thomas Sts., (800) 255-7932 or (206) 728-7666. **From I-5:** Take Exit 167 (Mercer St./Fairview Ave.). Keep to the left on the exit ramp and turn left at the light onto Fairview Ave. N. In 5 blks. turn right onto Denny Way. At Sixth Ave. N. (1 blk. beyond Aurora), turn right. Go 1 blk. to John St. and turn right again. The inn is on your left. Please do not park in the inn's lot.

Sponsor: F. S. Family Wanderers, 1715 28th Ave. W., Seattle, WA 98199

WASHINGTON

SHELTON ◆ Bay Walk

Dates: January 1–December 31   Alice Southwick (206) 426-2303

Description (2 +): This 11K walk will take you along Oakland Bay in South Puget Sound, in this town famous for oysters and Christmas trees.

Food and Fun: Oysterfest happens in early October, so join in if you're in the area. From November to mid-December arrange with the chamber of commerce, (206) 426-8678, to visit a Christmas tree packing shed loaded with the season's Christmas greens. Let the pine smell propel you into the holiday season.

Where Is It? Start at Mickey's Deli at Alder and First Sts., (206) 426-7662. **From I-5:** Take Exit 104 for Hwy 101 and follow signs to Shelton. **From 101:** Take the Shelton/Matlock exit and turn toward Shelton on Railroad. Take Railroad to First St. Turn left on First and go 4 blks. to Alder.

Sponsor: Capitol Volkssport Club, P.O. Box 977, Olympia, WA 98507

SPOKANE ◆ Scenic Parks Walk

Dates: February 1–December 31   Janet Carbary, (509) 459-4932/276-2867

Description (1): Paved sidewalks and pathways will take you through Riverfront Park, the former site of Expo '74. You'll pass the historic Browne's Addition, go into Coeur d'Alene Park and return to the downtown along the south side of the river.

See and Stay: Explore Riverfront Park, with its waterfall, carrousel, gondola ride, Japanese Garden, the Eastern Washington Science Center and planetarium, and the IMAX Theater with its five-story screen. Go back to the Flour Mill and explore its 24 shops and restaurants. See Walk in the Wild, a 240-acre park with a small animal collection and trained parrot shows.

Where Is It? Start at Deaconess Medical Center, 800 W. Fifth Ave., (509) 458-5800. **From I-90:** Exit at Lincoln St. Go east on Third Ave., and turn right (south) onto Wall St. Continue to Fifth and Wall and into the medical center's visitor parking lot.

Sponsor: Empire Health Services Volkssport Assoc., P.O. Box 248, Spokane, WA 99210-0248

WASHINGTON

SUMNER ◆ *Town Walk*

Dates: January 1–December 31 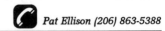 Pat Ellison (206) 863-5388

Description (1 +): Experience a small town with tree-lined streets and flower beds. Your route, primarily on sidewalks with some road shoulders, goes through city parks and lovely residential areas. You'll catch sight of Mt. Rainier along the trail.

See and Stay: Want another walk? Try the 10K in nearby Puyallup. Van Lierop Bulb Farms features colorful, seasonal displays.

This club also sponsors a bike route. Call Ellison for details.

Where Is It? Start at the Spartan Drive-In, 15104 E. Main. **From I-5:** Take Exit 127 for Puyallup and go on SR 512 to SR 410 east to the second Sumner exit. Turn left onto Valley Ave. and go to Main. Turn right and go 1 blk. The drive-in is on the right.

Sponsor: Daffodil Valley Volkssport Assoc., P.O. Box 1488, Puyallup, WA 98371

> If you want to walk in **Tacoma**, go to the Allenmore Hospital, S. 19th St. and Union. The walk is sponsored by the Evergreen Wanderers. Contact Ethel Roy, (206) 472-3236, 6210 S. Sheridan, Tacoma, WA 98408, for more information.

VANCOUVER ◆ *Ft. Vancouver Walk*

Dates: January 1–December 31   Marge Bickford (206) 693-6430

Description (1): Walk through this national historic site, which was the center of the Hudson Bay Trading Co. from 1825 to 1849, and the first U.S. military post in the Northwest. The unique Pearson Air Museum is on this 11K route, and you'll also get views of the Columbia River and Mt. Hood as you amble along paved paths.

Food and Fun: Sample the food in the Quay at the start point, or along the route in the Edelweiss for German food, and beware of the antique shops. The Red Lion offers discounts to volkswalkers. Visit the Ginkgo Petrified Forest State Park, which includes 7,470 acres of fossilized trees, the only petrified ginkgoes ever found.

Where Is It? Start at the Red Lion Inn, 100 Columbia at the Quay, (206) 694-8341 or (800) 547-8010. **From I-5 northbound:** Take Exit 1B (City Center). **From I-5 southbound:** Take Exit C (City Center). Go west to Columbia, then turn south. The hotel is just beside the river, next to the underpass below Interstate Bridge.

Sponsor: Vancouver USA Volkssporters, P.O. Box 2121, Vancouver, WA 98668

WASHINGTON

VANCOUVER ◆ Nature Walks

Dates: January 1–December 31 Daryl Pulley (503) 288-0148, days

Description (1+) (3+): Both walks include a mix of asphalt, sidewalk, packed dirt, and grass paths. Walk 1 includes 2.5K in a greenway, plus a park, and offers vistas of the Vancouver Lake lowlands. There is one steep hill, but strollers should be able to manage. Walk 2, an 11K, includes parks and a dedicated trail system that is too rough for wheeled vehicles.

🚲 This walking club sponsors three bike paths: a 25K into Vancouver Lake Park, a 41K along the channel and Columbia River, and a 50K combination of part of the other routes. Depending on your route, you'll see river traffic, many birds, and pastures. Helmets required.

Where Are They? Start at the AM/PM Store at the intersection of E. 39th and Main Sts. **From I-5:** Take Exit 2 (39th St./Hospital). Exit onto 39th and then turn left. Go 4 blks. straight to Main. At the intersection of 39th and Main, look for the ARCO Station-AM/PM Store on the southeast corner. Please park on the streets, not in the store's lot.

Sponsor: All Weather Walkers, P.O. Box 9810, Vancouver, WA 98668-9810

WENATCHEE ◆ Nature Trail

Dates: March 1–December 1 (seasonal) Gib Edwards (509) 663-3356

Description (1+): This walk on mostly paved pathways will take you to a graveled nature trail.

See and Stay: You're in the heart of apple growing country. Sample apples and juices at the Washington State Apple Commission Visitor Center at 2900 Euclid Ave. Walk through Ohme Gardens, just off US 97, where plants blend with rugged rock formations to create unusual effects. At nearby Rocky Reach Dam watch migrating fish climb the 1,700-foot-long fish ladder and enjoy displays of flowers and crafts.

🚲 This club sponsors two 25K bike trails. Call Edwards for details.

Where Is It? Start at the Orchard Inn, 1401 N. Miller. **From I-90:** Take the exit for US 97, a scenic highway that connects with I-90 just outside Ellensburg, north of Yakima. Go north on 97 and follow the signs for Wenatchee. The Inn is just off Wenatchee Ave., behind the Denny's Restaurant.

Sponsor: Bavarian Volkssport Assoc., P.O. Box 91, Leavenworth, WA 98826

WASHINGTON

YAKIMA ♦ *Parks Walk*

Dates: January 1–December 31    Millie Haupt (509) 453-8710

Description (1): Tour two parks on sidewalks and paved pathways.

See and Stay: See scenic Yakima Canyon from a restored vintage train car on a train to Ellensburg and have dinner to boot. The *Spirit of Washington* Dinner Train departs weekends for this 3-hr. round-trip ride. Call (800) 876-7245. The Yakima Area Arboretum, just off the I-82 exit, is a 40-acre reserve of native and non-native vegetation.

Where Is It? Start at the volkswalk stand in the main lobby of the Yakima Valley Memorial Hospital, 2811 Tieton Dr. **From I-82:** Take Exit 31 (White Pass/Chinook Pass, Hwy 12). You'll be going west. Take first exit south (16th Ave.). At the fifth stoplight (Tieton Dr.) turn right and go west to hospital. Turn right on 28th Ave. to a parking lot.

Sponsor: Yakima Valley Sun Striders, P.O. Box 10523, Yakima, WA 98909

Here are a few more Washington walks you might want to check out:

• From April 1 to October 31 in **Carnation**, you can walk from Remlinger Farms, 32610 N.E. 32nd. The walk is sponsored by the Hopkins Telephone Pioneers, and you can get details from Ruth Kalies, (206) 630-2728, 19905 S.E. 300th St., Kent, WA 98042.

• From April 1 to October 31 in **Fall City,** you can walk or bike from The Herbfarm, 32804 Issaquah. The walk is sponsored by the Emerald City Wanderers. Contact Virginia Davis, (206) 783-1858, 7348 20th NW, Seattle, WA 98117, for information.

• From May 1 to November 1 in **Leavenworth** in the Wenatchee Mountains you can walk from the Alpine Inn, 405 Hwy 2. The walk is sponsored by the Bavarian Volkssport Assoc. Contact Shirley Ward, (509) 548-7853, P.O. Box 296, Leavenworth, WA 98826, for information.

• From April 1 to October 31 in **North Bend**, you can do two walks or a bike ride from the Great Northwest Factory, 461 S. Fork Ave. SW. Contact Dorm Batson, (206) 927-2495/838-6981, at 35806 1st Ave. S., Federal Way, WA 98003, for information.

• From April 1 to October 31 in **Preston**, you can walk from Preston General Store, 30365 Preston Rd. The Tri-Mountain Volkssport Club sponsors this walk. For details contact Jennifer Littke, (206) 222-5715, 36002 S.E. 46th, Fall City, WA 98024.

• From April 1 to October 31 in **Snoqualmie**, you can walk from Isadora's, 132 Railroad Ave. The walk is sponsored by the Sea-Tac Volkssport Club, and Evelyn Wilton, (206) 839-1546, 30042 12th Ln. SW, Federal Way, WA 98023, can give you information.

Enclose a self-addressed, stamped envelope (SASE) with your requests.

WEST VIRGINIA

RICHWOOD ♦ *Cranberry Hill Walk*

Dates: April–November (seasonal) *Kitra Burnham (304) 846-2516/2201*

Description (2): You can choose to walk 10K or 20K through a forest wilderness that includes a cranberry bog—a remnant of the Ice Age—and a .5-mi. boardwalk nature trail in an area called Cranberry Glades. The path is fairly level on grassy trails and gravel roads.

Food and Fun: Visit Hillsboro, birthplace of Pearl S. Buck. Tour her home and eat at the Rosewood Cafe. Check to see if the Hillybilly Hikers have added another walk and bike trail in Lewisburg.

Hours: 9 A.M.–4 P.M.

🚴 The club sponsors a 30K and 55K bike route, open daily Memorial Day-Labor Day, and weekends only April-May and Sept.-Nov. There are also a 10K and 20K cross-country ski trails, Jan. 2–April 4.

Where Is It? Start at the Cranberry Mt. Visitor Center of the Monongahela National Forest, in south-central West Virginia, 23 mi. east of Hwy 39/55, (304) 653-4826. **From the west or north on I-79:** Turn on US 19 south and take Hwy 55 east at Muddlety. **From the south on I-77:** Take US 19 north at Beckley to Hwy 39 east at Summersville.

Sponsor: Hillbilly Hikers, P.O. Drawer D, Richwood, WV 26261

Mist and forested mountains envelop the New River near Richwood, West Virginia. Photo by Ralph Lauterwasser.

WISCONSIN

CEDARBURG ◆ City Walk

Dates: April 1–October 31 (seasonal) 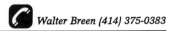 *Walter Breen (414) 375-0383*

Description (1 +): This walk on mostly city streets and grassy park lands meanders through the historic downtown, parks, and shopping areas.

See and Stay: With its downtown historic district, 1840s to 1920s architecture, artists' studios, quaint shops, and many festivals, Cedarburg is the state's second largest tourist attraction. Visitors will find a variety of good restaurants, elegant B&Bs, and attractions.

Hours: Daily 9 A.M.-5 P.M. Check-in/check-out times may be busy at the inn's desk.

Where Is It? Cedarburg is north of Milwaukee. Start at the Washington House Inn, a B&B at W62 N573 Washington Ave., (414) 375-3550.

From I-43: Take Exit 17 to Pioneer Rd. or Hwy C. Drive west on C to Hwy 57 or Washington Ave. Turn right on Washington and go 5 blks. to the inn, which is on the left, or west, side of the street. Please do not park in the inn's rear parking lot.

Sponsor: Deutschstadt Volkssporters, W51 N176 Fillmore Ave., Cedarburg, WI 53012

I Just Have To Exercise More!

Seems like everyone these days is "into" exercise. Having a healthier body is a great goal, but you're more likely to reach that goal if your road to success is paved more with smiles and laughter than with sweat and hunger. You should look for an exercise that offers

- a way to see and do new things
- a way to be with family and friends
- a physical challenge
- a way to reduce stress
- a chance to be outdoors
- a way to compete against yourself
- a chance to exercise almost anywhere for low to no cost

Hey, that sounds a lot like walking!

WYOMING

CHEYENNE ♦ Old West Museum Walk

Dates: January 23–December 31   *Carol or Mike Jennings (307) 632-9072*

Description (2): Your start card is your pass to the Cheyenne Frontier Days Old West Museum and its collection of western memorabilia dating from 1897. Indian artifacts, horse-drawn buggies, and railroad artifacts are included.

Hours: Mon.-Sat., 9 A.M.–5:30 P.M.

🚲 The walking club also sponsors a 25K bike route that starts at the Bicycle Station, 3515 E. Lincolnway in the Cheyenne Plaza. The store is open Mon.-Fri. 9:30 A.M.–6:30 P.M.; Sat., 9 A.M.–6 P.M.; Sun. 1:30 P.M.–4:30 P.M. Call Gaylord Fosdick (307) 638-8538 for details.

Where Is It? Start at Brown's Shoe Fit Company, 1701 Carey Ave. **From I-25:** Take West Lincolnway Exit 9. Take Lincolnway east to Carey. Go left on Carey 1 blk. **From I-80:** Take Exit 362 to Central Ave. Take Central to 17th St. (over viaduct). Go left on 17th; go 3 blks.

Sponsor: Cheyenne High Plains Wanderers, P.O. Box 5173, Cheyenne, WY 82003

CHEYENNE ♦ Historic Downtown Walk

Dates: January 2–December 31   *Carol or Mike Jennings (307) 632-9072*

Description (2): City sidewalks will take you through Wyoming's capital. You'll pass the historic Governor's Mansion, home to 19 first families from 1905 to 1976, and the capitol.

See and Stay: Experience Frontier Days, considered the world's oldest and largest professional rodeo. The batter for the pancake feed for more than 300,000 visitors is mixed in a cement truck. Be sure that you've made your hotel reservations if you're coming.

Hours: Summer, Mon.-Sat., 8 A.M.–9 P.M.; Sun., 9 A.M.–6 P.M. Winter, Mon.-Sat., 9 A.M.–6 P.M.; Sun., 10 A.M.–5 P.M.

✓ During Frontier Days, the last full week of July, the start moves to the Brown's Shoe Fit Company. (See above for times, directions.) The start returns to The Wrangler in August.

Where Is It? Start at The Wrangler, 118 Capitol Ave. **From I-25:** Take Exit 9 to Lincolnway, which is 16th St. downtown. **From I-80:** Take Central Exit 362 to Lincolnway. Go left to the red building on the corner of 16th and Capitol.

Sponsor: Cheyenne High Plains Wanderers, P.O. Box 5173, Cheyenne, WY 82003

From May 1–October 3 you can walk in **Newcastle** near the South Dakota border. The walk is sponsored by the Newcastle Area Chamber of Commerce. Contact Allen Ward, (307) 746-9429, P.O. Box 331, Newcastle, WY 82701, for details.

WYOMING

PINE BLUFFS ◆ *Archeological Digs Walk*

Dates: May 29–October 31 (seasonal) Sonja Carlson (307) 245-3301

Description (2 +): Walk at 5,047 ft. in the Bluffs Recreation Area on nature trails, and tour archeological digs. Archaeologists will be at the site intermittently during the season. Your walk also includes the High Plains Archeological Museum, the Texas Trail Museum, and the Pine Bluffs Recreation Wildflower Garden.

See and Stay: Visit during Pine Bluffs Trail Days, the first weekend in August; join in the dancing, barbecue, rodeo, melodrama, and the volleyball tournament. Make motel reservations in advance.

☑ This club also sponsors a 300-meter swim from May 29–Aug. 22. The outdoor pool is open Mon.-Fri., 1 P.M.–5 P.M. and 6 P.M.–8 P.M.; Sat., noon–6 P.M.; Sun., 1 P.M.–6 P.M.

Where Is It? Start at the Gator's Travelyn Motel, 515 W. Seventh at Parsons. **From I-80:** Take one of the Pine Bluffs exits. The motel can be reached by either exit. For the swim, go to 200 E. Eighth St.

Sponsor: Cheyenne High Plains Wanderers, P.O. Box 5173, Cheyenne, WY 82003

SUNDANCE ◆ *Town Walk*

Dates: May 29–September 6 (seasonal) Susan Worthington (307) 283-1677

Description (2): Enjoy a western town on this walk on blacktop, gravel, and some hard-packed dirt, which could get muddy. On the upward stretch to Mt. Moriah Cemetery, stop to enjoy the view of Sundance Mt., Crow Peak, Green Mt., and Terry Peak. Look for deer and wild turkey.

See and Stay: Harry Longabaugh, the Sundance Kid, took his name from this town after spending 18 months in the county jail. Go to the Crook County Museum and Art Gallery in the lower level of the courthouse where you'll find a re-creation of the courtroom as it looked when the Sundance Kid was sentenced.

☑ See if there's a new walk at Devil's Tower National Monument.

Hours: Mon.-Sat., no earlier than 9 A.M.; no earlier than noon on Sun.

Where Is It? Where you start in will depend on the day. On Mon.-Sat., start at Pamela's Shopper, 404 Cleveland (Hwy 14), (307) 283-2662. On Sun., start at the Country Cottage, 423 Cleveland, (307) 283-2450. Please don't park right in front of the stores. **From I-90:** Any of the three exits will take you into downtown. In a town of 1,000 people, nothing's too hard to find.

Sponsor: Northern Hills Walking Club, Box 189, Sundance, WY 82729

THERMOPOLIS ♦ State Park Walk

Dates: January 1–December 31   *Allen Cowardin (307) 864-2176*

Description (2): You'll walk in an urban park atmosphere at an elevation of 4,326 ft. on sidewalks and some gravel paths. This hot springs park contains four large springs, terraces, hot waterfalls, and one of the state's largest buffalo herds.

See and Stay: After the walk take a free dip in the hot springs pool. Explore the park with its many natural attractions. Bighorn Hot Springs, one of the world's largest hot mineral springs, releases four million gallons of water each day. Drive through Wind River Canyon to the south and admire the rock formations, including Chimney Rock.

Hours: Mon.-Sat., 8 A.M.–6 P.M.; Sun., noon–6 P.M.

Where Is It? Start at the State Bathhouse in the Hot Springs State Park, on the northeast edge of town on US 20 and SR 789. **From I-25:** Take exits for US 16 south of Sheridan or US 20/26 out of Casper. On US 16 go west until you reach US 20; go south to Thermopolis. On US 20/26 go until US 20 breaks off to the north, and follow it to Thermopolis.

Sponsor: Wyoming State Parks & Historic Sites, 2301 Central Ave., Cheyenne, WY 82002

FOUR WYOMING STATE PARKS WALKS

Dates: May 29–September 6 (seasonal)   *Carol Jennings (307) 632-9072*

Wyoming State Parks & Historic Sites, 2301 Central Ave., Cheyenne, WY 82002, sponsors summer walks in the state's various state parks. Each walk has a local contact person, but Carol Jennings, the state's volksmarch coordinator, also has information about the following four walks.

WYOMING

GUERNSEY STATE PARK

 Dusty Humphreys (307) 836-2334

Description (4): You'll walk at an elevation of 4,500 ft. on old CCC trails and on paved and graveled roads through an area offering views of wildlife, a lake, dam and spillway.

See and Stay: Visit the Oregon Trail Ruts State Historic Site, 1 mi. south on S. Wyoming Ave. from US 26 junction. Here you'll see well-preserved pioneer trails—some of the ruts are as much as 6 ft. deep.

Hours: Daily 10 A.M.–6 P.M.

Where Is It? Start at the Guernsey State Park Museum, (307) 836-2900. **From I-25:** Take the exit for US 26 and go east to Guernsey. The park is 4 mi. north of Guernsey.

☑ The Friends of Guernsey State Park Volksmarch also have a walk in this area. The walk goes from May 1–Sept. 6 and starts at the Bunkhouse Motel.

KEYHOLE STATE PARK

 Don Lester (307) 756-3596

Description (3): You'll walk along a lake, through woods and along grassy paths at an elevation of 4,200 ft. Watch for wildlife.

See and Stay: Enjoy the park's full recreational offerings, including camping, boating, boat rentals, fishing, swimming, water sports, lodging, cabins, and food services.

Hours: Daily 8 A.M.–6 P.M.

Where Is It? Start at the marina in Keyhole State Park, 8 mi. north of I-90 between Moorcroft and Sundance on the Pineridge Rd.

SINKS CANYON STATE PARK

 Darrel Trembly (307) 332-6333

Description (3): You'll walk at 6,500 ft., mostly on mountain trail, through a mixed coniferous forest and sagebrush meadows, and near the banks of the Popo Agie River. Watch for moose, elk, and bighorn sheep, and dramatic waterfalls, whitewater, and wildflowers.

See and Stay: Go into Lander and visit one of the state's oldest towns. Plan to visit Fort Washakie, northwest of town on US 26/287. There you'll find the grave of Sacajawea, the Shoshone woman who helped lead Lewis and Clark to Oregon. Just east of the fort, in Ethete, you'll find a public hot springs pool and bathhouse.

Hours: Start no earlier than 9 A.M.

Where Is It? Start at the Visitor Center of Sinks Canyon State Park, 9 mi. south of Lander on SR 131. Lander can be reached from I-80 by taking US 287 north at Rawlins.

SOUTH PASS CITY STATE HISTORIC SITE

 Ken Brecht (307) 332-3684

Description (4): At an altitude of 8,300 ft., you'll go up some steep rock and gravel paths, through trees, and along a creek. The trail passes historic mines and cabins—reminders of the town's mining days. Watch for wildlife.

See and Stay: You'll cross the Continental Divide as you go through South Pass City. This historic mining community is undergoing restoration, as seen in the many 1860s buildings you can visit. The saloon, jail, butcher shop, and livery stable are filled with mostly original artifacts. Catch a weekend melodrama at the Variety Theatre.

☑ Snowstorms above the timberline are common, even in July.

Hours: Daily 9 A.M.–6 P.M.

Where Is It? Start in South Pass City at the Smith-Sherlock Store. Turn off SR 28 at milepost 43 and follow the signs. The town is 35 mi. south of Lander between US 187 and US 287, both of which intersect I-80.

WHAT'S VOLKSWALKING?

Volkswalking was born in the mountain meadows of the Alps, where for centuries Europeans have walked within sight of snowcapped mountains and brilliant wild flowers simply for the joy of being outdoors. Back in the 1960s, weekend walkers in Germany, Liechtenstein, Austria, and Switzerland wanted walking alternatives to the popular pastime of volksrunning, a timed, competitive 10K (6.2 mile) outdoor race. Volksrunning discouraged walkers who had no chance of finishing, much less of winning, a race dominated by athletes who covered the route in less than 50 minutes and grabbed all the prizes.

Rather than give up outdoor sporting events, these walkers formed the International Volkssport Federation (IVV) in 1968 and rewrote the rules: Walking events will not be timed and anyone who completes the course earns an award. Congeniality replaced competition, and volkswalking quickly became a social, as well as a physical, activity. After walks, Alpine villages resonated with oom-pah bands and people lingered to dance, down beer and brats and relax with friends and family.

Volkswalking Today

Today the tradition of non-competitive, sporting events continues. The international membership roster has grown to about 20 countries, including most of Europe, Israel, Canada, and the United States. Biking, swimming, and cross-country skiing and snowshoeing events have been added. But walking, or wandering as it's sometimes called, remains the most popular event.

U.S. servicemen stationed in Europe brought volkswalks home to America. The first club was established in 1976 in Fredericksburg, Texas, and has been followed by almost 800 more clubs. All of these clubs belong to the American Volkssport Association (AVA), located in Universal City, Texas.

Each year these clubs host thousands of events, usually on weekends, and about 400 clubs sponsor a year-round or seasonal walk in their communities. More than 500,000 people participated in a volkswalk last year, and the numbers continue to grow.

Walking for Fun and Awards

Every AVA walking path is unique, but they all have a few things in common. The walks are free to anyone, but even the just-for-fun walker must sign in at the walk's start point and get a map of the route. Some walkers pay to walk. Some pay about $5 for the commemorative award that goes to anyone who completes the walk. These awards can be medals, patches, sun catchers, cane shields, hat pins, or even mugs or bookmarks. Many volkswalkers collect walking awards and display them on their clothing or in their homes.

Some walkers don't want the award, but they do want to earn credit for the number of events and distances they've completed. These walkers pay about $1.50 to have their IVV distance and event walking books stamped. These ink-stamped books give walkers an official record of their lifetime achievements. Anyone who's ever been a girl or boy scout can relate to the idea of earning a badge for specified activities. Some avid volkswalkers have walked more than 20,000 kilometers and have participated in more than 2,000 events.

How to Become Involved

Many people first learn about AVA walks from friends or local newspapers. When you go to your first event, look for the table where brochures on upcoming walks are displayed. These brochures will give you the dates and locations for the walks in your area.

You don't have to join anything to participate in AVA events, but once you get hooked on 10K walks, you might want to volunteer some time to a club in your area. If you don't know where the nearest AVA club is, call the AVA's national office. Some states such as Texas, California, Oregon, Washington, and Ohio have dozens of clubs, and other states have only have a few.

Volkswalking Etiquette

Volunteers make volkswalks possible, and the most necessary volunteers are the businesses that give space and employee time so walkers can check in and out of their walks. Please be patient if an employee at the start point can't help you right away. AVA members work on the principle that a business should always serve its customer first.

Some start-point employees are unfamiliar with volkswalking. All they may know is where the box of AVA supplies is kept. These self-start boxes almost always come with directions; so, if you're new to volkswalking, take time to read the directions and follow the steps for signing in. You may be asked to pay your fees before you start or after you return. When you finish, turn in your start card, and thank the business for its time. If you've had an unpleasant experience, don't complain to the employees; write and tell the club what happened.

If you're walking for an award or for credit only, most volkswalking clubs prefer you pay by check. If you don't have your checkbook with you, then try to have even change so that the start/finish point will not have to make change for you.

The American Wanderer

The American Wanderer, a bimonthly newspaper, lists every U.S. club and the location of every sanctioned year-round and seasonal walk, and gives the complete calendar of all volkssporting events in the country. It also includes articles about clubs, trails and special events.

A subscription to the *Wanderer* is included in the Volkssport Associate membership. Annual fees are $20 for an individual and $25 for a family. APO addresses should add $5 and foreign addresses $10. AVA members get special travel discounts and a few other perks.

For Information

For information about volkssporting, memberships, and local clubs, contact the AVA:

> AVA National Headquarters
> Suite 101, Phoenix Square, 1001 Pat Booker Road
> Universal City, TX 78148
> (210) 659-2112 FAX (210) 659-1212

More Walks

This book contains 405 walks, but we don't claim to have listed every AVA sponsored year-round or seasonal walk in the country. Volkswalkers have one thing in common—a passion for walking 10K trails, and they add new walks almost as fast as they can lace up their walking shoes.

Once you try a few volkswalks and get in touch with a club or two, you'll be learning about new trails on your own, and when you do, we hope you'll take a few moments to fill in the short questionnaire at the back of this book and tell us about them. Happy walking!

To Year-round and Seasonal Sponsors:

We hope this guide to the national network of year-round and seasonal volkswalk trails is the first of many. We will start working on the 1995-96 edition in late 1994, so look for our next questionnaire in November 1994. Until then, don't hesitate to send us updates about your year-round walks. We look forward to meeting you on the trails.

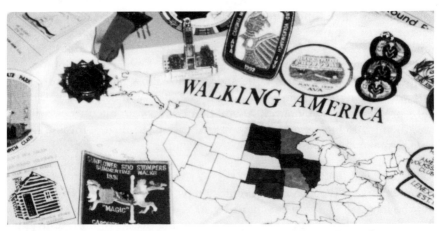

Many walkers collect awards as reminders of special trails and of their walking achievements. Photo by Judith Galas

APPENDIX

BIKE ROUTES

ARIZONA	Phoenix
CALIFORNIA	Carlsbad
	Homewood
	Los Gatos
	Monterey
	Sacramento
COLORADO	Colorado Springs
	Monument
FLORIDA	Coral Gables
	Pensacola
	Tallahassee
	Winter Park
GEORGIA	Stone Mountain
KANSAS	Lenexa
	Wichita (2)
MARYLAND	Columbia
	Wheaton
MASSACHUSETTS	Concord
	Martha's Vineyard
	Lincoln
	South Hamilton
MICHIGAN	Marquette
MINNESOTA	Mankato
	St. Paul
MISSISSIPPI	Ocean Springs
MISSOURI	Augusta
	Lees Summit
	St. Charles
	St. Peters
NEW YORK	Plattsburgh
NORTH CAROLINA	Winston-Salem
OHIO	West Carrollton
	Xenia
OKLAHOMA	Tulsa
OREGON	Albany
	Bend
	Eugene/Springfield (2)
	Fort Stevens State Park
	Lebanon
	Portland
PENNSYLVANIA	Kleinfeltersville
	Lancaster
	Ohiopyle
SOUTH DAKOTA	Brookings

SOUTH DAKOTA, cont.	Sioux Falls
TEXAS	Austin
	Boerne
	Dallas
	San Antonio—Missions
	Universal City
UTAH	Ogden
VIRGINIA	Jamestown
	Williamsburg
	Yorktown
WASHINGTON	Fall City
	North Bend
	Olympia
	Port Townsend
	Richland (2)
	Sumner
	Vancouver (3)
	Wenatchee (2)
WEST VIRGINIA	Richwood (2)
WYOMING	Cheyenne

CROSS-COUNTRY SKI TRAILS

CALIFORNIA	Tahoe City
WEST VIRGINIA	Richwood

SWIMS

FLORIDA	Coral Gables
GEORGIA	Stone Mountain
MISSOURI	St. Charles
NORTH CAROLINA	Winston-Salem
VIRGINIA	Williamsburg
WYOMING	Pine Bluffs

WHEELCHAIR-ACCESSIBLE ROUTES

ALABAMA	Montgomery
ARIZONA	Fort Huachuca
	Tucson
CALIFORNIA	Coronado
	Fresno
	Homewood
	Monterey
	Redding
	Redondo Beach

CALIFORNIA, cont.	Sacramento
	San Jose
	San Luis Obispo
	Sausalito
	Stockton
	Vacaville
	Yuba City
COLORADO	Aurora
CONNECTICUT	Wethersfield
FLORIDA	Cocoa Village
	De Land
	Melbourne
	Orlando
	Tampa
GEORGIA	Roswell
	Stone Mountain
INDIANA	Auburn
	Columbus
	Marion
KANSAS	Lawrence
	Topeka
	Wichita (2)
LOUISIANA	New Orleans
MAINE	Portland
MARYLAND	Baltimore
MASSACHUSETTS	Martha's Vineyard
	Sudbury
MICHIGAN	Marquette
MINNESOTA	Brooklyn Center
	Burnsville
	Lanesboro River
	Root State Park
	St. Cloud
MISSISSIPPI	Biloxi
MISSOURI	Augusta
	Hermann
	Lee's Summit
	St. Charles
	St. Louis
	St. Peters
NEBRASKA	Bellevue (1 mi.)
	Lincoln
	Omaha
	York
NEVADA	Incline Village
	Las Vegas
	Reno

NEW HAMPSHIRE	Portsmouth
NEW YORK	Plattsburgh
	Schenectady
OHIO	Xenia
OREGON	Hillsboro
	Joseph Stewart State Park
	Portland
	Roseburg
	Seaside
	Waldport
	Yachats
PENNSYLVANIA	Kleinfeltersville
	Valley Forge
SOUTH DAKOTA	Spearfish
	Yankton
TEXAS	Boerne
	Dallas
	Fredericksburg
	San Antonio—Sea World
	San Antonio—Fort Sam Houston
	San Antonio—Missions
	Universal City
UTAH	Provo
	Salt Lake City
VIRGINIA	Norfolk
WASHINGTON	Federal Way (2)
	Kirkland
	Richland
	Spokane
	Vancouver
	Yakima

WRITE TO US

We'd love to hear about your walk, about the interesting spots you visited nearby and about great finds in restaurants or accommodations. Did our descriptions hit the mark? Did we make a mistake? Your comments will make the 1995-96 edition of *Walking America* even better. Please feel free to photocopy this page and return your comments to: Walking America, P.O. Box 1971, Lawrence, KS 66044-8971

Town or city:
Route:
When did you walk?
Why did you like or not like this walk?

What tips do you have for others taking this walk?

Name: _____ (Optional)
Address: _____
_____

May we use your name and city if we use one of your comments or suggestions? __yes __no

— —

Town or city:
Route:
When did you walk?
Why did you like or not like this walk?

What tips do you have for others taking this walk?

Name: _____ (Optional)
Address: _____
_____

May we use your name and city if we use one of your comments or suggestions? __yes __no

More Comments or Suggestions

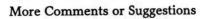

More Comments or Suggestions

If you'd like to order additional copies of *Walking America*, we'd be happy to fill mail requests.

ORDER FORM

To: **Walking America**
P.O Box 1971
Lawrence, KS 66044-8971
(913) 842-4958

Your name: _____
Address: _____
_____
City   State   Zip

For 1-9 copies:

_____copies of the 1993-94 edition of
Walking America @ $11.95
     $ _____

Sales tax (Kansas residents only) 5.9%
     $ _____
Shipping and handling:
                 1-2 books per address $2.50
                 3-5 books per address $4.50
                 6-9 books per address $5.50
            TOTAL $ _____

Bulk orders in lots of 10 only:

_____lot(s) of 10 books shipped to one address @ $100.00
     $ _____

Sales tax (Kansas residents only) 5.9%
     $ _____

Shipping and handling per U.S. address
     5.50

            TOTAL $ _____

Please ship to: _____
Address: _____
                           _____

Daytime phone no.   _____

Contact us about shipments to foreign countries.

Please make checks or money orders payable to **Walking America.**

ABOUT THE AUTHORS

Judith Galas works as a free-lance writer, and Cindy West works as a home-health nurse. What these Kansans really are, however, are recently converted long-distance walkers who have walked more than 1,000 miles since they hit the trails almost two years ago. Avid travelers, they never miss a chance to include as many 10K walks as they can in their travel itinerary. Still, they rarely walk more than 12 miles in one day, but they're working on their endurance; they're still overweight, but much less so; and they've only walked in 10 states, but plan to walk in all 50 before Judith reaches her 50th birthday in 1996.